Rejecting the 'pay through the nose' approach to conservation enshrined in the Wildlife and Countryside Act, this book demonstrates the urgent need to strengthen and extend the national parks system, and to introduce a 'Walkers' Charter' to enable more people to enjoy open country. Derived from the authors' highly acclaimed *National parks: conservation or cosmetics?* (1982), this new book is presented in a popular, illustrated form for a wider readership. Its publication is described by the Council for National Parks as one of the most important events in the Countryside Commission's National Parks Campaign.

The MacEwens believe that countryside conservation depends on reversing the trends that are intensifying the exploitation of land and natural resources and displacing people. They argue for conservation of landscape and resources to be made an integral part of social and economic development, and of government policy for town and country. They see the national parks not as specially protected oases but as experiments in integrated land management that could provide useful 'greenprints' for the harmonious management of the wider countryside.

This important book brings an urgent and challenging message, with implications going far beyond the national parks. It will be essential reading for anyone with a serious interest in the future of the countryside.

Ann and Malcolm MacEwen live in Exmoor and, although (as they say) they have only two good legs between them, are enthusiastic walkers. They are also leading authorities on the national park system. Ann is a planning consultant and (with Joan Davidson) wrote *The livable city* (1983) which forms part of the UK response to the World Conservation Strategy. Malcolm is a journalist and author, and a member of the Council for National Parks; he was a member of the Exmoor National Park Authority from 1973–81 and is a member of its consultative committee.

GREENPRINTS *for the* COUNTRYSIDE?

The story of Britain's national parks

By the same authors

Crisis in architecture, M. MacEwen (RIBA Publications 1974)

Future landscapes, M. MacEwen, ed. (Chatto & Windus 1976)

National parks: conservation or cosmetics?, A. & M. MacEwen (Allen & Unwin 1982)

The livable city, J. Davidson & A. MacEwen (RIBA Publications/ Kogan Page 1983)

New life for the hills, M. MacEwen & G. Sinclair (Council for National Parks 1983)

Countryside conflicts, P. Lowe, G. Cox, M. MacEwen, T. O'Riordan & M. Winter (Temple Smith/Gower 1986)

GREENPRINTS
for the
COUNTRYSIDE?

The story of Britain's national parks

Ann and Malcolm MacEwen

London
ALLEN & UNWIN
Boston   Sydney   Wellington

Allen & Unwin, the academic imprint of
Unwin Hyman Ltd
PO Box 18, Park Lane, Hemel Hempstead, Herts HP2 4TE, UK
40 Museum Street, London WC1A 1LU, UK
37/39 Queen Elizabeth Street, London SE1 2QB, UK

Allen & Unwin Inc.,
8 Winchester Place, Winchester, Mass. 01890, USA

Allen & Unwin (Australia) Ltd,
8 Napier Street, North Sydney, NSW 2060, Australia

Allen & Unwin (New Zealand) Ltd in association with the
Port Nicholson Press Ltd,
60 Cambridge Terrace, Wellington, New Zealand

First published in 1987

719.32

British Library Cataloguing in Publication Data

MacEwen, Ann
    Greenprints for the countryside? : the story of Britain's national parks
    1. National parks and reserves – England
    I. Title   II. MacEwen, Malcolm
    719'.32'0942   SB484.G7
    ISBN 0-04-719013-2
    ISBN 0-04-719014-0 Pbk   103172

Library of Congress Cataloging in Publication Data

MacEwen, Ann.
    Greenprints for the countryside.
    Bibliography: p.
    Includes index.
    1. National parks and reserves – Great Britain.
    2. Conservation of natural resources – Great Britain.
    3. Landscape protection – Great Britain.
    4. National parks and reserves – Government policy – Great Britain.
    5. Conservation of natural resources – Government policy – Great Britain.
    6. Landscape protection – Government policy – Great Britain.
    I. MacEwen, Malcolm, 1911–   . II. Title.
    SB484.G7M22 1987   333.78'3'0941   87-1022
    ISBN 0-04-719013-2 (alk. paper)
    ISBN 0-04-719014-0 (pbk. : alk. paper)

Typeset in 10 on 11 point Bembo by Computape (Pickering) Ltd
and printed in Great Britain by Billing and Sons Ltd,
London and Worcester

Preface and acknowledgements

In 1982 we published *National parks: conservation or cosmetics?*, which is still the only academic study of the national park system in England and Wales. It was well received and has been widely used here and overseas, not only by students and academics but by those who are involved in national parks as professionals or as participants in the voluntary movement for countryside conservation or recreation. By a happy coincidence our publishers, Allen & Unwin Ltd, suggested that the time was ripe for an up-to-date and popular version of our book at the same time as the Countryside Commission announced its intention to run a two-year compaign to make the general public more aware of the national parks. The campaign was launched in September 1985, and this book is a contribution to it. It is sponsored by the Council for National Parks, of which Malcolm MacEwen is a member; and the Countryside Commission has contributed generously by meeting half the costs of the research and travel needed to bring our information up-to-date. We have benefitted greatly from the help and advice of Fiona Reynolds, the Secretary of the Council for National Parks, who has read the entire draft in typescript. We are equally indebted to the Nuffield Foundation, which contributed the lion's share of the costs of research for our original book and has met half the research costs for this one. Adrian Phillips, the Director of the Countryside Commission made helpful comments on the final typescript.

So much has happened since the passing of the Wildlife and Countryside Act in 1981, the point at which the previous book stopped, that we had virtually to write a new one. This book retells the story up to 1981, but the greater part of it is intended to give the reader a lively picture of the extraordinary changes that have taken place since then. The movement for the conservation of nature, wildlife and landscape has burgeoned. The prospects for farming have changed out of all recognition as the impending collapse of the Common Agricultural Policy of the EEC has opened the way to new ideas and possibilities – some immensely hopeful, others highly threatening. We now take a more positive view of the national park

system than we did in 1981. Our title implies that it has gained
enough confidence and maturity to be able to offer useful guidance
on the conservation and management of the wider countryside. But
it still lacks the full commitment that only Government can give it,
and the powers and resources that the national park authorities need.
The question mark is asking whether the full potential of the
national parks will be realized, and whether the 'greenprints' they
offer will be used elsewhere.

We are indebted to many people for the help they have given us in
revising our information, exposing us to other points of view, and
helping us to develop our own ideas. Members and officers of the
Countryside Commission, the ten national park officers, members
and officers of the national park authorities, the principal adviser of
the Broads Authority and its staff and members have all been very
helpful. It would be invidious to single out one of them, but we
must make an exception for John Bradley, the National Park Officer
of the Brecon Beacons National Park from 1974 to 1986. John was a
planner, a climber and a naturalist. His death in February 1986 from
a heart attack on a high ridge of the Black Mountains robbed the
national park of an exceptionally gifted and dedicated officer. He
was always refreshingly open with us, as well as being helpful and
generous with his time and his ideas. We wish to thank Peter
Downing for advice on woodlands, Carys Swanwick for advice on
nature conservation and maps of 'open country', and Rachel Berger
for revising information on the White Peak and commenting on
integrated rural development. We must express a special debt to
Geoffrey Sinclair both as a professional colleague and a friend, for
writing the captions to the maps showing the physical features of
each national park, and for giving us the benefit of his unique
knowledge of hill farming and the uplands at a time of dramatic
changes and the emergence of new dangers. By reading drafts and
entering into a dialogue with us he helped us to reach some new
conclusions that are of central importance in this book.

John Anfield, Keith Bungay, Aitken Clark, Michael Dower, Ken
Parker, Tim O'Riordan and John Workman have read various
chapter drafts, and have helped both to eliminate errors of fact and
to shape our conclusions. But neither they nor any of the others we
have thanked are responsible for any errors that may remain, or any
of the opinions we express. We were old-fashioned enough still to
use a typewriter, so we have no thanks to offer to our word pro-
cessor, although that day has come. But we have been so well served
by Nicky Parnell and Jan Passmore, who typed the book from our
messy mixture of typing and manuscript, that we will probably
keep human company for some time to come. We must also offer a

'thank you' to Norman Nicholson for permission to publish his profoundly moving poem 'Windscale', from his *Selected poems 1940–82* (Faber & Faber). We acknowledge permission to reproduce copyright material from the Countryside Commission, the Broads Authority, the Dartmoor National Park Committee, the Exmoor National Park Committee and *The Times* newspaper. Ordnance Survey material was used in the preparation of the maps, and Crown copyright is reserved. Ruby and Waldo Barker and Kate MacAuliffe helped with some figures.

The following photographers provided the plates: John Darling © (1); Geoffrey Berry © (2, 3, 14, 15, 25, 26); David Doble © (4); Noel Habgood © (5); E. M. Tattersall © (8); Tom Stephenson © (9); Richard Denyer © (27–29). We also acknowledge the copyrights of The Crown (6); the Peak Park Joint Planning Board (10, 13, 18, 21); the Yorkshire Dales National Park Authority (11, 17, 19, 20); the Dartmoor National Park Authority (12, 23); the Snowdonia National Park Authority (16); the Central Electricity Generating Board (22); the Exmoor National Park Authority (24).

Ann and Malcolm MacEwen

We dedicate this book to the memory of John Bradley, mountaineer, champion of the national parks and National Park Officer of the Brecon Beacons from 1974 to 1986: his death on his beloved Black Mountains robbed the national park movement of an able and committed professional to whom we personally owe a great debt for his help and friendship.

Contents

PART TWO
Conservation and enjoyment

PART THREE
The National Park System – *running the show*

List of figures

List of plates

PART ONE

National parks –
then and now

Chapter One

National parks –

the dream . . .

THE NATIONAL PARK IDEA

The ten national parks of England and Wales are among the most beautiful, spectacular and popular stretches of countryside in the British Isles. Every year they attract many tens of millions of visitors, from every part of the world. The most famous and perhaps the best loved, the Lake District, has been given the rare distinction of nomination as a World Heritage site under an international convention. Yet it is said that the national parks of England and Wales are neither national (for they are not nationally owned) nor parks (for they include large areas of farmland and private ground to which the public has no right or even custom of access). Nor do they satisfy the internationally agreed criteria for national parks.

This is not because they are ranked lower than the national parks of other countries in terms of their beauty, wildlife or popular appeal. It is because they do not satisfy the two principal conditions laid down by the International Union for Conservation of Nature and Natural Resources (IUCN) for the recognition of national parks. The first is that they are essentially wilderness areas, extensive natural landscapes of great beauty or special scientific interest which have not been materially altered by human exploitation or occupation. The second is that they must be owned, or at least managed, by the government of the country concerned, primarily for the purposes of conservation, but also (although only on strict conditions) for public enjoyment.

The national parks in England and Wales (there are none in Scotland as we will explain later) are, on the contrary, landscapes that owe much of their character and interest both to the gifts of

nature and to hundreds, even thousands, of years of human occupation. They are farmed and afforested, criss-crossed by roads and
power lines, worked for their resources of water, rocks and minerals, and studded by hamlets, villages and even small towns.
Nearly 250 000 people live in them, and at the summer peak their
population reaches many millions. They are recognized internationally not as 'national parks' but as 'protected landscapes' and their
system, if successful, could be used to protect any inhabited
landscape where conservation and development are in conflict.
What the British call 'national parks' are intended not so much to
conserve uninhabited wilderness as to protect inhabited landscapes
where the land should be managed for a multiplicity of purposes –
conserving their character, promoting their enjoyment and supporting human life in many diverse ways. The purpose of this book,
therefore, is to describe a peculiarly British national park system,
and to assess how far it is successful in achieving these purposes. But
it has another purpose: to consider whether these national parks
offer what we call 'greenprints' for the integrated management of
the countryside.

National parks originated in the United States of America. The
nineteenth century saw the conquest and division of the globe by the
advanced industrial nations of the West, and the use of industrial
technology to exploit the natural resources of the world. In 1864,
George Perkins Marsh published *Man and nature*, a statement of a
new, ecological view that man must live with nature if he was not to
endanger the sources of life. While the Civil War was in progress,
Abraham Lincoln signed an Act of Congress in 1864 ceding the
Yosemite Valley and the Mariposa Grove of giant sequoias to the
State of California, to be used as a public park on condition that it
would be 'inalienable for all time'. In 1872 the first national park was
established at Yellowstone. The Federal Government assumed
responsibility for the ownership and management of national parks
in the National Park Service Act of 1916. The objective of the
system, which has expanded enormously since then, was defined by
the Act as being 'to conserve the scenery, natural objects and wild
life, and provide for their enjoyment in such a manner and by such
means as will leave them unimpaired for the enjoyment of future
generations'.

The central idea was a democratic one. The state would keep out
the freebooters of private (or public) enterprise and protect the
'natural scenery' for the enjoyment of the public. The American
concept was formally adopted by the IUCN in 1969, and national
parks that conform to its conditions have now been established all
over the world. But the IUCN concept in its purest form is now

increasingly questioned, for although it was possible in the 1870s for the US Army to remove the native Americans from Yellowstone, it has proved to be difficult (and often wrong) to prevent long established grazing and hunting practices elsewhere. The National Parks and Access to the Countryside Act of 1949, which established the system for England and Wales, was based from the start on the idea of reconciling conservation with the livelihood of the resident communities. But its objectives were based on the American model.

THE NATIONAL PARK MOVEMENT

The movement for the protection of the most beautiful scenery in England and Wales originated in the Lake District, which was the birthplace both of the National Trust, and of the pioneering amenity society, the Friends of the Lake District. The idea of a national park in the Lake District originated with the poet William Wordsworth, who lived by Rydal Water. His *Guide to the Lakes* published in 1810, concluded by saying that he and other 'persons of pure taste ... deem the district a sort of national property, in which every man has a right and interest who has an eye to perceive and a heart to enjoy'. Wordsworth had a deep understanding of nature, and a poetic vision of landscape, even if he also had a snobbish belief that the landscape would be ruined if 'artisans, labourers and the humbler class of shopkeepers', whose 'common minds precluded pleasure from the sight of natural beauty', were tempted by the new Kendal to Windermere railway to 'ramble at a distance'.

The Council for the Preservation (now Protection) of Rural England (CPRE) was formed in 1926 with the strong preservationist and rural bias its title implied. In 1929, Ramsay Macdonald's second Labour government appointed the Addison Committee to study the feasibility of national parks, and its report provided a platform around which a lobby was formed to exert pressure on government for national parks. On the initiative of the Friends of the Lake District, the CPRE and the Ramblers' Association, the Joint Standing Committee for National Parks, now the Council for National Parks, was set up in 1926, with the participation of nearly all the major open-air organizations. It rapidly became a formidable organization with strong bases in the countryside, where the CPRE and Friends of the Lake District had considerable influence among landowners and others, and in the towns, where the Ramblers' Association had working class and Labour associations. In *Freedom to Roam* Howard Hill has told the story of the campaigns in the 1930s for the right of access to open country. Men who confronted gamekeepers and police on the northern grouse moors were fined and sent to prison. These confrontations ensured that a Labour government would be under strong pressure from its supporters to secure the right to roam over open country.

World War II was the decisive factor that made the politically unattainable politically possible. The demand for a 'better Britain', to replace the Britain of dole queues, means-tests and massive unemployment, exerted pressure on the coalition wartime government to demonstrate that it contemplated some decisive changes when the war was over. By good luck one of the most prominent members of the Standing Committee for National Parks, an architect by the name of John Dower, was a wartime civil servant in the Department of Town and Country Planning whose Minister, Lord Reith, asked him to write a report on national parks. The Dower report on *National Parks in England and Wales* was published by the coalition government in April 1945, only three months before the general election brought into office a Labour government committed to the national park idea. Some of the new ministers had personal associations with the ramblers' movement – notably Lewis Silkin, the Minister of Town and Country Planning, and Hugh Dalton, the Chancellor of the Exchequer.

Within days of taking office, Lewis Silkin appointed Sir Arthur Hobhouse, chairman of the County Councils' Association, as chairman of a Committee on National Parks in England and Wales, charged with making specific recommendations arising out of the Dower report. But the Committee had two offshoots, a Committee on *Footpaths and Access to the Countryside*, with Sir Arthur in the chair; and the Wildlife Special Conservation Committee, with the scientist Sir Julian Huxley as chairman, on *The Conservation of Nature in England and Wales*. All three committees reported in 1947, and this led in turn to the passing of the National Parks and Access to the Countryside Act 1949. In the event, as we will see in the next chapter, the Act proved to be a grievous disappointment to the national parks and access lobby, while fulfilling the highest hopes of the scientists whose main interest lay in the conservation of wildlife.

THE 1949 ACT:
assumptions and consequences

The National Parks Act was the last in a series of statutes by which the postwar Labour government curtailed the rights of property by establishing the principle that the use and development of land should be planned and controlled in the public interest. The principle had been accepted by the wartime coalition government and in the provisional legislation of 1944. The Town and Country Planning Act of 1947 gave the county councils the power to control all development (with some exceptions) in accordance with policies laid down in their development plans, which had to be approved by central government. Urban sprawl, ribbon development along main roads and garish advertisement hoardings were then seen to be the main threats to the landscapes of national parks, and the remedy was seen to lie in development control. The National Parks Act of 1949 therefore entrusted the responsibility for national parks to the county councils as the local planning authorities (with special arrangements for joint planning boards where parks lay in more than one county).

Unfortunately, the thinking behind the Act was based on some mistaken assumptions, which had been spelt out in the Scott report on *Land utilisation in rural areas* in 1942 and accepted by the Dower and Hobhouse reports of 1945. One was the firm belief that development control would ensure a harmonious, well-ordered and well-designed countryside without interfering unduly with the rights of property owners. The other was that farming operations and afforestation need not be subject to development control, because farming would preserve both the rural landscape and the rural communities. The Scott report firmly declared that 'there is no antagonism between use and beauty', and herein lay its fatal contradiction. For it failed to anticipate the course of postwar farming and the consequences for the rural landscape and community, not because the signs were invisible but because it failed to see them.

The acceptance by John Dower and the Labour government of the philosophy of the Scott Committee and its assumptions go a long way to explain why the 1949 Act proved to be such a big disappointment to the supporters of national parks. Both farming and forestry were exempted from the new development control system set up by the 1947 Town and Country Planning Act, although this exemption has been modified over time. The 1950 Landscape Special Development Order, which introduced a modicum of control over farm buildings in three national parks, was extended in 1986 to bring the design, materials and siting of farm buildings and roads in all national parks under an expedited form of planning control. But the basic philosophy that excludes agriculture and forestry operations from control remains unchanged. So, when modern farming and massive afforestation came to be seen in the 1970s not as benign activities but as major

threats to landscape and wildlife, the national park authorities were
powerless to deal with them.

THE DESIGNATED AREAS

John Dower recommended that national parks should be extensive
areas of beautiful and wild country, consisting largely of mountains
and moors (with the associated farm lands of their valleys and
fringes), heaths, rocky and infertile coastlines and the rougher parts
of numerous downs, hills and forests. His definition was accepted
by the Hobhouse Committee. Part 2 of the 1949 Act defined the
areas to be designated as 'extensive tracts of country' characterized
by 'their natural beauty', and by 'the opportunities they afford for
open-air recreation having regard to their character and to their
position in relation to centres of population'. The purposes of
designation were defined as 'preserving and enhancing their natural
beauty and promoting their enjoyment by the public'. What is
common to the successive definitions of a national park is that the
areas to be designated include, however worded, extensive tracts of
'open country' which are now statutorily defined as mountain,
moor, heath, down, cliff or foreshore, together with woodlands,
rivers, most canals and strips of land on the banks of tow-paths.
Open country, so defined, has the park-like attribute that the public
can have access to it. It is also likely to have an above-average
scientific interest for nature conservation.

Ten national parks were designated by the National Parks Commission (now the Countryside Commission) and confirmed by the
Secretary of State between 1951 and 1957. They are shown in Figure 1
and listed in Table 1. The boundaries exclude large settlements such
as Whitby in the North York Moors and degraded landscapes such
as the limestone quarries near Buxton and the slate quarries at
Blaenau Ffestiniog in Snowdonia, but not the artillery ranges of
Northumberland, Dartmoor and the Pembrokeshire Coast. To this
list could be added the Norfolk and Suffolk Broads, which have had a
status 'equivalent' to that of a national park since 1985. Legislation
was pending as we went to press in the summer of 1986 to establish
the Broads Authority, but it has broken the national park mould
established by the 1949 Act and later legislation, and we have
devoted the whole of Chapter 17 to it.

A couple of clauses in the 1949 Act provided for the designation of
Areas of Outstanding Natural Beauty (AONBs), of which 37 have
now been designated (Fig. 1). They have been drawn, in practice,
from 52 'conservation areas' proposed by Hobhouse. They were

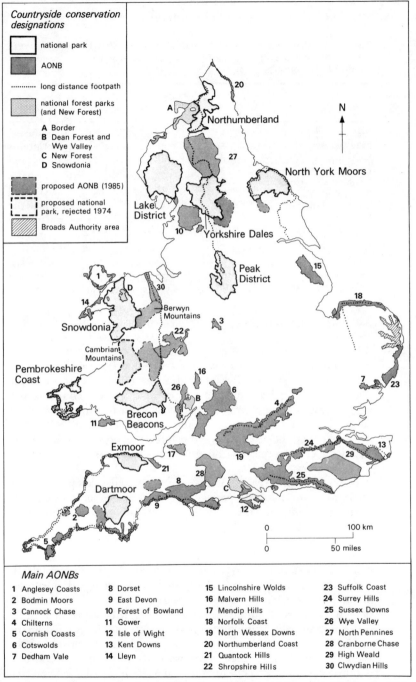

Countryside conservation designations

- national park
- AONB
- .... long distance footpath
- national forest parks (and New Forest)
  - A Border
  - B Dean Forest and Wye Valley
  - C New Forest
  - D Snowdonia
- proposed AONB (1985)
- proposed national park, rejected 1974
- Broads Authority area

N

Northumberland

North York Moors

Lake District

Yorkshire Dales

10

Peak District

20

27

15

18

Snowdonia

Berwyn Mountains

30

1

14

D

3

22

Cambrian Mountains

16

26

B

6

Pembrokeshire Coast

Brecon Beacons

11

Exmoor

17

21

Dartmoor

8

28

19

C

12

4

24

29

25

13

7

23

9

2

5

| 0 | | 100 km |

| 0 | | 50 miles |

Main AONBs

1 Anglesey Coasts	8 Dorset	15 Lincolnshire Wolds	23 Suffolk Coast
2 Bodmin Moors	9 East Devon	16 Malvern Hills	24 Surrey Hills
3 Cannock Chase	10 Forest of Bowland	17 Mendip Hills	25 Sussex Downs
4 Chilterns	11 Gower	18 Norfolk Coast	26 Wye Valley
5 Cornish Coasts	12 Isle of Wight	19 North Wessex Downs	27 North Pennines
6 Cotswolds	13 Kent Downs	20 Northumberland Coast	28 Cranborne Chase
7 Dedham Vale	14 Lleyn	21 Quantock Hills	29 High Weald
		22 Shropshire Hills	30 Clwydian Hills

Figure 1 National parks, Areas of Outstanding Natural Beauty and the area of the Broads Authority (Crown copyright reserved).

Table 1 National parks in England and Wales (from 1981 census, adjusted in Brecon and the Peak District by the National Park Authority, and in Broadland by the Broads Authority).

Park	Area designated (mile²)★	(km²)	Date of confirmation	Population (1981)
Peak District	542	1404	1951	37 368
Lake District	866	2243	1951	39 835
Snowdonia	838	2171	1951	23 761
Dartmoor	365	945	1951	29 139
Pembrokeshire Coast	225	583	1952	21 531
North York Moors	553	1432	1952	24 599
Yorkshire Dales	680	1761	1954	16 842
Exmoor	265	686	1954	10 438
Northumberland	398	1031	1956	2 219
Brecon Beacons	519	1344	1957	32 170
Totals	5251	13600		237 902

Broadland's 'executive area' is 109 mile² (283 km²), and its population in 1981 was 5300.

★As metric measurements are often used in this book the following conversion table will be useful to readers: 1 mile² = 2.59 km², 1 km = 5/8 mile and 1 hectare = 2.47 acres.

given no nature conservation or recreational functions, although recreational use could be inferred from the power to provide wardens. Their administration was entrusted to the county councils. Despite the proximity of many of them to centres of population, and recreational use as intensive in some AONBs as in national parks, they received (and still receive) no special funding in any way comparable to the government grants now paid for national parks.

In Scotland, where the potential for national parks is greatest, the movement for national parks failed to achieve legislation. The Ramsay committee, the counterpart of Dower, Hobhouse and Huxley in England and Wales, produced *National parks: a Scottish survey* in 1945 and a report on *National parks and the conservation of nature in Scotland* in 1947. It came much closer to the American concept of a national park 'owned or controlled by the nation'. It firmly recommended that land required for national park purposes, including the open moorlands, be designated for free public access as of right, and also acquired outright, if possible by agreement but if not, compulsorily. But national parks in Scotland foundered on the resistance of the landed interests to the radical proposals of the Ramsay report. Five areas proposed by the Ramsay report as national parks in Scotland lingered on as 'National Park Direction

Areas', within which proposals for development were notified to the Secretary of State for Scotland. But their national park status was never confirmed, and the title 'national park' served only as a buoy to mark the scene of the wreck and to recall the ideas of the 1940s. The Secretary of State finally extinguished National Park Direction Areas in 1980, and put in their place 40 National Scenic Areas which are a complete reversal of the ideas of the 1940s, and a purely aesthetic and cosmetic concept. These areas enjoy no special protection for their natural or wildlife interest. Nor are there any special arrangements for their management or administration, apart from a slight tightening in development control and a greater possibility of intervention by the Secretary of State for Scotland. Responsibility for planning control rests with the regional councils whose primary concern, understandably, is to promote development. Scotland cannot yet, unfortunately, have any place in a book on national parks.

Chapter Two

National parks –

the reality

THE FLAWS IN THE ACT

The reasons for the disappointment of national park supporters, and the cynicism of the civil servants who administered the 1949 Act, are not hard to understand. They can be summed up as lack of powers, gross underfinancing and confused or divided authority. The so-called 'authorities' that were put in charge of the national parks could acquire land by agreement either to protect landscape or to promote recreation, but they could only do so compulsorily for the purpose of securing public access to 'open country'. They had no last resort powers either to make orders to prevent damaging farming or forestry operations, or to acquire land for the primary purpose of preserving or enhancing its 'natural beauty'. Yet Dower and Hobhouse had both regarded the public acquisition of land in national parks as an indispensable weapon in the national park's armoury to be used unhesitatingly wherever planning control seemed unlikely to achieve the objectives of conservation or recreation. The Hobhouse report recommended that £50 million should be spent over ten years by the new national park authorities on acquiring land. The money was to come from the National Land Fund (now the National Heritage Memorial Fund), set up by Hugh Dalton in a short-lived mood of financial euphoria in 1946, with an initial capital of £50 million – equivalent to perhaps £2500 million in 1986. Not a penny of it reached the national parks until 1979. The county councils, which had already become the planning authorities for the areas to be designated as national parks, were determined not to surrender their new powers. Nor was the Government in any mood to quarrel with them, and the National Parks Act made the county councils the national park authorities. But the county councils continued their resistance even after the Act had been passed. They opposed the designation of every park by the National Parks Commission, except in Dartmoor and Northumberland. Even in Northumberland there was a prolonged wrangle between the Commission and the county council, the Commission wishing to designate the Hadrian's Wall area and the council the Cheviot moors, before they agreed to include both in the Northumberland National Park.

The county councils were not very worried about the three single-county parks (Dartmoor, Northumberland and Pembrokeshire Coast), which would be run by a county council committee served by county council officers. They objected to the loss of control involved in the administration of the seven multi-county parks by semi-autonomous joint planning boards. But the Act left a loophole by which 'in exceptional circumstances' national parks could be run by separate county council committees, one for each bit of a park, with a powerless joint advisory committee for the whole park. This arrangement defeated the basic principle that each park should be planned and managed as a geographical entity. When the National Parks Bill was going through Parliament firm pledges were given that the parks would be managed as single units.

The first park to be designated by the National Parks Commission was the Peak, which lies in no fewer than six counties and plainly could not be run as six separate parks with a joint committee to oversee the whole. It could only be managed by a joint planning board, and Hugh Dalton, by then Minister of Town and Country Planning, overruled the objections of the Labour-controlled Derbyshire County Council when he made the order establishing the Peak as a national park in 1951. It was administered from the start by a joint planning board with its own national park officer and staff, and thereby gained a start over the other national parks which it has never lost. He weakened over the Lake District, which then lay in three counties, conceding that the board need have neither a national park officer nor staff of its own and agreeing that the three constituent county councils would control its expenditure.

The retreat turned into a rout in Snowdonia, which now lies in one county but then lay in three, where the new Minister of Housing and Local Government, Harold Macmillan, surrendered to the pressure of the Welsh county councils. He found that there were 'special circumstances' (actually, a room full of demonstrating Welsh councillors) that justified him in agreeing to this 'more efficient administration' of Snowdonia by no fewer than four committees – three separate county council committees and a powerless joint advisory committee. In Exmoor he gave in over the joint board and agreed that the national park should be run by three committees. The exception became the rule and the same system was followed in the other multi-county parks, even in Brecon Beacons which extended over three counties and had no fewer than four national park committees. In this atmosphere the movement to designate national parks was brought to a halt. The only park to be designated since the Brecon Beacons Park was constituted in 1957, the Cambrian Mountains National Park in mid-Wales, was turned down by the Secretary of State for Wales in 1973 without even holding a public inquiry.

THE GREAT DIVIDE

Another basic flaw in the 1949 legislation was the establishment of two separate conservation agencies. The Nature Conservancy (now the Nature Conservancy Council) was made responsible for 'nature conservation', and 'nature' was defined in its Royal Charter of 1949 as 'the flora and fauna of Great Britain'. The 1949 Act made the National Parks (now Countryside) Commission responsible for the preservation and enhancement of 'natural beauty' which was also defined to include 'flora, fauna and geological and physiographical features'. In practice, the Nature Conservancy took the conservation of nature for its province and 'natural beauty' came more and more to be equated by the National Parks Commission with landscape and the *appearance* of the countryside. This arrangement departed from one of Dower's central tenets that landscape and nature conservation should be in the same hands.

The National Parks Commission, was given no executive, administrative, landowning or land managing functions. Apart from designating national parks and AONBs (subject to ministerial confirmation), its role was entirely advisory and supervisory. The Commission contained no full-time members and only its chairman and vice-chairman were paid. Unlike the Nature Conservancy, it was staffed by civil rather than public servants, in the choice of whom its freedom was severely restricted. It was given no local role or staff at all. One-third of the members of the national park boards or committees were appointed not by the Commission (as Dower and Hobhouse proposed) but by ministers. They were in no sense the representatives or nominees of the Commission, whose advice on these appointments was often disregarded.

The Nature Conservancy, on the other hand, was given an independent status, executive functions and appropriate powers to provide scientific advice on the conservation of natural fauna and flora, to manage National Nature Reserves (NNRs) and to develop research and scientific services. It could also designate Sites of Special Scientific Interest (SSSIs), although these enjoyed no statutory protection until 1981. It was given powers to enter into agreements with landowners for the management of nature reserves, to buy land for this purpose (compulsorily if need be) and to make bylaws for their protection. It was free to recruit the most suitable people. It is hardly surprising in the circumstances that the Conservancy went forward to establish a national and international reputation, whereas the Commission turned out to be a weak and ineffective body.

The emphasis placed today on the protection of the whole environment, not merely the reserves or areas of scientific interest, necessarily calls in question both the political wisdom and the scientific validity of the split between nature conservation and landscape, and the limited role of the Nature Conservancy Council (NCC) – as it became in 1973. The loss of the Conservancy's research branch, hived off to form the Institute of Terrestrial Ecology (ITE) in 1973, breached the basic principle of the Conservancy that research and practice should be combined in the same hands. Today the responsibility for the conservation of nature and landscape is in fact split between four agencies if the ITE is included, for a separate Countryside Commission for Scotland was set up in 1967, while the Nature Conservancy Council remains responsible for nature conservation throughout Great Britain. The need to reunite landscape and nature conservation is discussed in Chapter 9.

FOOTPATHS AND ACCESS

The access provisions in Part 5 of the 1949 Act, which apply throughout England and Wales, stood the principles of the Scott, Dower and Hobhouse reports on their heads. The Hobhouse report on *Footpaths and access to the countryside*, in particular, had firmly recommended that the public should have a legal right to walk (subject to certain conditions and exceptions) over all open or uncultivated land. The Act, however, provided that the public should have legal rights of access to open country only where an access agreement had been made with the landowner or, in default of agreement, an access order had been made by a local planning authority and confirmed by the Secretary of State. The county councils were required to review their areas and to advise what action was necessary to secure public access. With few exceptions, the county councils reported that little or no action was needed.

Access agreements have not been used widely outside the Peak District National Park, and orders have hardly ever been made. The last review, made in 1973, showed that in the whole of England and Wales only 98 access areas covering 35 260 ha (86 625 acres) had been created, of which 80% were in national parks and 56% in the Peak. There has been no substantial increase since then. The consequence of this limited use of the Act was not so much to deny the public access (although it does, as the Ramblers' Association campaign for access to *Forbidden Britain* shows) as to confuse the public and to reduce public expenditure for the public's benefit.

The provisions of the 1949 Act on public rights of way were intended first to identify and protect the public's rights of way that had been built up over centuries and then, where necessary, to adapt the system of footpaths and bridleways to the needs of modern recreation. County councils were required to survey their areas and to prepare maps which would become statutory, definitive maps of rights of way after objections had been disposed of. The county councils were given powers also to close or divert existing paths, to create new rights of way by agreement or compulsorily and to pay compensation. But when the Sandford Committee on national park policy reported in 1974 it found that after 25 years three county councils in national park areas had not even completed the definitive maps of existing rigl.ts of way. We can now see, with nearly 40 years of experience behind us, that the intentions of the Government were seriously frustrated by the complexity of the procedures designed to protect private interests, and by the failure of the county councils as highway authorities to provide either the will or the resources to implement the Act – an issue to which we return in Chapter 8.

REORGANIZATION: 1972

The flaws in the 1949 Act were soon exposed when the austerity of the late 1940s gave way in the 1950s to the more affluent, mobile, consumer postwar society. Successive governments were too deeply committed to the satisfaction of the new demands for water, power, materials and recreation to be reliable protectors of threatened environments. The national park authorities were faced by pressures and demands far greater than even Dower had anticipated, but they lacked the resources, the powers and often the will to control them. National parks were obliged to accommodate massive new installations on a scale far exceeding anything that had happened in prewar years before designation – an oil port and refineries in Milford Haven, a nuclear power station in Snowdonia, high-tension transmission lines and television and radio masts all over the place, vast new reservoirs and quarries. The main impetus for destructive change came from government and the public authorities. Lord Strang, chairman of the National Parks Commission, summed up the experience of 12 years in 1962 by saying: 'Where a government department has had plans for erecting large installations of one kind or another in a national park, I can remember no case where it has been diverted from its purpose by anything that the Commission might say'.

By the end of the 1950s, government was already promising that some of the more glaring weaknesses of the 1949 Act, particularly its financial terms, would be remedied at some unspecified date. But the action when taken in the Countryside Act 1968 was to transform the National Parks Commission into a Countryside Commission, and to shift its interest from a concentration on national parks and AONBs towards recreation in the countryside as a whole. The Act did little to remedy the flaws in the 1949 Act. The government made what proved to be an empty gesture in the direction of conservation by imposing a pious duty on every Minister, government department and public body to 'have regard to the *desirability* of conserving the natural beauty and amenity of the countryside' (our italics). But even this feeble 'duty' (which had no practical effect) was counterbalanced by the duty on national park authorities to have 'due regard to the needs of agriculture and forestry and to the economic and social interests of rural areas' in the exercise of their functions under the Act. The net effect was to make it more difficult, not easier, to resist damaging agricultural operations.

National parks could hardly be left forever in the limbo to which the 1968 Act consigned them. A political wrangle between the Association of County Councils (which wanted to retain the *status quo*) and the Countryside Commission (which wanted every national park to be run by a board on the Peak model) produced a compromise that was enacted by the Tory government in the 1972 Local Government Act. The Countryside Commission settled for a unified administration of every park and statutory requirements that every park authority should appoint a national park officer and prepare a national park 'management plan'. The two boards were retained in the Peak and Lake District. Elsewhere there was to be a committee of the county council as before in single-county parks; but in multi-county parks there was to be a joint committee of several councils (as in Brecon) or a committee of the council with the largest part of the park, to which the council with the minor interest would send representatives (as in Exmoor, North York Moors and

Table 2 Composition of national park authorities 1986–7

Park boards	County council	County	District	Appointed	Total
Peak	Cheshire	2			
	Derbyshire	8			
	Staffordshire	2			
	Barnsley★	1	18 4	11	33
	Kirklees★	2			
	Oldham★	1			
	Sheffield★	2			
Lake District	Cumbria	16	2	9	27
Single-county committees					
Dartmoor	Devon	12	2	7	21
Northumber-land	Northumberland	15	3	9	27
Pembroke Coast	Dyfed	10	2	6	18
Snowdonia	Gwynedd	14	4	9	27
Multi-county committees					
Brecon Beacons	Dyfed	2			
	Gwent	2	14 4	9	27
	mid-Glamorgan	2			
	Powys	8			
Exmoor	Devon	4	12 2	7	21
	Somerset	8			
North York Moors	Cleveland	2	14 4	9	27
	North Yorks	12			
Yorkshire Dales	Cumbria	1	13 3	8	24
	North Yorks	12			
Totals		138	30	84	252

★ Metropolitan district councils, which for national park purposes have the status of county councils, replacing the metropolitan county councils of Manchester, South Yorkshire and West Yorkshire abolished in 1986.

the Yorkshire Dales). The 2 : 1 split between elected and appointed members was retained. The district councils failed to win statutory representation, although they did so in the 1981 Wildlife and Countryside Act.

A NEW START: 1974

The result of these reforms, together with the financial settlement that followed, was to leave the 1949 Act concept intact but to remedy some of the worst defects that had arisen both from the Act and from its application by central government and the county councils. New life was breathed into what had been, in at least eight of the ten parks, an ineffective and even a moribund system. The national park officer was the only statutory appointment, but he became the leader of a professional team whose exclusive concern was the planning and management of the national park. The unified authority, whether board or committee, was able to think of the park as a whole, regardless of political boundaries. The requirement to prepare a national park management plan created an indispensable instrument for building up information, developing ideas and translating them into practical programmes. The two boards retain the unique advantage of combining in one authority both the land use planning function of the county councils and the development control functions that are normally exercised by district councils. In the other parks the county councils remain the local planning authority, but the 1972 Act makes the national park committees responsible for development control within the policy framework of the county council structure plans (see p. 197).

The 1972 settlement was a remarkable cart-before-horse exercise, for the government settled the principles of reorganization a few weeks *after* it had appointed a committee chaired by Lord Sandford, the countryside Minister, to review national park policy. The Sandford Committee's report, published in 1974, recommended toughening up development control, but it shrank from recommending any controls over farming, preferring to rely on co-operation with farmers and landowners by means of voluntary management agreements. It recommended that the park authorities should have power to acquire 'open country', compulsorily if need be, for the purpose of preserving or enhancing its natural beauty and to control afforestation of 'bare land'. But the most significant aspect of the report was its confirmation of the criticisms made since 1949 of the failure of the national parks to realize their objectives. It found that there had been a marked tendency to subordinate long-term benefits to short-term considerations – so much so that it wanted the presumption against development 'to amount to a prohibition to be breached only in the case of a most compelling national necessity'. The whole emphasis of the report, albeit in carefully measured phrases, is on the shortcomings over the entire range of issues – the government's priorities, development control, highways and traffic management, recreational facilities, the management of footpaths and commons, agricultural reclamation, afforestation and quarrying, and administrative, financial and staffing arrangements. It confirmed that more had been achieved in the Peak and to a lesser extent in the Lake District, by their semi-autonomous planning boards, but taken as a whole, the record of the parks in positive work and management before 1974 was shown to be pitiful.

After 20 years, in 1971–2, expenditure was running at £1.2 million a year, which was equivalent to about one-third in real terms of the figure that Hobhouse had recommended. Nearly half of this total was spent in the Peak and the Lake District, and the government's contribution was little more than a third of the meagre total. It is hardly surprising that Sandford called for the budgets of the national park boards to be doubled in real terms by 1978 or 1979 and for those of the committees to be trebled, and for both to continue to rise thereafter, although more slowly. This would have raised total expenditure to less than £4 million a year, an amount so modest that the committee hardly felt called upon to justify it.

The Labour government responded to Sandford by accepting a host of minor recommendations while rejecting or failing to implement most of the more important. A joint circular issued by the Departments of the Environment and Transport in 1977 advised highway authorities to consult national park authorities and make environmental quality the 'primary criterion' in planning road systems and traffic schemes. Another circular issued by the Department of the Environment and the Welsh Office in 1976 agreed that priority should be given to conservation where there was an irreconcilable conflict with recreation, but took no steps to give the principle statutory force. The government accepted that the social and economic wellbeing of national parks was 'an object of policy', but rejected a suggestion from the Snowdonia National Park Committee that this should be made a statutory purpose of the national park authorities. It refused to give the authorities powers to buy land compulsorily for purposes of conservation or to control afforestation. Nor would it agree to a quinquennial review of defence sites in national parks. The financial expectations raised by the Sandford report were not realized. In real terms national park expenditure peaked in 1976–7 (see Fig. 16), at a level that was not reached again until the settlement for 1987–8.

A CHANGE IN THE CLIMATE

In retrospect, the reforms of 1972 and 1974 and the good intentions of the Sandford Committee, however circumspect, mark a temporary peak in the fortunes of the national park system. The reforms were, by later Tory standards, decidedly 'wet' and reflected the readiness of the Heath administration to jack up public expenditure in this field. The reforms put the park authorities into business, and gave them a status and a structure that enabled them to weather the tough years that followed, emerging with enhanced prestige and a track record of achievement.

There have been no fundamental reforms or even major changes in the national park system since the Local Government Act of 1972. Later chapters will examine the implications of the Farm Grant Notification Scheme (for national parks and SSSIs) 1980, the Wildlife and Countryside Act 1981 and the amending Act of 1985, the extension to all national parks of the Landscape Special Development Order 1951 (LASDO) and the Government's proposals to introduce Landscape Conservation Orders in national parks. The overall effect has been to offer national parks a special if limited protection denied to the rest of the countryside, at a time when it has been Government policy to relax planning controls generally. These changes have subtly modified the national park system, and have raised to the level of a principle the 'voluntary approach' by which conservation is achieved by buying off at high prices farmers and others who propose to damage the environment. The Government's policy seems increasingly to make national parks and SSSIs islands of conservation in a sea of spreading *laissez-faire*. But, as later chapters will show, there are limits to the extent to which the Thatcher government will exempt even the national parks from the general trend of its policies.

Chapter Three

Resources:

their use and abuse

CLIMATE AND ROCKS

The resources of the uplands and the severe handicaps from which they suffer both arise from the combination of geological processes, weather, climate and human activities. The hills and mountains that provide the spectacular scenery, the rocks, minerals and water that men need, and the habitats for plant and animal life, also provide the harsh conditions in which the hill farmer has to wrest his living from the ground. The poor, acid soils, short growing season and difficult communications in remote areas have been among the most significant factors driving the native populations down the valleys and into the cities.

Weather conditions vary immensely between and within the parks according to altitude, latitude and distance from the westerly winds of the Atlantic. The combination of these factors can produce extraordinarily severe weather conditions in the higher parts of the more northern and northwesterly parks, where the wet, chilling winds inhibit the growth of vegetation and can rapidly reduce the body temperature of human beings (unless they are properly shod and clad) to dangerously low levels. In southern parks – Dartmoor, Exmoor, Pembrokeshire Coast and Brecon Beacons – the climate is somewhat warmer, reflecting latitude and the tempering influence of the Gulf Stream. Looking at all the parks, the areas with the warmer and drier climates and the most favourable conditions for both agriculture and holiday-making are the North York Moors, Exmoor, the White Peak and Pembrokeshire Coast. In the latter two, most of the land is enclosed for agriculture as are extensive tracts of the North York Moors and Exmoor.

Figure 2 Relief and rivers of England and Wales (Crown copyright reserved).

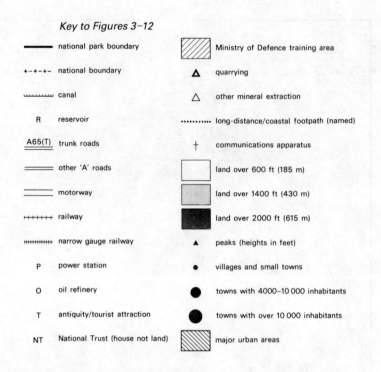

Key to Figures 3–12

———	national park boundary		Ministry of Defence training area
-+-+-+-	national boundary	▲	quarrying
⊔⊔⊔⊔⊔⊔	canal	△	other mineral extraction
R	reservoir	··········	long-distance/coastal footpath (named)
A65(T)	trunk roads	†	communications apparatus
=====	other 'A' roads		land over 600 ft (185 m)
=====	motorway		land over 1400 ft (430 m)
++++++	railway		land over 2000 ft (615 m)
⋈⋈⋈⋈⋈	narrow gauge railway	▲	peaks (heights in feet)
P	power station	•	villages and small towns
O	oil refinery	●	towns with 4000–10 000 inhabitants
T	antiquity/tourist attraction	⬤	towns with over 10 000 inhabitants
NT	National Trust (house not land)		major urban areas

Figure 3   North York Moors National Park   This is the only park east of the Pennines: its Jurassic rocks are younger than those of the other Palaeozoic parks; it is the driest; and though cold in winter, it is tractable enough for substantial land-use change around its moorland core. In the south and east there has been substantial afforestation, and locally moorland cultivation, both spreading upwards out of the shallower dales. Nonetheless, the landscape pattern is striking, simple and powerful, and more than in any other park is dependent on semi-natural vegetation cover. A central and extensive plateau of rolling heather grouse-moor is intersected by a complex system of valleys, whose upper slopes carry an almost continuous fringe of bracken. The dale floors are well-walled and contain far more arable land than in other parks, completing the visual contrast from the apparent infinities of the moorland world to the contained orderliness of the in-bye dales.

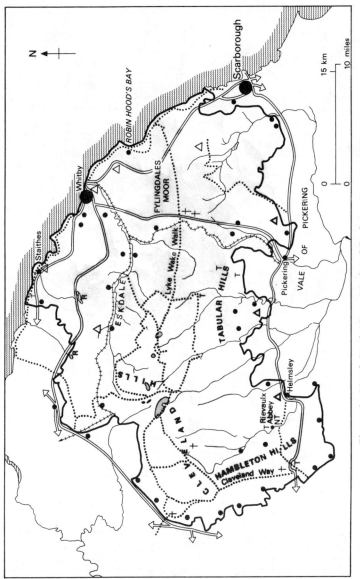

Figure 3 North York Moors National Park (caption opposite)

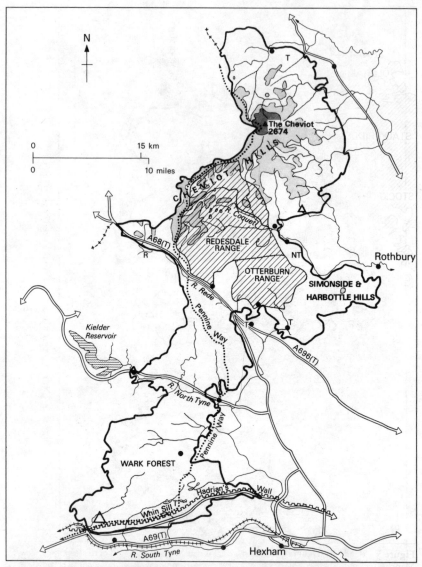

Figure 4　Northumberland National Park　Wide-open and empty, the park has four distinctive landscapes which are more typical of the southern uplands of Scotland. The Whin Sill escarpment provides an emphatic boundary above the South Tyne valley, and a natural site for Hadrian's Wall. To its north grassy moorlands, extensively forested in the west, blend into the open valleys of the North Tyne and Rede; they stretch into the Otterburn and Redesdale army ranges, and merge into the drier heather and bracken of the Simonside Hills. The deep valley of the Coquet marks the change to the Cheviots: huge rounded close-grazed hills dissected by bracken-sided intricate valleys make marvellous walking country, not yet afforested.

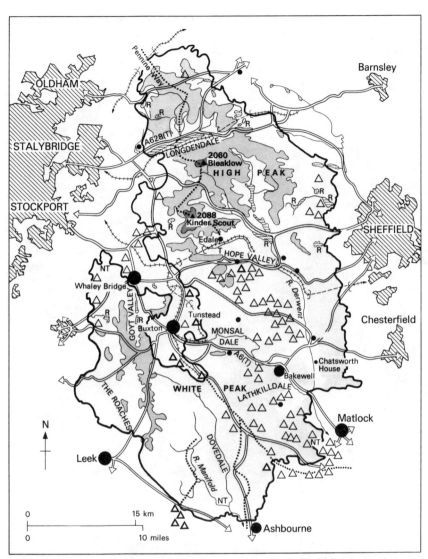

Figure 5 Peak District National Park This southernmost section of the Pennines between Manchester and Sheffield performs a vital recreational role for these conurbations. It is, however, neither a uniform district nor typified by a peak. The 'High Peak', forming a crescent in the west, north and east of the Park is characterized by peat-covered eroding plateaux and gritstone edges, but is also known in part as the 'Dark Peak' from its heather moorlands and gritstone walls. Contained within the arc of the crescent is the 'White Peak', a lower limestone plateau of white-walled pastureland threaded by narrow fescue-bent covered dales. Limestone quarrying and associated cement works occur around Buxton, in an enclave partly excluded from the Park, and in the Hope Valley. Fluorspar and other vein mineral workings – an extensive industry in the past – are found in the east.

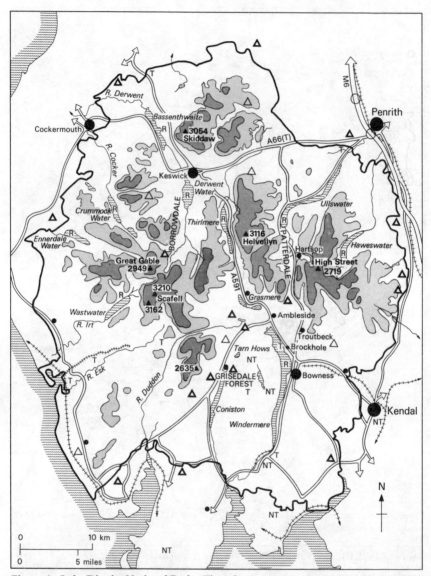

Figure 6 Lake District National Park The only mountainous English park, formed from a complex dome of volcanic and sedimentary rock surrounded by a broken rim of limestone. Glacial activity scoured and deepened the valley floors and deposited debris where the dales widened to create linear lakes. Bracken dominates lower dale sides above which the matt-grass gives a dull whitish cast to upper slopes and hill shoulders. Western fellsides carry the tussocky purple moor-grass, while heather and bilberry form a scenic contrast on crags and rocky sites – also occurring on some eastern fells managed as grouse moors. Several valleys have natural broadleaved woods, and there are intrusive prewar conifer plantations, although forestry on lower ground in the south has created a more attractive landscape.

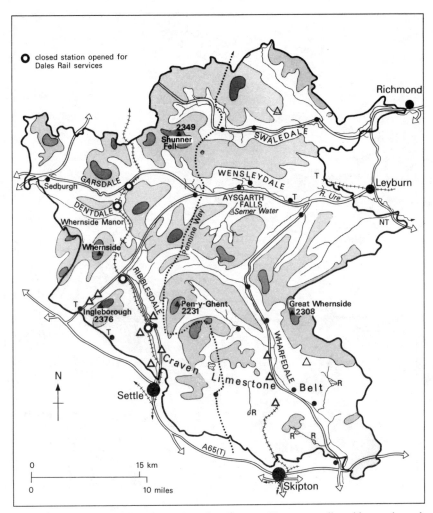

Figure 7 Yorkshire Dales National Park Chequered by stone walls and barns, the park straddles the central Pennines between the Aire Gap on the south and Stainmore on the north. The landscape is dominated by limestones, sandstones and shales of the carboniferous age which dip gently eastwards. Like all upland Britain, the watershed is near the west, where short steep valleys drain the Three Peaks of Pen-y-Ghent, Ingleborough and Whernside. In the centre, straight broad dales gradually open out towards the Vale of York, their stepped profiles reflecting the alternating rock bands. Woodland cover is sparse, though there have been some recent intrusive straight-edged plantations. The landscape of the plateau moorlands between the dales gradually changes, as altitude and rainfall decrease eastwards, from cotton-grass to heather (especially where managed for grouse). The Craven limestone belt dominates the south-west with its green fescue-bent swards, caves, pavements, crags ... and quarries.

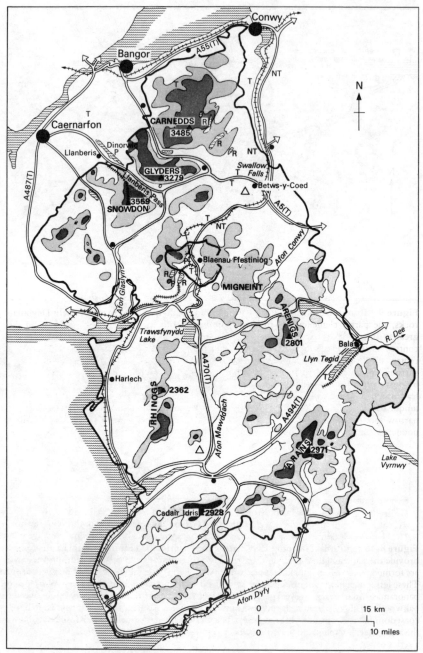

Figure 8 Snowdonia National Park (caption opposite)

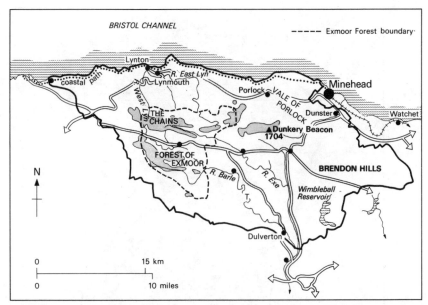

Figure 9 Exmoor National Park In the mild south-west, and made of shaly Devonian rocks, the park's clemency has ironically produced both its characteristic verdure and the greatest threat to its semi-wild landscape. Once dubbed 'Ex-moor', its regrettable and controversial period of subsidized moorland reclamation now appears to have ended. The park's centre, originally a royal hunting forest, is now a landscape of purple moor-grass. It is surrounded and contrasted by a series of heather landscapes, which, though much fragmented by postwar cultivation, still blend with deep oak-filled combes and beech-hedged in-bye, and lead into the wooded valleys of the Exe and Barle. But the abiding Exmoor memory has to be its unique coastline. From Lynton to Porlock the most spectacular road in any park twists round narrow hump-backed hills topped by heather and gorse, tantalizing even the Sunday after-nooners with airy vistas of South Wales and panoramas of Exmoor's heartland.

Figure 8 Snowdonia National Park (facing page) Although the high northern mountains provide the park's name and fame, the Arenig, Aran, and Cadair Idris ranges complete a giant arc formed from volcanic rock, enclosing the ancient and rugged sedimentaries of the Rhinogs. These lesser-famed mountains lie back from their neighbours in more isolated grandeur. Their panoramas embrace extensive grassy moorlands (heather in the east), rocky valleys with oakwoods, rushing torrents, lakes, and intricate estuaries penetrating a rocky or dune-lined coast dominated by the dramatic seaward skylines of the Lleyn Peninsula. Add: Coed-y-Brenin, the acceptable face of upland forestry; the slate-industry at Llanberis and Blaenau Ffestiniog and a series of scenic private and state railways. Result: a microcosm of the national parks system.

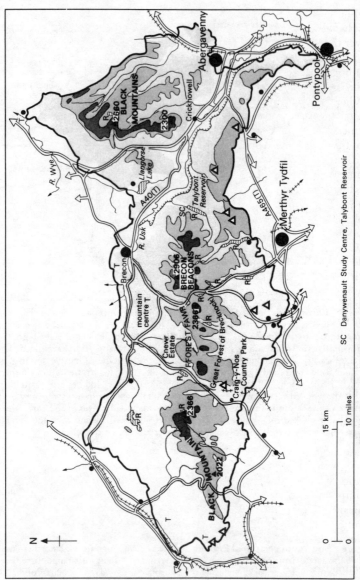

Figure 10 Brecon Beacons National Park (caption opposite)

SC Danywenault Study Centre, Talybont Reservoir.

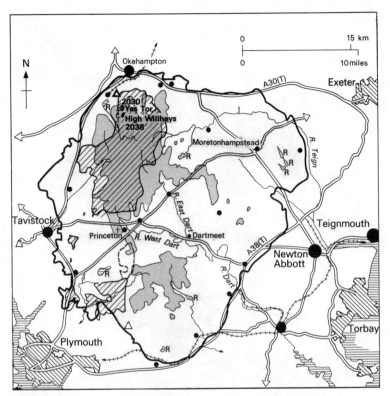

Figure 11 Dartmoor National Park The major granite upland in the parks, topped by tors and rising round and robust out of pastoral Devon, the moor proper is mostly common land. As a result its landscapes of heather, gorse and purple moor-grass, though in some areas overgrazed, have remained more intact than those of Exmoor, and convey a real sense of wilderness. Many southern and eastern valleys retain substantial natural oakwoods, and several persist at high moorland sites. Exploitation of the park's natural resources has always been controversial: quarrying in the north-west, china clay extraction in the south-west, military training over most of the northern moor, and the construction of the Okehampton bypass. Dartmoor has the most important archaeological heritage of any of the parks.

Figure 10 Brecon Beacons National Park (facing page) The park's mountains present a formidable, though discontinuous, north-facing escarpment of old red sandstone to the Twyi, Usk and Wye valleys, and a long moorland dipslope tailing off into the South Wales coalfield. The Beacons proper and the Fforest Fawr are dominated by grassy plant communities, interrupted by an extensive area of commercial forestry in the south. As the names suggest, though rather confusingly, their western extremity the Mynydd Ddu (Welsh for The Black Mountain) has some heather, but the Black Mountains across the Usk valley in the east are classic heather–bilberry–bracken hills and ridges cleft by deep bosky valleys. A belt of carboniferous limestone runs across the central southern section of the park, and, lying nearest to populous areas, is heavily used for caving.

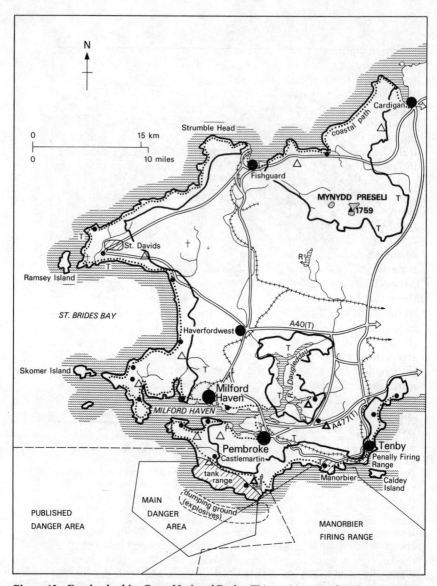

Figure 12 Pembrokeshire Coast National Park This maritime tip of south-west Wales is a wave-cut platform raised in successive stages from former sea levels. Its complex geology thus bears little relation to the generally bland interior land surface, but produces a spectacular and varied coastline of rocky outcrops, islands, massive cliffs and 'drowned' estuaries. The undulating coastal strip of gorse, heather and flower-rich grassland is narrow but packed with interest and served by a long-distance footpath, while the Daugleddau estuary at the head of Milford Haven is more sheltered and well wooded – in contrast to the oil port downstream. Although this is the only lowland park, it does have a more typical upland aspect in the Preseli hills, rolling heather and gorse Common Land crowned by rocky summits.

The upland resources that attract the visitor, the second-homer, the commuter and the retired, cater for an almost limitless range of recreational interests and attract the mining companies, the water authorities, the Central Electricity Generating Board (CEGB), the 'improving' farmer, the commercial forester, the grouse moor proprietor and the Ministry of Defence. Conflicts over land use are built into the landscape by nature itself, not least by letting loose on it the human species, and equipping us with rather less understanding of our impact on the natural world than the boastful title *Homo sapiens* might suggest.

We ask readers to study the maps, one of England and Wales showing relief (Fig. 2) and one for each park (Figs 3–12) to enable them to form a picture in their minds of the main characteristics of each park. The different landforms of the parks reflect the properties of the underlying rocks and the changes effected over geological time by rain, wind, ice and snow. Except for the North York Moors, the Palaeozoic rocks of the uplands are older and harder than those that form the lowlands and it is to their resilience, as much as to the earth movements that raised them in the first place, that the mountains and hills of the parks owe their existence. The glaciers of the last Ice Age, that melted a mere 10 000 years ago, created the steep-sided valleys and lakes, the hanging valleys and waterfalls and the small basins or cwms in the spectacular mountains of Wales and northern England. The dome-like masses of Dartmoor and the Cheviot Hills are granite or other coarse igneous rocks, the chemical and physical structures of which make them susceptible to surface weathering and result in a smooth, undulating terrain. They provide a complete contrast to the bare rocky crags of the highest mountains in the central Lake District and Snowdonia formed from hard volcanic rocks; these, in turn, are different from the lower hills in both these national parks which are formed of softer shales and slates. The spectacular gorges, the flat 'pavements' and the subterranean rivers of the southern or White Peak, parts of the Brecon Beacons and Yorkshire Dales are characteristic of limestone country. Sandstone country gives rise to the scarped mountains of the Brecon Beacons, the Millstone Grit edges of the High Peak, as well as the rolling plateaux of the North York Moors and Exmoor.

In the Peak, geology has created two contrasting worlds to form a single national park. To the north lie the heather moors and the cliffs or 'edges' to which the climbers flock from Manchester and South Yorkshire. South of the gritstone moors, the white walls of the small dairy farms of the White Peak criss-cross a green, almost treeless and undulating plateau broken only by the odd clump of hardwoods planted 100 years or so ago and by enchanting limestone dales. Their names are as evocative as their scenery – Dovedale, Monsal Dale, the Manifold Valley, and many others. The Pembrokeshire Coast, the smallest of the parks, is in a class by itself. A great diversity of rocks – faulted, folded and contorted – is exposed in the cliffs, while at their base the sea has worn away the softer materials to leave a much peninsulated coast. As John Barrett has put it, 'the complicated intricacies of larger headlands and little promontories constantly conjure views at unexpected angles across wide bays, sandy coves or deeply indented estuaries ... the cliff-tops support such a profusion of flowers that almost any square yard would win the rock garden prize at Chelsea'. On the other hand, the geology that creates such dramatic forms also gives rise to the acute conflicts over the extraction of rocks and minerals that are discussed in Chapter 13.

MOORLAND, SOILS AND VEGETATION

Oliver Rackham describes the British Isles in his latest book *The history of the countryside* as 'the world's great moorland countries', and moorland as 'with heath the most distinctively British kind of vegetation' that foreigners come to see. In the uplands the effects of a general deterioration in climate about 3000 BC, and the clearance of forest by early man contributed to the infertile, acidic soils and the heath vegetation that we see today. But Rackham argues that while there may be some justification for the notion of moorland as 'wet desert' in some areas 'this is not true of moorland as a whole, with its varied and complex plant and animal communities, especially in the smaller moorland areas'. For the moorlands have acquired a wildlife interest of their own. Once man moved down from the hilltops to the more productive environment of the lowlands, his use of the uplands for rough grazing allowed the soils to develop by natural processes in the main and the vegetation has continued to be self-generated despite some management by man.

It is in contrast to the soils and vegetation of the lowlands, which are largely man-made after centuries of cultivation, drainage and fertilization, that the semi-natural systems of the uplands take on a special significance. The uplands and coasts are the most extensive areas left in England and Wales in which to study natural processes and to find out what happens to wildlife in a relatively natural environment. The severe physical conditions of the uplands have limited man's scope for changing the natural environment. This is what makes the soils and vegetation of the mountains and moors of such interest to natural scientists and makes the national parks of special significance to everyone.

The peaty, acidic moorland soils have severe limitations when looked at simply as factors of agricultural production. They support grasslands of varying palatability to livestock, heathlands which merge into wetter moorlands and bogs, and woodlands or bracken on the hillsides. On the Agricultural Land Classification map of England and Wales, the uplands stand out as the areas where the lowest grades are concentrated. Land of these qualities is shown to be suitable only for low-output enterprises and is generally under grass or rough grazing. The natural handicaps of the uplands are the main justification for the subsidizing of both hill farming and afforestation. It is the permanent natural handicap imposed by the infertility of the land that qualifies the hills and uplands for livestock subsidies under the EEC Less Favoured Area (LFA) scheme. Its aims are to conserve the countryside and arrest depopulation by supporting those farmers who labour under handicaps. A substantial part, more than half, of the farms in the LFAs of England and Wales are in the national parks.

The semi-natural vegetation of the national parks has been divided into five categories by Geoffrey Sinclair: woodland (including planted forests); bracken and gorse; heather and bilberry moors; grasslands; and bogs. A rough calculation based on Sinclair's work shows that semi-natural vegetation covers more than half the area in only five of the parks – Northumberland (where apart from forestry plantations there is hardly any cultivated land), Snowdonia, Yorkshire Dales, the Lakes and Dartmoor. Heather moors epitomize the uplands for many people, but they are far from being the major component of the semi-natural vegetation. Even in the North York Moors, where it is indeed possible to walk for 40 miles on heather from one side of the park to the other, the heather core is in effect an elongated strip poking thin fingers between the valleys, up the sides of which bracken creeps relentlessly. Every national park has heather moorland, but grassland is the dominant vegetation in the Brecon Beacons (the southern slopes of which are covered in the most extensive area of purple moor-grass (*Molinia*) in England and Wales), the Lakes, the former royal forest of Exmoor, Snowdonia, the Dales and Northumberland. Dartmoor and Exmoor probably have no more heather, even taken together, than the North York Moors, which makes their heather moors a precious resource in South-West England.

WATER

Upland reservoirs and streams supply about a third of all the public water used in England and about 60% of that used in Wales,

Yorkshire, the north, the north-west and the south-west. The national parks with 137 reservoirs and a water surface of more than 18 square miles are, according to a study by Dr Mark Blacksell of Exeter University, major suppliers. The Peak District with 54 reservoirs serving the Midlands and Yorkshire, 32 of them built before 1900, seems to have hardly a valley left un-dammed. The water authorities own about a seventh of the park. But the Lake District's 17 reservoirs hold more water and cover a larger area, many of its large natural lakes having been turned into reservoirs. The City of Manchester ruthlessly dammed whole valleys and removed communities to create new reservoirs at Thirlmere and Haweswater, and then supplemented its supply from Ullswater and Windermere before handing over to regional water authorities in 1973. Kielder reservoir, on the boundary of the Northumberland National Park, was opened in 1979 and is said to be the largest man-made lake in Europe. Intended to serve the growing industries of North-East England, which were then on the verge of collapse, Kielder is now a successful though grotesquely expensive water sports and leisure centre. South Wales has been supplied from 14 reservoirs in the Brecon Beacons. Reservoirs have long been part of the Snowdonia scene, 10 of its 26 dating back to the nineteenth century.

The CEGB also controls seven lakes and reservoirs in Snowdonia to supply two pumped storage hydroelectric schemes, and one nuclear power station. The turbines at Dinorwic on Lake Llanberis have been hidden under a mountain of slate in what is said to be the largest man-made cavern in the world. An equally ambitious pumped storage scheme at Longdendale in the Peak has been deferred by the CEGB, although not abandoned, after five years of intense opposition by the Peak Board.

The exploitation of water and water power has generated many conflicts. The concentration of water authorities in larger units, technical advances in dam construction and demands for economies of scale have led to reservoirs continually increasing in size and depth, with corresponding increases in the environmental damage they inflict. The 19 reservoirs built since the national parks were designated contain more than half as much water as the 118 constructed before designation, and cover nearly half the area. They transform the landscape and the ecology and can severely disrupt public access, although they also offer opportunities for sport and recreation and, in some cases, have even enhanced the landscape.

The extravagant forecasts of demand on which the water authorities traditionally based their case for more and bigger reservoirs can no longer be sustained. Water consumption has been falling for 15 years and investment in modernizing water mains (now so leaky that they are more accurately described as underground irrigation systems) and water metering could reduce consumption still further. Present and planned resources are expected by Government to satisfy demand until the year 2000 and beyond.

The defeat of the proposals of British Nuclear Fuels and the North-West Water Authority to raise the levels of Wastwater and Ennerdale in the Lake District in 1983, and the earlier defeat of the Swincombe reservoir in Dartmoor, suggest that the danger is receding. In 1985 the Welsh Water Authority decided not to build a new reservoir in the Brecon Beacons when faced by opposition from the park authority. However, the year 2000 is not very far away, and the Lakes Board warned in 1985 that 'there is no guarantee that a scheme in a national park will not prove to be the cheapest available source of supply yet again'. There is equally no guarantee that the CEGB will not revive its pumped storage scheme at Longdendale in the Peak District.

The uplands suffer from the continuing increase in farm-based pollution: from fertilizers leached into water courses, sprays, silage and slurry run-off. Farmers are now the main source of water pollution in rural areas, but they are exempt from prosecution under some parts of the Control of Pollution Act 1974 so long as they observe a voluntary code of good agricultural practice. The number of water pollution 'incidents' caused by farmers and reported to the water authorities has increased from 61 in 1974 to 2828 in 1984 and 3510 in 1985, but only 159 farmers were prosecuted in 1985. The Secretary of State for the Environment has proposed setting up a powerless Water Pollution Inspectorate, with a very small staff, which will have to rely on 'guidance and persuasion', but the Government has rejected most of the proposals made by the Royal Commission on Environmental Pollution for controlling agricultural wastes.

Farm run-off and (until recently) pollution from domestic sewage have been among the many factors that have been causing the biological death of Llangorse Lake in the Brecon Beacons, whose wildlife interest is unique in Wales (for a fuller account see *National parks: conservation or cosmetics*. A. & M. MacEwen 1982, pp. 170–2). It has become a classic example of the inability of the national park authority, the local authorities, and the Nature Conservancy Council to prevent the gross over-use by sporting interests of a small but polluted lake of great beauty, which is an SSSI, a Grade I Nature Conservation site and of National Nature Reserve status. The Lakes Board is worried about the eutrophication (or enrichment) and acidification of the lakes from several sources, including farm run–off and domestic sewage (see page 211). It is looking to the North-West Water Authority to improve the Windermere sewage system, and hopes it will insert a plant to remove the phosphates that are a major cause of eutrophication from domestic sewage. But will a North-West Water Authority – public or private – that will have to find £2.5 billion to clean up the Mersey alone, readily choose to purify the water of Windermere?

The present government's plan to turn the ten regional water authorities in England and Wales into private profit-making companies has been postponed in the face of widespread public criticism. The official reason given was the technical difficulties involved in drafting the complex legislation. But there was also serious concern on the Tory back-benches over the political impact, in the run–up to a general election, of the sale of such a basic monopoly. It is the government's intention however, to proceed with privatisation 'as soon as practicable' and the threat will remain so long as a major political party undervalues public service, and seeks to turn even the water we drink into liquid gold to be exploited for private profit. The government takes pride in the fact that the water authorities have already been transformed into 'ten modern businesses', with substantial improvements in efficiency and performance as measured by staff and cost reductions. This may have made them a more attractive prospect for privatisation, but it has clearly taken priority over the basic task of raising the standards of water quality in our polluted rivers, lakes and coasts, or making good decades of underinvestment in the dilapidated water and sewage systems. Francis Jacobs, Professor of European Law at King's College London, has advised the CPRE that it would almost certainly be illegal under EEC law to place the control of water pollution in hands of private companies. But government pressure has also produced an alarming change in the attitude of the water authorities to the sale of land, which we discuss in Chapter 9.

THE UPLAND PROFILE

One key to understanding the natural life of the uplands and its changing relationship to land use and scenery is the 'upland profile' (Fig. 13). By this we mean the cross section from valley bottom to moor or fell and mountain top. The essential characteristics are everywhere the same – a transition from relatively fertile soils and diverse vegetation on the valley bottoms to poor soils and less stratified vegetation at the top. As one goes up the hillside the soil and vegetation change, providing habitats for different fauna and

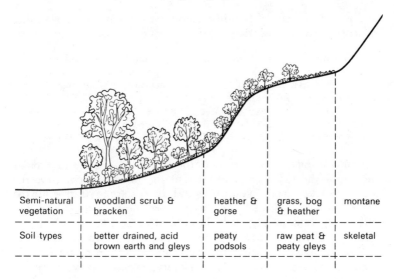

Semi-natural vegetation	woodland scrub & bracken		heather & gorse	grass, bog & heather	montane
Soil types	better drained, acid brown earth and gleys		peaty podsols	raw peat & peaty gleys	skeletal

Figure 13   The upland profile.

flora. But the line between them shifts up or down the hill in response to man's changing objectives and techniques of management, and local geological conditions and aspect produce an infinite variety in the characteristics of the profile.

The profile may begin at sea level, which it does in five of the parks, with coastlines that offer (in Pembrokeshire Coast, Exmoor and the North York Moors particularly) a remarkable combination of marine, coastal and terrestrial life with spectacular scenery. Ecologically, the wildlife of the coast is often as fragile as the mountain fauna and flora at the other end of the profile. Away from the coast, the traditional hill farm uses the full profile, as it climbs up the hill from the sheltered farmstead and enclosed fields (or 'inbye'), originally cleared from woodland, on the better soils of the valley and its lower slopes, through the enclosures of rough pasture on the upper slopes (variously known as allotments, intakes, new takes or ffridd), to the rough grazing, sometimes managed for grouse, in the open moor or fell. The enormous popular appeal of the national parks lies in the changing scene and the wealth of different environments as they unfold from level to level.

The range between the extremes astonishes foreign visitors and takes many British townspeople by surprise. Even in the benign climate of Exmoor with its modest altitudes and easy climbs, what Tim Burton (author of the best book on Exmoor) calls 'the high forbidding plateau' of the Chains is a world away from the teashops and putting greens of Lynmouth, only 1500 ft below and 4 miles distant. Between the valleys of the Exe and the Barle

> lies the boggy tableland which only the deer and stout-hearted walkers can cross. The lonely heights are lashed by frequent gales – even on a summer's day the wind stirs here. The rainfall is heavier than anywhere else on the moor; the land is sour, peaty, awash. There are no trees, only the coarse matted grass. Yet the desolation and the silence culminate in a sublimity that makes the Chains, for a very few, one of Exmoor's finest scenes. (*Exmoor*, by S. H. Burton 1970, p. 4)

Many of the natural features of the greatest scientific and popular interest – the caves and potholes of the limestone country, the seashore, lakes, dales, woodlands and rivers – are to be found at the lower or intermediate levels. So too are the towns, villages and interesting buildings. Stately homes, such as Chatsworth in the Peak, or villages, like Dunster in Exmoor with its castle and intact mediaeval layout, are often the most powerful tourist attractions in the park. The easier walks and much picturesque scenery, the major lines of communication and nearly all the facilities for servicing both the local people and the visitors – hotels, caravan and camp sites, hostels, restaurants, museums, information centres, car parks – are located on the lower ground. It is here that visitors come most sharply into conflict with farming as they make their way across the enclosed inbye land, or drive their cars up narrow lanes to the valley heads to reach the fells and moors above.

At every level of the upland profile, there are disturbing signs of the reduction in the extent and diversity of the semi-natural vegetation. A study of upland landscapes carried out for the Countryside Commission showed that for 100 years up to 1967 there was little change in the total area of semi-natural vegetation. Between 1967 and 1978 the rate of decrease went up elevenfold. Deterioration is the price being paid in all the national parks for whatever benefits are derived from modern commercial agricultural and forestry techniques, neglect (often caused by an acute shortage of labour on farms and estates), mismanagement and inappropriate or excessive use. The herb-rich meadows on the lower land are going fast, as the result of spraying, ploughing and draining. A survey of hay meadows carried out in the Yorkshire Dales National Park in 1981 showed that only 4.9% could be regarded as herb-rich and of these only a third (60 meadows) had the plant diversity to qualify for protection.

The semi-natural woodlands that are critically important elements in the natural life and scenery of the combes and valleys of the national parks are under serious threat. Every survey made of the woodlands confirms the statement of the Nature Conservancy Council in 1980 (and repeated in much the same terms in its strategy report of 1984) – that since 1947 some 30–50% of all ancient, semi-natural woodland in Great Britain has been lost, mainly to agriculture and commercial afforestation, and that the rest of it (outside reserves and other specially protected areas) will be eliminated by the year 2025 if the trends continue. Grazing of woodlands and shelter belts prevents natural regeneration. Former woodlands on well-drained hillsides once cleared for grazing are now being overrun by bracken and gorse as sheep replace cattle and shepherding declines. In the Brecon Beacons and Snowdonia about two-thirds of the woods are grazed, many of them heavily. The seriousness of the situation is highlighted in *Coed Cymru*, a report on broadleaved woodlands in Wales (1985): 'It seems likely that many broadleaved woodlands, perhaps the majority, will continue to deteriorate and may eventually disappear completely unless remedial action is taken soon'.

On the peaty moorland soils, heather can produce a continuing supply of nutritious food for sheep, deer and grouse by means of carefully controlled burning. In the North York Moors and parts of the High Peak, Northumberland and Snowdonia, the management of heather for grouse shooting has been a major factor in its conservation. Repeated burning, however, produces a heather monoculture which favours grouse but impoverishes the moorland flora and soil. Similarly, the burning of grassland and mixed vegetation communities, when skilfully carried out, can enhance their value for grazing. But when, as often happens, it is done ineptly (or intentionally) it can destroy the desired (or unwanted) species or even the peat itself. Investigations in the Peak District have shown that 8% of the moorlands is now bare ground or severely eroded as the result of intensifying environmental pressures. A major vegetation change which may have been critical in promoting erosion is the disappearance of bog moss (*Sphagnum*) over the past 200 years. This phenomenon has been associated with atmospheric pollution from the surrounding industrial areas in the nineteenth century. Recolonization is now hampered by a combination of grazing animals and acid rain.

The wet and relatively mild climate of the British uplands often makes it possible to grow coniferous species more rapidly than is possible in their native habitats. Firm scientific evidence about the long-term effects of afforestation on upland soils is lacking, because there is an alarming lack of information. The NCC does not accept the claim of the forestry interests that coniferous afforestation replaces a uniform habitat by a more diverse one. It takes the view that the most serious losses of plant communities and species are suffered when wet ground and upland peat bogs are drained and planted. Its report (1986) on *Nature conservation and afforestation* asserts that there is a 'basic incompatibility' between afforestation as currently practised and the conservation of heaths, grasslands and peatlands. More generally, in its strategy report (1984) the NCC challenges the forestry interests to demonstrate their support for conservation by making the necessary changes in silvicultural practice and foregoing maximization of growth

The most contentious conflicts of interest and changes in vegetation at the higher levels are produced by military training, reclamation of heather and grass moorland for agriculture and afforestation, overgrazing by sheep and excessive trampling of fragile soils and vegetation by human feet. All these problems arise from the suitability of the terrain for activities that can easily diminish the semi-natural vegetation and its associated wildlife. For, as the profile diagram illustrates, there is a relationship between the severity of physical conditions and resilience to use: the more severe the environmental conditions the less diverse is the vegetation and associated wildlife, and the greater their susceptibility to damage as a result of intensive use. Their acid soils, cold, wet wind and short growing season limit the capabilities of the uplands for self-renewal and repair.

This suggests that over a major part of the national parks the ecosystems are easily damaged, and if they are to be conserved, should be used or managed in ways that respect their ecological characteristics. Just how damaging the changes described here are to the landscape and natural life of the national parks and what the management options are will be discussed in Chapters 5 and 6. In the meantime we go on to follow the story of the human resource in the uplands and the parks.

Chapter Four

People and the paradox

THEN AND NOW

The national parks have a rich history running in a continuum from man's arrival after the Ice Age, through pre-history and historical times to the present day. The evidence of man's progress and conflicting interests is to be seen everywhere – in archaeological remains, field boundaries, the lines of communication, the settlement pattern, place names, ancient buildings, forts, castles and churches. The very remoteness of the uplands has preserved much of the evidence. But the past has more than historical or archaeological interest, for it survives into the present-day in language and dialect and in the habits of thought and independence of mind of the people, as well as in the landscape.

Evidence of life in the Neolithic, Bronze and Iron ages, from about 3000 BC to the Roman invasion, is to be found in all the parks, although it is thin on the ground in some. In Dartmoor the antiquities are so numerous and their setting so relatively unchanged that they still give an intelligible picture of early man in relation to his environment. The Romans also left their mark on the upland parks, mainly in the form of military forts and a linking road system. Hadrian's Wall, the central part of which is in the Northumberland National Park, is the most outstanding Roman monument in Britain.

From the early English period – the sixth to the eleventh centuries – the English uplands have inherited their pattern of villages and place-names, their systems of mixed and of hill farming and the dialects of today which derive from the language of the early Anglo-Saxon, Danish and Norse invaders. Few buildings survive, but in the long, narrow S-shaped fields still surviving in parts of the Dales, North York Moors and the Peak (notably at Chelmorton, Plate 10) one can see the pattern of the early English strip cultivations.

During this period Wales remained a Celtic kingdom and was affected very little by the English and Scandinavian invasions. The Welsh spoke their own language, maintained their own laws and customs and, from the sixth century, developed a literature of their own. In spite of the English conquest at the end of the thirteenth century, much of the old way of life continued in Wales until the Tudor succession. It was Tudor policy to assimilate Wales which, as the official guide to the Snowdonia National Park says, smoothed the way for ambitious Welshmen to proceed to the English Court, but was socially disastrous: '... the leaders of the native Welsh society became gradually anglicised in speech and habit and between them and the mass of ordinary Welshmen there opened a gulf leading to two separate social classes, different in language, in religion and in politics'.

It is against this background and the subsequent attempts to eradicate Welsh as a living language that the present-day nationalist movement, opposition to second-homers from England and the fierce resistance put up in Snowdonia to a national park board has to be understood. The Snowdonia park guide itself, while admitting that tourism makes a significant contribution to the local economy, makes it clear how offensive to many Welsh people is the indifference of visitors and second-homers to the culture and language of Wales. Snowdonia is located in Wales, but primarily it is a park for the English.

The economic development of the uplands was retarded by ferocious forest laws which operated to preserve extensive tracts of land as hunting grounds for the king and severely restricted the rights of local people to cultivate and use the land. But development was accelerated by the activities of the great monastic orders. The monasteries, such as Rievaulx Abbey in the North York Moors (Plate 8), established farms and sheep walks and grew rich on the wool trade, thereby coming into conflict with local people and depriving them of grazing, fishing and hunting rights over large tracts of wild country. However, it was the enclosures that finally settled the fate of many peasants and small farmers, whose survival depended upon the ability to graze animals or to take turf and wood for fuel from privately owned land over which they held rights of common.

Every part of the uplands was affected by the parliamentary enclosures of the eighteenth and nineteenth centuries. The results are still visible in mile upon mile of stone walls running up hill and down dale, giving their distinctive character to the fells and moors of northern England and in the earth and stone banks of the south-west. But the discerning traveller will notice that there are large areas in all the national park uplands that have not been enclosed. The enclosures were incomplete, mainly because the less fertile upland commons were less attractive to the enclosers, but also because it was not so easy, for reasons of land tenure and the independent attitudes of upland folk, to ride roughshod over the commoners. The consequence is that by far the greater part of the 600 000 ha or so of remaining commons are to be found in the uplands, where they are a major resource for livestock farming, wildlife and recreation.

It is now 44 years since the Scott report drew attention to the urgent need to restore commons management where it had collapsed and to provide legal rights of public access, and nearly 30 years since the Royal Commission on Common Land recommended legislation. The Commons Registration Act was passed in 1965, but a quarter of a century later the process of investigating claims and registering rights is still incomplete. Common rights continue to be extinguished, overgrazing and neglect are rife through non-management or mismanagement, and public access is insecure. There is now a real prospect of early legislation to halt these trends as a result of agreement between the interested parties in the Commons Forum in 1986 (see Ch. 8).

Often it is forgotten that the uplands have had mixed economies in the past, the evidence of which is still to be seen in old mines, drifts, mills and quarries, and the farmhouse spinning galleries of the Lake District. In the eighteenth century, water power, now almost totally neglected despite its potential for small-scale enterprises, attracted the northern textile manufacturers into the valleys and established a widespread spinning industry in the Lake District, the Yorkshire Dales and the Peak. When the centres of industrial activity shifted to the major coalfields a prolonged depression in agriculture set in. Throughout the era of cheap labour, cheap food and free trade, the upland economy became less and less self-sufficient, more marginal and increasingly dependent on a weakened hill farming industry. At the same time, with the coming of the railways, local cultures were exposed to the influence of nascent tourism and the influx of the new rich seeking second homes or sporting estates. The scene was being set for the recreational explosion, the transformation of communications, farming, forestry and industry in the mid-twentieth century – changes that have exposed the uplands to a more intimate relationship with the lowlands and the cities than ever before, and pose problems of an entirely novel kind for the physical, social and cultural environment.

THE CYCLE OF DECLINE

Looking back over history, one can see the uplands as marginal areas, continually changing in response to economic, technological, social and political trends. But in the past their remoteness and the harshness of the environment that depressed living standards also protected them from some of the worst excesses of human exploitation experienced more acutely in the lowlands. More recently, the national parks have been by and large the more economically handicapped parts of the least prosperous regions of England and Wales – the industrial north, Wales and the predominantly agricultural south-west. The parks rely even more heavily than do their counties on the primary industries, in which employment has been falling sharply. They have benefited little from the measures taken within the depressed regions to promote economic growth or provide infrastructure at key growth centres. These measures have been concentrated on the larger enterprises and on settlements in the lowland areas where communications and the availability of labour can more easily attract business enterprises. Furthermore, these measures have aggravated the social and economic problems of the remoter uplands by drawing people away from them. There are, of course, exceptions to this general picture. The Lake District as a whole is more prosperous than the towns of the Cumbrian coast which are in a state of acute decline.

In 1977 Joan Davidson and Professor Gerald Wibberley described the uplands as consisting of 'interlocking vicious circles of natural, economic and social difficulties which act and interact upon each other in ways which are hard to change with any degree of permanence'. They showed the hill farmer caught in a cycle of decline from which there is no escape, as harsh natural conditions, limited agricultural opportunities, uncertain markets, lack of alternative jobs, low incomes and limited social and cultural opportunities forced young people to leave, caused the deterioration of rural services and reinforced the downward spiral. The Wibberley cycle can be adapted to take into account the enormous public and private investments that have been made in the uplands since 1945, and the counter-trend of immigration. The conclusion we have reached is that the measures taken to intensify the exploitation of the resources of the uplands have tended on the whole to effect the same end as the cycle of decline described above – that is, to lead to depopulation and the deterioration of social and economic life. What we have had since 1945 is the cycle of intensification and decline (Fig. 14). The

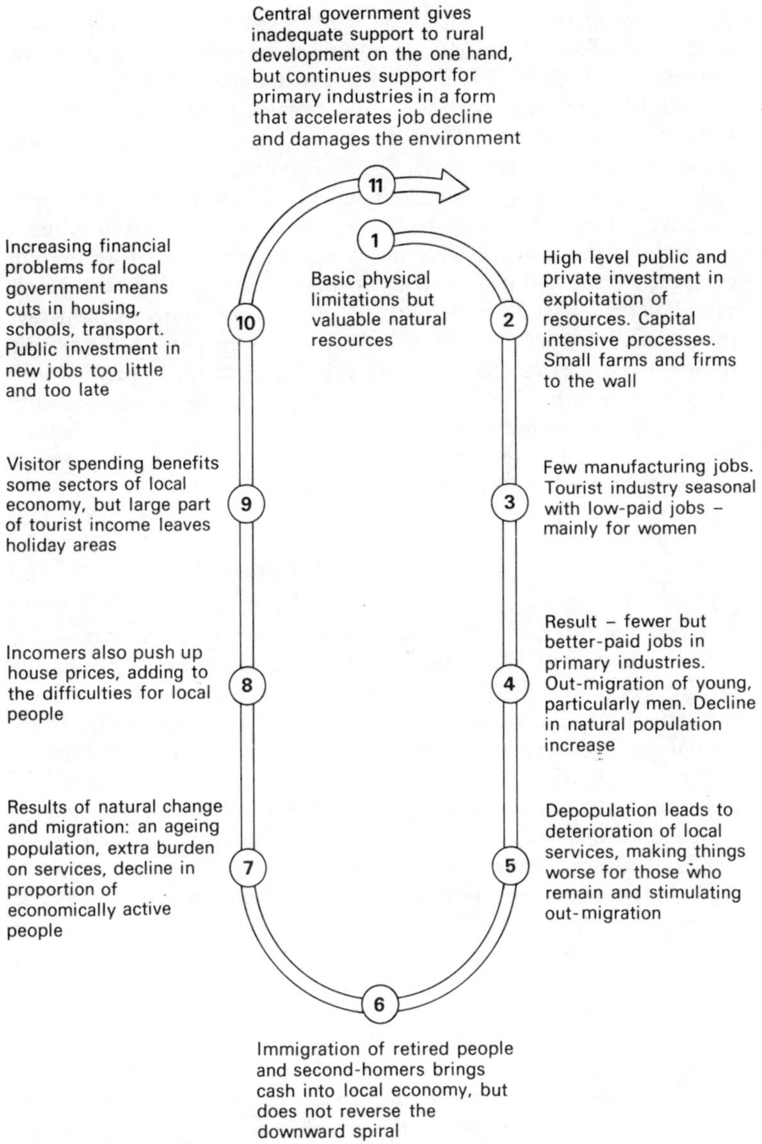

Central government gives inadequate support to rural development on the one hand, but continues support for primary industries in a form that accelerates job decline and damages the environment

Increasing financial problems for local government means cuts in housing, schools, transport. Public investment in new jobs too little and too late

Basic physical limitations but valuable natural resources

High level public and private investment in exploitation of resources. Capital intensive processes. Small farms and firms to the wall

Visitor spending benefits some sectors of local economy, but large part of tourist income leaves holiday areas

Few manufacturing jobs. Tourist industry seasonal with low-paid jobs – mainly for women

Incomers also push up house prices, adding to the difficulties for local people

Result – fewer but better-paid jobs in primary industries. Out-migration of young, particularly men. Decline in natural population increase

Results of natural change and migration: an ageing population, extra burden on services, decline in proportion of economically active people

Depopulation leads to deterioration of local services, making things worse for those who remain and stimulating out-migration

Immigration of retired people and second-homers brings cash into local economy, but does not reverse the downward spiral

Figure 14 Cycle of intensification and decline.

starting point of the cycle is the combination of severe physical limitations allied to the natural resources described in the previous chapter. The high level of public and private investment has not, on the whole, been made with the aim of breaking out of the cycle, but rather to satisfy urban needs and to achieve a medley of national and personal goals associated with resource exploitation.

The way in which highly capitalized enterprises lower unit costs but shed jobs can be illustrated by examining the trends in mineral extraction, the construction industry, farming and forestry. In Chapter 13 we will discuss the enormous changes that have taken place over the past 30 years in the control of the minerals industry, the scale of its operations and the techniques employed. The small mines and quarries that used to provide part-time jobs for hill farmers have gone. Farming policy, which is more closely analyzed in Chapter 14, provides a classic example of the process by which large-scale capital investment has contributed to the process of demographic, social and landscape decline.

THE UPLAND PARADOX

The cycle of intensification leads, in fact, to the upland paradox – that the measures taken to exploit the resources of the uplands have on the whole had the reverse of the desired effect, if the aim is to conserve both the human and the natural resources. The more capital has been invested, the more rapid has become the cycle of decline. Some of those who remain enjoy higher standards of life, but others are relentlessly squeezed. There are no longer enough people on the land to support the necessary services, or to maintain the landscape that attracts the visitor.

In this situation attention is now focused on alternative ways of creating new jobs. The best prospects are seen in forestry and tourism. But forestry is on the same capital-intensive technological treadmill as farming or quarrying. An analysis of afforestation figures by Peter Melchett has shown that as the Forestry Commission has extended its conifer plantations, so the number of people it employed has declined. Between 1955 and 1985 the area of land owned or controlled by the Commission and planted with conifers doubled; in the same period the number of people it employed declined by about 60%. On this basis forestry would have to expand very much faster than in the past even to keep pace with the loss of jobs through mechanization.

Tourism, the other widely canvassed source of jobs, is the business of making money out of satisfying the demand (which may have to be artificially stimulated if the business is to succeed) for recreation. Tourism is important to the economies of all the parks and is being actively promoted by the tourist boards – a development we will examine in Chapter 7. It is probably the major industry for the Pembrokeshire Coast, but accurate information is hard to come by. Insufficient is known about the 'multiplier effect' by which the income from tourism is passed on to others in the area, or about the reverse process by which a large part of the tourist income leaves the tourist areas to pay for the profits of externally based enterprises and the wages of seasonal employees from outside the area. Visitors certainly help to keep marginal village shops and services going, but they can also push up prices and stimulate the change from convenience to specialist shops. The jobs are seasonal, mainly for women and low paid.

Welcome as the extra income undoubtedly is to local people – and it makes the difference between survival and defeat on many hill farms – tourism cannot be the answer to the employment problems of the national parks. The season could be extended but there is no realistic prospect of a winter sports season. In moderation tourism may be benign; in excess it can have cataclysmic or corrupting effects on the physical, social and cultural environments. Whatever else tourism may do, it will not halt the emigration of young people, particularly young men, who will stay only if there is a prospect of reasonably paid employment the whole year round.

The results of the upland paradox are reflected in the changing population structure of the park counties. The natural increase of population through an excess of births over deaths has been declining in nearly all of them, in line with national trends. Moreover, the natural trend towards an ageing population has been exacerbated by the pattern of migration. The younger people of the working and child-bearing age groups have been forced to leave by lack of jobs or have been attracted by the opportunities of city life. They have been outnumbered by the inward flow of people of retirement and pre-retirement age, attracted by the remoteness, peace and beauty of the park counties. The emigration of the young masks the true level of unemployment and the lack of job opportunities, and the growth in towns and large villages masks the decline in the remoter upland valleys, some of which can no longer reproduce their population.

In common with most rural areas, the picture in the parks is one of decline in shopping and transport services, the closure of schools and an acute failure to meet local housing needs. External pressures on the housing market combined with inflation have taken house prices beyond the reach of local people, particularly the young, while the 'right to buy' is lowering the stock of local authority houses. A special report to the National Park Board in 1984 sums up the situation for the Peak: 'the park can be seen as a haven of prosperity and affluence and increasingly so over the past decade. Houses are larger and more expensive. There are fewer houses to rent, and such local authority rented housing as exists is being sold off even faster in the park than elsewhere'. The report goes on to say that the poorer members of village society are in danger 'of losing the option of following their traditional way of life'. The acute housing problem in Snowdonia, where one house in five is now a second home (40% in some areas) is one of the main reasons why the National Park Committee has repeatedly asked for powers to deal with social and economic problems. The Housing and Planning Act 1986 has made the situation worse by increasing the discount available to sitting tenants who buy council homes to 70%. It even gives the housing authorities powers to move tenants out of pleasant saleable houses into inferior houses that may not easily be sold.

Lacking, as they do, any powers to deal with the housing problem directly the national park authorities have clutched at straws in their attempts to ensure that there are some homes to rent or sell at low prices. Their attempts to use development control for this purpose could at best only have alleviated the problem, but they have been totally frustrated by central government. Both Labour and Tory Secretaries of State struck out of the Peak Structure Plan its policies for limiting new homes to local needs, on the specious argument that planning powers should not be used to achieve social aims. Between 1962 and 1976 the Lake District Board allowed 5000 houses to be built for a static population, only to find that the net effect was to increase the number of second and retirement homes. It then insisted on developers signing agreements under Section 52 of the Town and Country Planning Act 1972, restricting the occupation of new houses to people who live and work in the national park. By 1983 some 650 new dwellings were subject to these agreements, but the Secretary of State then deleted all references to restrictions on occupancies from the joint Structure Plan for Cumbria and the Lake District. He followed this up by upholding appeals by developers against the conditions and thereby destroyed the one policy the Board had to keep homes in the occupation of local people.

The effect of all this on local life and culture should not be ignored. Nobody who is familiar with the work of Arthur Raistrick could entertain for one moment the notion that nothing would be lost if the indigenous population of the Yorkshire Dales were to be submerged completely or displaced by incomers. But, although the uplands are repositories of local customs, traditions, crafts, skills and dialect, local culture is discussed in English policy documents, if at all, in terms of its value as a tourist attraction. Well-dressing ceremonies, town criers in eighteenth century costumes, villagers (or actors) dressed up to enact the Lorna Doone story, and morris dancing on the green may amuse visitors, but once local culture is valued in these terms it is being deprived of its true purpose – which is to transmit human experience.

In Wales the inward migration of English-speaking people with higher incomes and the impact of English-language television are seen by Welsh speakers as threatening a deathblow to a language and culture that have proved astonishingly resilient under centuries of English domination. Snowdonia is in the Welsh-speaking heartland and it has the only national park committee in Wales where the proceedings are in Welsh (with an English translation for non-Welsh-speaking members), all documents are printed in both languages and a knowledge of Welsh is essential for most officers. It is here that the cultural changes being wrought by tourism and by second- or retirement-homers are felt most deeply and the national park is perceived by some as a factor that undermines the Welsh position.

SCRATCHING THE SURFACE

It would be wrong to give the impression that nothing has been done at national or local levels to counteract the effects of the cycle we have described. But in setting up national parks as playgrounds for the nation, governments and parliaments treated them initially as a free resource, calling for negligible investment or maintenance. They saw no need for special policies to sustain a social and economic structure that would conserve the resources that nature and man had provided, because it was assumed, as we saw in Chapter 1, that traditional farming would do so. The water, electricity, quarrying and other interests were not expected to put much, if anything, back into the areas that they were exploiting. The small amount of help the national parks received in the past from the Department of Industry's assisted area programmes for tourism and job creation was heavily cut by the government's decisions in 1980 and 1984 to reduce the extent of development and special development areas, and to concentrate the money on a few heavily depressed industrial areas.

In recent years the main responsibility for rural development has been placed on the Development Commission and its agent the Council for Small Industries in Rural Areas (CoSIRA) and its Welsh counterparts. All the English national parks fall to a greater or lesser extent within the Commission's Rural Development Areas (RDAs), in the case of Northumberland, the Yorkshire Dales and Exmoor entirely so. The RDAs have generated many promising initiatives in the provision of 'craft homes', workshops, support for village shops, community transport, grant-aid for village halls, housing associations and the conversion of redundant buildings for tourism or workshops. But the influence of these programmes on the national parks and other upland areas, with their increasingly heavy emphasis on tourism, has matched neither the scale nor the character of their problems. The Mid-Wales Development Board takes in most of the Brecon Beacons and all but the northern parts of Snowdonia, but excludes the Pembrokeshire Coast. A scheme announced as far back as 1980 to promote small-scale employment projects in selected villages in mid-Wales has made little or no progress in the few villages selected in Snowdonia.

The Development Commission's initiatives are often linked to those of the Manpower Services Commission. The latter's 'community programmes', although primarily designed to camouflage the unemployment statistics by giving temporary jobs to the long-term unemployed, have been the largest source of new funds for footpath maintenance and similar work in the national parks (see Ch. 10). The usefulness of individual projects should not obscure how small the efforts are in relation to the scale of the problem. The Development Commission, to take one example close to our home, is investing £750 000 to create mini-workshops in five places in West Somerset, two of them in villages in the Exmoor National Park. It is hoped that all five workshops will create 100 new jobs. This hope should be set against the reality that 6000 people have been out of a job for more than a year in Somerset, quite apart from the much larger numbers who are registered as out of work or have not registered because they see no hope of a job. The programmes all assume that employment on the land will continue to fall, at a time when the land, if it had a voice, would be crying out for more people to be settled on it and to care for it. We return in Chapter 16 to the wider issue of integrated rural development, and the fears that many of the hopes raised by the rural development programmes may be cruelly disappointed.

The Upland Landscapes Study by Geoffrey Sinclair and others, of which a summary was published by the Countryside Commission in *The changing uplands* (1983), provided irrefutable evidence of the trends we have described. It persuaded the Commission to undertake a nationwide consultation with interested parties, and to publish a report – *A better future for the uplands* – in 1984. Although its policy recommendations were characteristically mild (no doubt to avoid giving offence to the Government) the kernel of its message was the need to integrate conservation with development and to reconcile the conflicts between competing government policies. This, in turn, led the Commission and the Government to include for the first time a heading 'Support for the local community' on the forms in which the national park authorities submitted their annual budgets and bids for National Park Supplementary Grant. The result was to expose in the starkest manner how little the park authorities have been able to support their local communities – mainly because it forms no part of their statutory responsibilities.

In their revised estimates for 1986–7 (see Fig. 18) most of the park authorities had to scrape the barrel to find items of expenditure that could be presented as 'support to the local community'. Some, by 'creative accountancy' or by transferring items from other headings, contrived remarkable increases in spending for the local community when compared to their original estimates made a year before. Northumberland's estimate was nil, the two Yorkshire parks each estimated £5000 and the others, with the exception of the Peak, ranged between £10000 and £49000 – mere drops in the local communities' buckets. The Peak expected to spend £158000. In addition it budgeted £81000 for support to public transport (which drew in an even larger sum from other sources) and provided staff and other facilities for the pioneering Integrated Rural Development Programme which we describe in Chapter 16.

The Peak Board has always shown a keen awareness of the need for a healthy local community. It was among the first to take advantage of the Development Commission's scheme for building small advance factories. It is assisting the formation of housing associations, with support from the Development Commission and the Housing Corporation, to buy run down property and let it at low rents. It uses its ranger service with its radio communications and cross-country vehicles to provide emergency assistance in case of fires, blizzards, floods, moorland rescue, animal disease and water pollution. In Chapter 8 we describe the bus and rail services and co-ordinated time-tables it promotes and publicizes, although its efforts may well be destroyed by the 1985 Transport Act and the abolition of the metropolitan counties. It has surveyed village shops and other services, and publishes information about them. This gives some idea of the effort that an enterprising and, let it be emphasized, autonomous authority has been able to make despite the lack of statutory powers to provide local services.

Until now, the national park authorities have only been able to scratch at the surface of social and economic problems. But, as we will see, there are good reasons for believing that they have a unique but undeveloped potential for co-ordinating, integrating and assisting local initiatives.

PART TWO

Conservation and enjoyment

Chapter Five

The meaning
of conservation

LANDSCAPE CHARACTER

Parliament gave the national park authorities the job of conserving
and enhancing the 'natural beauty' of the national parks, and it
defined that term to include nature in its broadest sense. We use the
term 'living landscape' to express the integration of all the factors –
geological, climatic, vegetational and human – involved in the
creation of the visual scene, and the word 'scenery' to describe the
appearance of the countryside. The interdependence of scenery and
nature and the wide overlap between areas of great scenic beauty and
areas of great wildlife value have long been acknowledged. The
Nature Conservancy Council said in 1976 that

> the natural scenic beauty and amenity of the countryside depends to a
> large extent upon the maintenance of physical features with their cover
> of soil, vegetation and animals, these in turn being an expression of
> patterns of land use evolved by man over the centuries ... National
> parks, chosen as the outstanding areas of natural beauty, necessarily
> express this relationship with the basic ecological features to an
> especially marked degree.

The NCC went on to say that national parks contain 'some of the
least disturbed and developed country in England and Wales and
encompass a substantial part of the country's wildlife resources'.
    In these words, the NCC has put its finger on the first essential
characteristic of the national parks – their appearance of wildness.
They are not wild, in the sense that they have never been used or
exploited by man, but within them natural features and processes
are dominant and it is still possible to experience the natural world
face-to-face with its qualities of wildness and renewal intact. It
is precisely the relative ascendancy of the natural world that

characterizes the uplands of these islands in general and can be experienced to an exceptional degree in the national parks of England and Wales. We call this characteristic semi-wildness, and it is from this that the beauty of the park landscapes is derived.

The uplands are also unique repositories of Earth and human history as is clear from the previous two chapters. Not only are their mountains and rocks visible and tactile links with the Earth's beginnings all those unimaginable aeons ago and a reminder of the natural forces of ice, water and wind that moulded them; the uplands also reveal the continuity of geological, vegetational and human history. For, as the last great geological event in the shaping of the landscape – the great Ice Age – was coming to an end around 9000 BC, the first Stone-age peoples are known to have reached the Pennines. They lived in caves and left little trace, but from around 5000 BC, onwards the patterns of successive human occupations are etched on upland hills and valleys. The various kinds of semi-natural vegetation that contribute so much to the scenic beauty of the parks are also of historic interest. Moorland has characterized the uplands since the end of the Iron Age, and there are many ancient woodlands in the national parks.

It is true that the countryside everywhere contains elements of previous landscapes. What distinguishes the historic landscapes of the uplands is the time-span and physical extent of the record of past use that they contain. Whereas in the lowlands much of the evidence of human activity since earliest times has disappeared under towns, tarmac, the bulldozer and the tractor, the evolution of upland landscapes can be more readily detected on the ground. This does not make upland landscapes more valuable than lowland landscapes, but rather reinforces the need for a broader interpretation of what is meant by landscape conservation for both. It is not enough to know about archaeological sites, important though these are. There has to be an understanding of the way landscape as a whole has changed and developed from earliest times to the present day. This adds another dimension to the concept of the living landscape. It calls, according to Mick Aston of Bristol University, for new insights on the part of the archaeological and associated disciplines if they are to be able to give sound advice to landowners and managers. It calls, too, for any conservation strategy to embrace not only the maintenance of historic buildings and conservation areas but also the care and maintenance of all our towns and villages.

To the landscape characteristics of semi-wildness and historic continuity we would add three more to which conservation is relevant. The uplands contain valuable natural resources; they offer open space and freedom that cannot be found elsewhere; and although people have left their mark, and have sometimes done so with a brutal disregard for natural systems and scenic beauty, their relationship with nature is, in contrast to much of the lowlands, relatively harmonious.

THREATS AND THEIR EFFECTS

However, this relative harmony is itself being continuously threatened and eroded. The description in Chapter 4 shows that the natural resources of the national parks are being managed for a variety of purposes that can be in the sharpest conflict with the conservation of landscape and nature. The conclusion we reached in our original book that 'incremental changes induced by man's activities are threatening the living landscapes of the national parks' was also reached in the wider context of the Countryside Commission's Upland Landscape Study, the full report of which was edited by Geoffrey Sinclair in 1983. It concluded that, taken together, the decrease in semi-natural vegetation and woodland, increase in the area under crops, grass and conifer plantations, enlargement of fields, replacement of walls, banks and hedges by wire-fencing and the neglect of old farm buildings, constituted 'significant, accelerating and generally deleterious change in the upland landscape, producing uniformity where previously there was diversity'. The report went on to say that if present trends continue the existing upland landscape is in jeopardy.

In scenic terms the effect of these changes is profound. The essential character of the traditional landscape is clear from the description of the upland profile in our third chapter. What strikes the eye is the contrast between the intimacy of the green fields, farmsteads, villages, wooded valleys and waterways of the lower land and the openness, conspicuous colour and texture of the heather moors above, or the soft tones of grass moorlands as the case may be. There are infinite variations on the scene depending on whether or not it embraces the magic ingredients of lake, mountains or coast; on the spatial relationship between inbye and moorland; on how well defined is the moorland 'edge' between the two, and on the subtle hues of the vegetation that change with the seasons. But in addition to their beauty the numerous upland landscapes each have a consistent character that is typical of a particular tract of countryside. One still knows from the nature of the vegetation, building and walling materials, trees and hedgerows, as well as from the topography, whether one is in Swaledale in Yorkshire, Porlock Vale in Exmoor, a valley in the Brecon Beacons, or in the Dark or the White Peak.

It is this combination of consistency and diversity that is at risk. The improvement of rough grazing, whether by treating the traditional enclosures or taking in new moorland, means that green fields and crops stretch from valley bottoms far up the hillsides and even over the tops, at best breaking the continuity of the moorland vegetation, at worst eliminating it as a crucial element in the upland scene. The wire fence is not only ugly in itself and inhibits walkers, its universality diminishes the indigenous character of every location in which it is used. New buildings tend to make farmsteads in one valley look like those in another and both to look like lowland farms. As for afforestation, no-one has described the visual effects of its worst excesses better than Nan Fairbrother in *New lives, new landscapes*:

> crude and unnatural patterns of straight lines and sharp angles on flowing hills, block planting of geometric patches of forest on bare hillsides, chequer-board arrangements of different species, straight rows of trees ruled up and down slopes and extraction roads like wounds slashed across the hills ... blanket planting in small scale scenery smothering the landscape in a uniform dark fleece of trees.

In the lowlands, according to the Countryside Commision's second report on Agricultural Landscapes (1984), it is increasingly unusual to find landscapes which have a consistent character typical of any area. This is not yet the case in the uplands but the trends give cause for concern for the landscapes of the national parks.

There is concern as well over the conservation of nature. The NCC, in defining its new strategy in its report *Nature conservation in Great Britain* (1984), did not attempt to conceal the fact that since 1945 the failures of conservation had been 'even more striking' than its successes. It published what it called 'a stark assessment of the dwindling heritage of nature' by cataloguing the 'dramatic' losses in habitats of every type in recent years – only 3% either of lowland herb-rich meadows or of limestone pavements in northern England left undamaged; 71–77% of chalk downland lost between 1934 and 1972; 46% of ancient broadleaved woodlands in 23 counties of England and Wales lost between 1933 and 1983; 30% of upland grasslands, heaths and blanket bogs lost or significantly damaged between 1950 and 1980 through coniferous afforestation, hill land 'improvement' or reclamation, burning and overgrazing; and damage that is hard to measure to lakes and rivers by pollution, water abstraction, land drainage and acidification.

It was hardly surprising, in these circumstances, that the NCC concluded that 'economic forces are increasingly pressing the managers of land into practices inimical to nature conservation'. It went on to say that although compromise was essential to a democratic society 'in nature conservation the great compromise has been made already through the surrender of so much of our heritage of nature to development for the national good'. The time had come, the NCC added, for other interests to pay regard to the needs of nature conservation because 'in some parts of Britain there is little if anything to compromise about'.

The Wildlife and Countryside Act of 1981 (see Chs 6 & 12) has slowed down the rate of damage to SSSIs since the NCC's figures were first published, and the rate at which moorland has been reclaimed in national parks has also been slowed down. But the NCC (which is committed to the government's 'voluntary approach' to conservation) has made it abundantly plain that the process of degradation is far from being halted. Since two glaring loopholes in the Act (of which some unscrupulous farmers had not hesitated to take advantage) were closed in 1985 the NCC can stop any potentially damaging operation in an SSSI for three months, and, if the government will make the necessary order, for 12 months. But farmers or landowners are under no obligation to enter into the management agreements that the NCC is obliged by the Act to offer to them. Once the notice has expired they are free to do as they please, unless the NCC is prepared to find the money from its limited capital resources to buy the land compulsorily. The NCC itself still emphasizes that 'SSSI status is no guarantee of adequate protection'. Moreover, the National Nature Reserves (which do enjoy a high degree of protection) constitute well under 1% of the land areas of the national parks. Even complete protection for SSSIs would leave most of the national parks at risk, protected only by voluntary arrangements. The conservation of the totality of the resources of the national parks is still a long way from realization.

However, as the NCC itself explains in *Nature conservation in Great Britain*, the NCC's sphere of responsibility was restricted by lack of powers and resources from its inception in 1949, and still is. Far from being able to translate into reality 'the broad and integrated concept of conservation' which was 'the great vision' of the Dower and Huxley reports of 1945 and 1947, the NCC was forced to concentrate on what it calls the protection and management of wild flora, fauna and physical features for 'cultural' purposes only. The economic or even environmental consequences were not its concern. The conservation of the fertility of the soil, surely one of the most fundamental aspects of resource conservation for the future of mankind, is the responsibility of the Ministry of Agriculture which cut its grant to the Soil Survey by 50% in 1985 and was only restrained by public protest from stopping it entirely. The Ministry of Agriculture, Fisheries and Food (MAFF) has never accepted responsibility for researching the long-term consequences of short-term profitability and productivity.

CONSERVATION AND RESOURCE USE

This brings us to the World Conservation Strategy (WCS), which was launched in 1980 by the International Union for Conservation of Nature (IUCN), and the wider challenge it has opened up. It showed that over-exploitation of resources, loss of genetic diversity and damage to ecological processes and life-support systems have dangerously reduced the planet's capacity to support people in both developed and developing countries. It sought a new partnership between conservation and development to meet human needs now without jeopardizing the future, and called upon each country to prepare a national conservation strategy tailored to its own particular problems and conditions to achieve this. In Britain the lead was taken, not by government, but by a consortium consisting of the World Wildlife Fund, Royal Society of Arts, Council for Environmental Conservation, the two Countryside Commissions and the NCC. Work started in 1981 and the report, *The Conservation and development programme for the UK*, was published in 1983. It consists of seven separate and detailed reports on the industrial, urban, rural and marine aspects of the integration of conservation and development, and on its international, educational and ethical implications.

The rural report by Timothy O'Riordan, the professor of environmental studies at the University of East Anglia, is the one most relevant to the subject matter of this book. It concluded that there is a serious absence of information about what is happening to the ecological fabric of the UK and that there can certainly be no sweeping assumption that the ecologically sustainable use of rural resources is taking place. The evidence in the report is that certain resource use practices, including agricultural improvements, afforestation, quarrying and major construction projects, are incompatible with the conservation of nature and landscape. While seen as a step in the right direction, the Wildlife and Countryside Act is strongly criticized because of its inadequacies in protecting the wider countryside and the danger that it will make the sustainable use of rural resources a purchasable commodity, with all the overtones of legalized greed.

The weighty (in every sense) *Conservation and development programme for the UK* in which the problems of integrating conservation and development were highlighted, contrasts sharply with the government's official response to the WCS published in May 1986. This slim document, entitled *Conservation and development: the British approach*, was presented at – and no doubt prepared for – the international conference on implementing the WCS held in Ottowa at the end of the same month. It cannot be regarded as a response to the WCS because it is in no sense the strategic programme that the WCS called for. It was written in the Department of the Environment without consulting either of the agencies appointed by Parliament to advise the Government on conservation. It does not draw on the earlier *Conservation and development programme for the UK* in which these agencies and other bodies had set out evidence and recommendations that were in sharp conflict with many aspects of government thinking and policy.

The British approach is a glossy public relations brochure with a portrait of Mrs Thatcher crowned with what appears to be a halo as its frontispiece. It oozes complacency and congratulates the government on its splendid performance, while evading all the tricky issues. To claim, as *The British approach* does, that 'the spirit of the World Conservation Strategy is manifest in the Wildlife and Countryside Acts' is manifest nonsense. As this book will show, even in the national parks (which the government claims to be 'probably the single most effective tool for conservation') it has not been possible to achieve more than a very moderate degree of integration of conservation with social and economic development. The economic forces, government policies and financial incentives have been, and still are, pulling too strongly the other way.

The national parks cannot, however, be isolated from the wider national environment of which they form part. Their survival depends on sound policies for the integration of conservation and development, in accordance with WCS principles, being adopted throughout the United Kingdom. It follows that the first statutory purpose of the national park authorities – the conservation of 'natural beauty' – does not go nearly far enough. It should be the duty of the NPAs to conserve natural resources, as well as nature and all aspects of landscape. In particular they should have the power to ensure that non-renewable resources such as rocks and minerals (and renewable resources such as water) are not squandered by wasteful use and pollution or by uses for trivial or non-essential purposes.

Essentially therefore, conservation is an attitude of mind that runs counter to the prevailing ideology of consumerism. It implies a commitment on the part of public and private owners and users of land that goes far beyond cosmetic gestures. To husband energy and materials while enhancing natural processes and landscape must touch some pockets too, for at the most fundamental level it changes the conventional wisdom that never-ending growth and increasing material wealth are intrinsically desirable and attainable goals.

POSSIBLE OPTIONS FOR
THE FUTURE

A shift from the conservation of scenery (and some islands of nature) to the conservation of nature, natural resources, the living landscape and the built heritage opens up a range of options for management or non-management for upland areas like the national parks. What is common to them all is that although they may or may not involve changes in scenery over time, they are all designed to conserve or enhance (perhaps we should say enrich) the living and the man-made landscape. One option is of course traditional hill farming. It is practised under severe natural handicaps and has evolved as a way of rearing store sheep and cattle from a reservoir of hardy breeding stocks, with economy of resources, for finishing in the lowlands. The stocking levels on the unimproved land on the hillsides and tops is dictated partly by the grazing capacity of this land and partly by the ability of the small areas of the more resilient bottom land to produce hay, silage and other crops for winter feed. If practised with a minimum of well-controlled grass or heather burning, and attentive shepherding (in contrast to the present trend towards overburning and little or no shepherding) hill farming maintains some of the diversity of vegetation and wildlife. As a low input farming system it is suitable to the uplands where soil and other conditions preclude a maximum response from costly inputs such as fuel, phosphate and nitrogen. When the world comes to terms with the need to make intelligent use of one of its most plentiful resources – human labour – and to minimize the use of energy and other finite resources, it will perhaps recognize the advantages of agricultural systems such as hill farming that can combine conservation with food production.

There could, however, be some place in the national park landscapes for non-management. Particularly in the British Isles, where man's interference has been so widespread, there is a case at suitable (and very carefully selected) places for letting nature take its course and allowing the natural vegetation of moor and woodland to develop without interference until it reaches its climax. Non-management of heather moorland would change the scenery as the heather grew high and woody, and scrub appeared. It might impair access and appear unsightly to those who like the managed land-scape. Often untidiness is equated with mismanagement in the minds of those who regard all scrub clearance as an act of virtue. But in the right place a regime of non-management could, we suggest, be consistent with sustaining the semi-wild landscapes in the parks. Moorland can be viewed also as a degraded landscape, characterized by nutrient-poor acidic soils, or even as Britain's first, man-made, ecological disaster. Geoffrey Dimbleby has argued that the long-term aim should be to restore the fertility of the degraded moorland soils, and this offers another management option. Doubts about the long-term effects of continuously taking crops of conifers off moorland soils were voiced many years earlier by W. H. Pearsall. He suggested that long-term forestry policy should be directed towards the restoration of the natural fertility of moorland soils, by a combination of fertilization and the gradual introduction of deciduous hardwood species that would enrich rather than deplete the soil. Such a policy is ruled out today by the financial encourage-ment given to quick returns from coniferous afforestation.

Yet another possibility is suggested by Nan Fairbrother's idea of creating a 'man-made wild'. In some of the less exposed parts of the parks there may be scope for increasing the diversity (and hence the resilience) of the vegetation to create a landscape designed to take recreational pressure. It would be new 'scenery' but also a usable semi-wild landscape, designed with a full understanding of the ecosystem where eventually natural processes would be allowed to operate. A long-established example of a man-made landscape of this kind is to be found at Tarn Hows, said to be the most popular beauty spot in the Lake District. The Tarn itself, a small lake of only 13 ha in a 20 ha site, was created by a dam in 1865. The plantations on the lake shore and the island, which are a major feature, date from the same time and are coniferous – Scots pine, larch and fir. It is a living demonstration of the fact that people, if tourist figures are anything to go by, can sometimes do as well as nature in creating beautiful places.

Even to suggest the exploration of some of these options could stir up controversy. But they are no more than part of a range of possibilities, each of which could have a role to play in the strategy of conservation. The fact that the uplands of Britain have the special characteristics that we associate with semi-wildness, and therefore need appropriate conservation measures, does not mean that they are more important than other parts of the country. It means that they are different and should be conserved for their specific qualities.

Chapter Six

Conservation in practice

FROM 'PERSUASION' TO 'PAY THROUGH THE NOSE'

The park authorities have been faced from the outset by a continuing decline in the number of people working on the land, and
an acceleration in the rate of environmental losses caused largely by
agricultural, forestry and other policies that they were unable to
control. Their job, until now, has been to try to stop the rot, and
to slow down the pace of damage to the environment caused in
part by social and economic change. Despite a range of conservation programmes and some substantial achievements since 1974
none of the authorities would claim in 1986 to have brought the
situation fully under control. It was hardly surprising, therefore,
that our study of the first national park plans raised the question in
our minds whether the park authorities were not attempting the
impossible. 'They rely almost entirely', we wrote, 'on persuasion,
negotiation, influence, public relations, encouragement and hope
to protect some of the finest landscapes in England and Wales
against a formidable battery of threats and pressures which are
largely financed by public funds and promoted by public agencies'.

The main hope lay in radical changes in agricultural and forestry
policies, but the Peak was almost alone at that time in identifying
them as the root cause of its problems. The Tory government, like
the Labour government before it, set its face, until 1984, against any
changes in the financial incentives it was offering to farmers and
foresters. It rejected controls as well, and pinned its faith entirely on
the voluntary or 'persuasion approach' to resolve the conflicts
generated by its policies. The Wildlife and Countryside Act of 1981
created, as will be seen in Chapter 12, a statutory framework for a

one-sided system that was, indeed, almost entirely voluntary for landowners and farmers but compelled the conservation authorities to 'pay through the nose' to conserve threatened sites or landscapes.

When we resurveyed the scene in 1986 the political and economic framework that had seemed to be set in concrete ten years earlier was clearly flexing under the pressures of the conservationists, the bankruptcy of the Common Agricultural Policy, the weakening grip of the farming lobby on the Ministry of Agriculture and the Government's determination to cut agricultural subsidies and present a greener image to the electorate. But the old destructive forces were still at work and such changes as had been made only affected the situation at the margins. The situation was pregnant with fear, uncertainty and hope.

In this climate the park authorities are feeling their way, almost by trial and error, towards a more coherent and effective set of conservation policies and programmes. But real shifts in direction are discernible. The authorities are asking more and more insistently for changes in the farming and forestry support systems that would help them to promote a more integrated approach to land management. There is something approaching unanimity in the emphasis laid on the need to buy land and to have the power to make a Landscape Conservation Order when other solutions fail. There is also a growing emphasis on the role of experiments and demonstration projects to show what can be achieved in conservation terms. Those parks with large areas of commercial forest, or large areas of technically plantable land, want afforestation to be brought under planning control, and the Lake District Board wants replanting of existing forests to be controlled in the same way. The process by which policies are evolving is, perhaps inevitably, very haphazard as the authorities react to new threats or respond to legislation or policy decisions forced on them by government. And they are hindered by the Government's meanness and lack of commitment, the immense paperwork generated by having to justify everything they do, and the failure of government and its agencies to do the things that only they can do in good time; listing buildings, scheduling ancient monuments or designating limestone pavements to name but three.

Nevertheless, the park authorities are in a stronger position than in 1974 to develop effective conservation policies, and to make them stick. There is a groundswell of public opinion in support of conservation measures. Some parts of the farming community have begun to adopt a more sympathetic attitude to nature and landscape, and the farming lobby has begun to see conservation or alternative farming techniques as possible sources of income. The need to respond to farm grant notifications since 1980 has brought farmers and the park authorities much closer together. Farm grant notifications, the statutory duty imposed by the Wildlife and Countryside Act to prepare maps of moor and heath, and the need to support bids for national park grants with 'functional strategies' have all forced the park authorities to undertake more surveys, to get to know their parks much better and to develop firmer conservation policies.

THE LIVING LANDSCAPE

Two of the fields in which the park authorities have found it necessary to extend their knowledge are nature conservation and landscape character. Without more information and more understanding of the distinctive qualities of the different parts of a park, it was proving difficult for policies and decisions on land management to be sensitive to the living landscape. The NCC was unable in 1986 to give us figures for the extent of SSSIs and National Nature Reserves in England, but 20.5% of the land area of the three national parks in Wales were designated sites. Park-wide surveys to identify the full range of habitats have been carried out, or are planned, in all the parks. They are being undertaken by the park authorities, the NCC, the county trusts for nature conservation and other bodies, using remote sensing, infra-red photography and other techniques. But in the Lake District, with its exceptionally rich diversity of habitats, basic surveys of this kind cover no more than two-thirds of the park area. For the major part of the Yorkshire Dales there is as yet no comparative study of wildlife and scientific interest although, as in other parks, the sites of national and international importance have been described in detail in the NCC's *A nature conservation review* 1977. In some parks surveys to evaluate individual sites have been completed, in particular for habitats under pressure such as hay meadows and woodlands. The concern for nature conservation over the whole park, and not just in nature reserves and SSSIs, is common to all park authorities. In the Lake District designated sites cover only 13% of the park area, and the ecological surveys carried out since 1974 have established how extensive are the valuable habitats outside them.

The art of landscape appraisal is not as well established as are the more quantifiable techniques for assessing natural habitats and this has left the park authorities on their own in this difficult field. Progress has been made in landscape understanding, but there is a lack of consensus about how landscapes should be interpreted and priorities defined. In their desire to take nature conservation more seriously, the national park authorities have taken onto their staffs more ecologists and naturalists, who tend to focus on the scientifically classifiable and measurable. In policy documents and statements there is often a reluctance to be specific about exactly what it is in each landscape that makes it so highly-prized, which is in contrast to the relative ease with which the park authorities address more specific and easily handled topics, such as agriculture, forestry, nature conservation and recreation. There has been, in particular, a diffidence about landscape beauty. In none of the park plans or other documents is there anything to fire the imagination of the reader with the visual magic of the landscapes that draw people to the national parks.

Most of the initial park plans settled for broad statements about conserving the 'traditional character' of the park. Some went on to identify broad landscape zones and related equally broad policies directly to them. There are now signs of an increasingly positive attitude to the visual aspects of landscape conservation and several of the revised plans contain descriptions of the park landscapes. Some authorities are finding it necessary to have a detailed analysis of landscape character against which to assess agricultural, afforestation and other development proposals. The revised park plan for the Yorkshire Dales, for example, identifies the different landscape characteristics of each of the zones into which nature, with some help from man, has divided the park. This provides the basis for afforestation policies and takes the place of an abortive afforestation map on which no consensus could be reached with the landowning and forestry interests.

There are obvious overlaps and conflicts between these landscape 'character maps' and the 'threat maps' and related policies that provide the other approach to landscape conservation policies. What we call the 'threat maps' were an attempt to resolve conflicts over afforestation and moorland reclamation, in the absence of any powers to control these developments. In essence they identify those bits of threatened areas that it was thought most important to conserve. First, from 1962 onwards, came the afforestation maps of several parks, which merely recorded the highest measure of agreement that could be reached between the Forestry Commission, the park authorities and the timber growing interests on presumptions for or against the afforestation of 'bare ground'. Next came Exmoor's map of moorland that was 'critical to amenity', which was born out of the conflict over moorland ploughing. Negotiated in 1969 between the park committees of that time and the National Farmers' Union and the Country Landowners' Association, it was replaced in 1981, as we will see in Chapter 11, by two maps agreed between the same parties. These were followed by a map that all national park authorities have had to publish, under Section 43 of the 1981 Wildlife and Countryside Act, of those areas of moor and heath that they think it is 'particularly important to conserve'. Section 3 of the amending Act of 1985 extended these maps to include 'mountain, woodland, down, cliff or foreshore' (that is, to all 'open country') and required the Countryside Commission to provide guidance on the criteria to be adopted in preparing them.

The Section 43 maps were typical of the legislative dog's dinner served up by the Parliamentary cooks. The authorities were not required to have any policies for the areas of moor and heath. Nobody knew why they had to be prepared in every park, for moorland is far less significant and less vulnerable to change in some parks than it is in Exmoor, Dartmoor and the North York Moors. No criteria were laid down, so some parks produced moorland maps based mainly on aesthetic criteria while others gave equal weight to a range of conservation and recreation factors. The Section 3 maps embracing all 'open country' should be based on consistent criteria suggested by the Commission, but they will omit altogether some precious and vulnerable habitats such as wetlands and hay meadows that fall outside the statutory definition of 'open country'. The draft guidelines circulated to national park authorities by the Countryside Commission in February 1986 urge the holistic approach: 'the concern is not so much with the details of topography, historical or archaeological features and natural habitats or individual components of the landscape, but with the way in which these elements come together to make up the whole scene'. Yet the Section 3 maps omit not only certain habitats but the entire farmed landscape, which interlocks with the 'open country' to which the maps are confined.

Despite these criticisms the overall effect of the Section 43 maps was to strengthen the policies for conserving the moorland. The Countryside Commission's guidelines for Section 3 maps are clearly intended to encourage the park authorities to look at the whole landscape when they are considering which parts of 'open country' should be designated, and to devise appropriate conservation policies for them. The maps could be extended to include additional features, and provide the basis for a statutory notification system without which the power to make Landscape Conservation Orders will not be of great value. Section 3 maps, in spite of their shortcomings, should prove to be useful additions to the park authorities' defences.

The park authorities' increasing knowledge and resolve have been accompanied by a major expansion in practical conservation programmes. The Lake District sees conservation projects and plans for individual farms as critical to the maintenance of the network of habitats in its park. The Peak District's study of moorland erosion and experiments in techniques for controlling it are not untypical of the new, more scientific approach. The North York Moors have engaged in a series of moorland and other programmes that combine experimentation with practical restorative work. Nearly every national park authority has schemes for grant-aiding woodland management, with the main emphasis on neglected woodlands of high wildlife value. The Yorkshire Dales and Lake District are giving priority to the restoration of stone walls and other man-made features of the landscape. Other authorities have special projects for particular habitats that are peculiar to their area, such as hay meadows, lakes, estuaries, bogs or wetlands. They rely on offers of grant-aid, sometimes farm plans, an input of expert skills and co-operation from increasingly interested farmers or landowners. A start has been made, and the potential for further progress is immense. However, the more park authorities become involved in practical conservation on the ground, the more they are moving into area-based management plans and projects. These provide the basis for integrating conservation with recreation and with measures to promote local prosperity, and are discussed in Chapter 16 in the context of integrating conservation with development.

BUILT AND LANDSCAPE HISTORY

Care of the built environment has been the cinderella of conservation in the national parks. When the Countryside Commission drew the attention of the government in 1985 to the potential for 'very substantial additional expenditure' in this field it was, we believe, the first time that it had done so. Development control has been seen as the main means of protecting individual buildings, although all it can do is to prevent the demolition or alteration of listed buildings. Most park authorities, though not all, have grant-aided the repair of listed buildings on a very modest scale, illustrated by the Lake District's expenditure of £5000 on historic building grants. Substantial numbers of conservation areas have been designated in towns and villages, but many more remain to be designated and the funds allocated for their enhancement have in most cases been negligible in proportion to the need. Most park authorities expect the 7600 listed buildings in the 10 national parks to be doubled by mid-1987, which will mean an increased demand for grants to maintain them and for staff to deal with applications to alter or demolish them. Any concentration of listed buildings also gives rise to the need for the comprehensive treatment of the area in which they stand. A few park authorities would like more town schemes, by which they can contribute to the costs of repairs of groups of unlisted buildings in conservation areas. Several promote village improvement schemes, in which parish councils and other local bodies can be helped to carry out small projects to enhance the appearance of any village and increase its attractiveness to visitors.

In this field, as in so many others, the Peak Board is in a class by itself. It budgeted nearly £250 000, or 6.5% of its total expenditure, for conserving the built environment in the bid for grant it submitted for 1986–7, although even in the Peak the amount asked for was inadequate to meet the demand. Elsewhere the sums budgeted for are pitifully small in relation to the scale of the problems. When the park authorities have to look for cuts, the built environment is usually one of the first items to suffer. The 1986–7 grant settlement forced both the Peak and the North York Moors to cut this element in their budgets severely, although the 1987–8 settlement included a modest increase for this purpose in all parks.

More is now known about the archaeological resources and historic landscapes of the parks and they are being given greater prominence in conservation policy than was the case ten years ago when the first park plans were prepared. But, as the park authorities are aware, their protection is still not getting the expert attention and investment priority that is needed. Nor is it helped much by recent legislation. The 1979 Ancient Monuments and Archaeological Areas Act does strengthen the protection afforded to scheduled monuments and provides a new basis for management agreements. Unfortunately, in most of the parks, only a small part of their archaeological wealth is scheduled. In Dartmoor for example, only some 430 out of 6000 sites identified on the Devon Sites and Monuments Register are scheduled. The progress being made by English Heritage and its Welsh equivalent, CADW (meaning 'Protect') – since 1984 the central bodies concerned – is extremely slow. Dartmoor is the only park authority to employ a full-time archaeologist on its staff, although the Peak District and Snowdonia have access to part-time professionals. Elsewhere the authorities rely on the county council's archaeologists.

The archaeological work done in the parks, particularly in Dartmoor, the Lake District, Snowdonia and the Yorkshire Dales, has, however, shifted the focus of attention away from individual monuments and sites and towards the concept of whole archaeological

landscapes as the basis for protection, conservation and interpretation. Several authorities have identified historic landscapes, or will
soon do so, but this has no statutory significance and the intention is
to secure protection by means of agreements with landowners. The
Peak Board is negotiating a management agreement to protect a
mediaeval landscape at Chelmorton (Plate 10) by paying the landowner to maintain the characteristic stone walls. But will the
'massive injection of resources' the authority believes to be needed
be forthcoming?

There are, in theory at least, other management options. The 1979
Act makes provision under Part II for local authorities to designate
Areas of Archaeological Importance (AAIs) within which certain
land use changes can be controlled and archaeological investigations
regularized. But so far the Secretaries of State for the Environment
and for Wales have limited designations to small areas in a few
historic towns. No AAIs have been designated in the countryside as
the Act allows. Under the same Act local authorities can enter into
Guardianship Agreements with landowners to protect and allow
access to ancient monuments, a power that can be delegated to the
national park committees, but not to the two boards. All the park
authorities are willing to acquire archaeological sites if this appears
to be the only way to secure protection, but not many have done so.
A rare example is the acquisition by the North York Moors
authority of Cawthorn Roman Camps for which it has prepared a
management plan. Hadrian's Wall is; of course, the outstanding
historic monument in any of the national parks, but it is a special
case – so special that we argue the case in Chapter 19 for an
exceptional solution.

There are some general points to be made about the conservation
policies of the national park authorities. The first is that without a
continuous and substantial increase in resources the policies of the
more forward-looking authorities will remain unattainable pipe
dreams. There is still a big gap between the needs even of the
better-off authorities and the resources available to them.

Our second point is that neither structure nor national park plans
reflect the need to husband energy and other natural resources. Even
today, although several plans express concern about the demands
for minerals and water and some mention the World Conservation
Strategy, the overriding concerns are still amenity and recreation
rather than resource conservation. If the national park authorities are
to realize the potential they undoubtedly have to conserve the
human and natural resources of these infinitely precious and beautiful areas, conservation in the broadest sense needs the full weight of
government behind it and the full backing of popular opinion.

This leads us to our third conclusion that the plans, policies and first functional strategies were all written (as was our original book) in a period that is now rapidly passing into history. The impending collapse of the farming policies pursued since the 1940s, all aimed at maximizing productivity with huge investments of public money, have created an entirely new situation that we will examine in Chapter 14.

Chapter Seven

Enjoyment

WHO ENJOYS
THE NATIONAL PARKS?

The preservation and enhancement of natural beauty – the first statutory purpose of the national parks' legislation of 1949 – was not an end in itself but a means to an end. The countryside was to be protected so that the public could enjoy it. The 1949 Act struck a political compromise over access to open country, but none of those concerned foresaw the full extent of the changes that were to take place between 1945 and the mid-1970s when the new park authorities took over. Real disposable income per head had doubled, energy costs fell in real terms, the number of private cars increased eightfold and nearly half the manual workers were entitled by 1978 to at least three weeks' holiday – another third being entitled to four weeks or more. As these benefits moved down the social scale, so did ordinary people take increasingly to the countryside. According to the Countryside Commission Recreation Survey of 1984 (data from which is used throughout this chapter), not only was countryside recreation still growing in popularity but over half the trips to the country were made by clerical or skilled manual workers.

It is often suggested that the mass demand for countryside recreation comes from the new motorists, the white-collar workers and those from manufacturing and service industries, who simply want to relax by their cars, with a nice view in front of them, the radio and their dogs for company and a *News of the World* on their laps. The scene at innumerable car parks by riversides or viewpoints on hot summer Sundays would seem to confirm this cynical view, and there are facts and figures to support it. But visitors include many elderly and disabled people, mothers with very small children and men and women whose daily work gives them all the exercise they want. Add the pleasures of idleness, sunbathing, picnicking and paddling and unfamiliarity with the countryside, and one can understand why so much countryside recreation is passive.

The evidence that many people enjoy passive recreation has been used, however, to create the myth that the great majority of townspeople (and in particular the working classes) do not appreciate the 'real' countryside, and are happy to remain by their cars near the 'tarmac corridor'. This attitude was openly expressed by the English Tourist Board in 1985 in its Exmoor Tourism Development Action Programme which assumed that the Exmoor landscape appeals to 'the long-holiday up-market', but is of 'only limited interest to the long-holiday mass-market'.

An interesting collection of studies of rural tourism edited by Mary Bouquet and Mike Winter (*Who from their labours rest*, 1986) argues that the passivity of many tourists is actually encouraged by the high level of investment in facilities for car-borne visitors. They attribute the concentration on such provisions as picnic sites and country parks to the 'rural planning orthodoxy' that gives agriculture an overriding priority and therefore seeks to locate leisure activities as far out of agriculture's way as possible. The Countryside Commission itself conceded in 1986, in a paper on future recreation policies, that too much of its own attention had been concentrated on country parks, picnic sites and a few long-distance routes, and too little on the wider countryside and the nation's 120 000 mile network of footpaths and bridleways. The most significant change in recent years, which will be discussed in the next chapter, has been the increase in the number of people whose favourite recreation is a country walk. Surveys by the Commission and others have shown that at least 20% of the people visiting the countryside now take a walk of two miles or more.

These 'middle distance walkers', to use a convenient phrase to describe those who fall between the two extremes of athleticism and passivity, are responding to the call of Norman Nicholson, the Lakeland poet, who said in 1975:

> to see the Lakes clearly ... we must penetrate the living landscape behind the view. We must get out of our cars, feel the rock under our feet, breathe the Cumbrian air, and learn to know something, at least, of the complex organic life of grass, herb and tree, something of the changing pattern of the weather, water and rock, and something of the way man has helped to shape the landscape in the past and is shaping it today.

The Countryside Commission survey also confirms what Joan Davidson and Gerald Wibberley and others had shown, that opportunities for countryside recreation are circumscribed sharply by income and social class. What holds the unskilled worker back is low pay, inaccessibility of the countryside from the inner city, chronic unemployment (or conversely, weekend work or overtime), and lack of a car or the means to run it for leisure trips, as well as unfamiliarity with the countryside. In present economic circumstances it seems likely that the working and lower middle classes will in fact get less access to the countryside, not more. This trend can and should be reversed. We hope to persuade the reader that the national parks, although overcrowded at times and places, have under-used space to provide part of the additional recreational capacity that will be required.

What information there is for the national parks suggests that in most of them visitor numbers fell from a peak in the early 1970s to a plateau in the second half of that decade and have fluctuated around this level since. But even though visitor levels are fairly static overall, about 1¼ million of the 18 million or so people who are taking their leisure in the country on a fine Sunday will be in the national parks. The national park authorities have all made guess-timates of the number of visitors, which range from about a million visitor days annually in Northumberland or Exmoor to 16–20 million in the Peak and the Lake District. But even in intensively used parks, such as Snowdonia, there are both large tracts of mountain or hill country that are little used, and very intensively used areas such as Snowdon itself or the coast. Every park has 'honeypots'. The Swallow Falls in Snowdonia, Tarn Hows in the Lake District, Aysgarth Falls in the Yorkshire Dales and Dovedale in the Peak are each visited by half a million or more visitors a year.

There is a wide variation in the use of the parks for day trips and holidays. The Peak, within an hour's drive for 16.5 million people, is far and away the park most heavily used by day visitors. But day visitors also outnumber visitors on holiday in the Brecon Beacons (on the doorstep of what was once industrial South Wales) and the Yorkshire Dales, (within 90 minutes' drive of eight million people in Yorkshire and Lancashire). Snowdonia, Pembrokeshire Coast and Exmoor are predominantly holiday parks. In the Lake District (within a three-hour drive of the northern conurbations), the North York Moors and Dartmoor the balance between the two kinds of use is more even. Northumberland is really two parks. The Roman wall, the only major 'honeypot' in the national park, is an outstand-ing tourist attraction which draws a quarter of its visitors from South-East England and a fifth from overseas, while the Cheviots are the least used part of any park and take day trips on a modest scale, mainly from the conurbation of Tyne and Wear.

There is a common tendency to denigrate the day visitor who has little money to spend. In reality, both the day trip and the holiday satisfy important needs, although there are contrasting views about the relative quality of the different experiences they offer. Frederick Law Olmsted, the American landscape architect who as long ago as 1865 began to formulate policies for national parks, took the view that natural places had to be experienced 'at length and at leisure'. The same spirit moves A. W. Wainwright the author of those inimitable, personal, handdrawn and handwritten guides for walkers to the Lake District and other fells. In one of the television programmes on the walks he describes, he took the viewer through the Lakeland mist to one of his favourite corners, the 1900 ft Haystacks – 'a place appreciated by those who go there to linger and explore'. Wainwright is not one of those who wants to get from A to B as fast as he can, or to break records. 'For a man trying to get a substantial worry out of his mind the top of Haystacks is a wonderful cure.'

On the other hand, for people living in big cities there is enormous value in having areas of wildness and beauty relatively nearby where, as Patrick Monkhouse the editor of the original Peak park guide said, they are most needed and most appreciated: 'living so near at hand they do not need to stay for weeks at a time, as they might in North Wales or the Lake District. They come for the inside of a day, taking nature in sips'. Far more opportunities are needed for people in the great conurbations, particularly in London, to make short day trips to open and accessible countryside. If national parks are for people of every class and kind, there is a need not only for cheap transport and easy access from towns within day-trip distance, but also for cheap holiday accommodation for those who are beyond the day-trip range – in fact, for social recreation policies.

PROVIDING FOR ENJOYMENT

The language of the specialists in countryside recreation, with its classifications and marketing terminology, tends to remove from whatever pursuits are being described all the magic of the actual experience. One such breakdown is that between active and informal recreation which does nothing to conjure in the mind's eye the enormously wide range of enjoyable activities the national parks have to offer, or to distinguish between pursuits that are compatible with the semi-natural world of the uplands and those that are not. The classification obscures some important differences between the two kinds of enjoyment, not the least of which is that between activities that yield a profit to the private entrepreneur and those that do not. The trouble is that the tourist trade, in contrast to the park authorities, will provide whatever goods and facilities the public will pay for, whether or not these are necessary for the quiet enjoyment of the parks. But the trade contributes little or nothing to the maintenance or enhancement of the resource and it looks to the public authorities to solve the problems that its activities generate.

The term 'informal recreation' covers both the more or less car-tied or passive visitors, and the people who use their vehicles to get to the points from which they can get out and explore 'the living landscape behind the view' on foot. It is not surprising that the park authorities, faced as they were with the rapid postwar growth in the number of car-borne visitors, should have focused their initial recreation strategies on the former; that is on management schemes for honeypot areas, the provision of facilities for car-borne visitors and the protection of the more remote and fragile areas from cars and caravans. Nor is it surprising that they have concentrated their very limited resources on parking, picnicking, public conveniences, information and an immense range of well-designed interpretive material, mainly for the less active visitors.

The park authorities have had very much less success in controlling the motor vehicle and in traffic management than they have had in providing facilities for car-borne visitors. Schemes to restrict motor vehicle access on particular lengths of public highway have been few and far between. This may have something to do with the problems associated with the necessary Traffic Orders, which can arouse local opposition, are difficult to enforce and time-consuming to prepare. Dartmoor has not got very far in its attempts to persuade motorists not to take their cars into the high moor. In two cases where weekend restrictions have been successfully imposed – the Goyt and Upper Derwent Valleys in the Peak – the roads in question give access only to reservoirs and forests. Over 15 years have passed since the Goyt Valley was first closed to cars and the Peak Board provided a mini-bus for non-walkers. Visitors welcomed the scheme, but as time went by fewer and fewer used the mini-bus and in 1982 it was discontinued altogether. An experiment which started on the principle of park-and-ride has become a park-and-walk scheme with facilities for the disabled.

The Derwent Valley with its three reservoirs and surrounding plantation woodlands has long been one of the most popular places in the Peak. Virtually all the land is owned by the Severn Trent Water Authority, the Forestry Commission and the National Trust. A management experiment was begun in 1981 which involves the owning bodies, the Peak Board, local authorities, the Countryside Commission, the Nature Conservancy Council and the Sports

Council. In addition to much conservation and recreation provision, six and a half miles of road have been freed from traffic and
there are cycles for hire, a mini-bus service and toilets for the
disabled. There have also been impressive achievements in the
management of 'honeypots' like Dartmeet in Dartmoor, Malham in
the Yorkshire Dales, Tarn Hows in the Lake District and Dovedale
in the Peak. But against this record of achievement two glaring
weaknesses in the provision for walkers that we identified in 1982
(and discuss in the next chapter) remain. Neither the footpath
network nor the arrangements for the public to have access to open
country measure up to the standards that can reasonably be expected
of a national park.

The long-distance fell walkers, climbers, cavers and other
countryside athletes or enthusiasts who come to enjoy the natural
features of the park in their various ways cause relatively few
problems. They are well served by the voluntary organizations to
which many of them belong. They need little in the way of facilities
beyond transport, car parking, somewhere to stay and access to the
resource and rescue services if things go wrong. They do not attract
large crowds. It is to the public authorities that these individuals or
organizations must turn if essential facilities are lacking or deficient,
or beyond the resources of the voluntary bodies, because there is not
much money to be made out of them.

Other active pursuits require a greater degree of management,
however, if the needs of the different users are to be met and the
environment and quiet enjoyment of others are to be safeguarded.
For example, water sports can be noisy and conflict with more
peaceful pursuits such as fishing. The noise of power boating and
water skiing reverberating between the hills can disturb entire
valleys. One of the few special powers possessed by national park
authorities is to make byelaws for the use of lakes and rivers, and
good use has been made of them by the Lakes Board to reduce, if not
yet entirely to eliminate, the nuisance of noisy water sports. The
park authorities also help active enjoyment by providing gliders,
sailors and others with special facilities they need in order to use
their equipment. For example, public launching places are provided
on Windermere for the use of people with their own boats.

The land-based motorized sports are noisy and often destructive
of the terrain. Motor-bike trail-riders flagrantly disregard the law
and can be an unmitigated nuisance unless a special area can be set
aside for them. Other sports, such as pony-trekking, are peaceful in
themselves; but if intensively pursued (as in the Brecon Beacons and
Exmoor) they can erode footpaths seriously, destroy vegetation and
be a nuisance to others while making no contribution to the costs

they impose on others. Hang-gliding and gliding are also quiet in themselves but attract crowds and may need large car parks and base installations. Competitive events or sponsored walks, such as the Lyke Wake walk across the North York Moors or the Three Peaks walk in the Yorkshire Dales are destructive of soil and vegetation. Stag hunting in Exmoor and the Quantocks causes intense bad feeling when (as happens occasionally) deer are killed before the eyes of children and other holiday-makers or (as happens all the time) dozens of motor vehicles follow the hunt over open country shattering the peace and eroding the vegetation.

All the park authorities face the problem that they have few powers to control active sports however destructive of the environment or of its peaceful enjoyment they may be. Private owners are free to permit the use of their land for noisy or cruel sports. The National Trust tolerates not only stag hunting on some of its land but even the cavalcades of motorized hunt followers. Motor rallies on public roads are the responsibility of the Royal Automobile Club. The Lake District was threatened in 1985 with regular tourist helicopter flights based on Carlisle Airport, but the park authority can only control the points at which they land or take off in the park.

In addition to providing facilities and management, much else has been done by the park authorities to enhance visitors' enjoyment. Every park except the Yorkshire Dales now has a full-time youth and schools liaison officer to handle the immense number of groups which come to field study centres or on day visits. Ranger and warden services have been transformed since 1974, and have been augmented by large numbers of volunteers and part-timers who now provide most of the face-to-face contact at busy times between the park authorities and the public. This has freed full-time staff to undertake, or to organize, what the Lake District was the first to call its Upland Management Service that helps visitors and farmers alike by waymarking and repairing footpaths and bridges, and coping with problems that arise at local stress points.

The strategies for visitor management are essentially unchanged in the latest revisions of the national park plans, but two shifts of emphasis are clearly discernible. First, the severe limits on capital spending have led the park authorities to give a much lower priority to investment in new visitor facilities. Expenditure is now concentrated on maintenance, urgent remedial works and low-cost low-key management. Secondly, high levels of unemployment and the Government's belief that the main hope of new jobs lies in the tourist and other service industries is producing a more positive attitude to tourism.

HOLIDAYS FOR THE HAVES
AND THE HAVE-NOTS

With memories of mass unemployment and hunger marches fresh in their minds, Dower and Hobhouse saw the provision of cheap accommodation as one of the keys to making the national parks accessible to everyone. They saw this as the job of voluntary or charitable bodies such as the Youth Hostels Association, which now has one hundred hostels in or close to the national parks; but the main providers were to be farmers and householders offering bed and breakfast or full board, and private enterprise developing more guest houses and hotels. The park authorities were empowered to provide holiday accommodation, but only where existing facilities were inadequate and their contribution, though useful, has been relatively small. The huge increase in incomes, and in motor cars, caravans and camping, and the response of the private sector in providing accommodation, were only dimly foreseen. Today the holiday and tourist business has changed out of all recognition. Even the YHA, whose *raison d'être* was to provide the cheapest, simplest accommodation for walkers, and which turned walkers who arrived by car away, is now adapting its policies to cater for a more affluent, motorized membership. A study group set up by the Trades Union Congress and the English Tourist Board in 1974 did identify a huge gap in our social services, which do not recognize holidays as a social need, but nothing came of it.

When we wrote our original book in 1980–1, the main problems facing the park authorities, as they saw them, were not so much shortage of accommodation as the huge upsurge in touring caravans (whose numbers more than doubled between 1969 and 1976) and the spread of static caravans which covered huge areas on the coasts of Pembrokeshire and Snowdonia and threatened to blight many inland areas. In the event the expected increase in touring caravans failed to materialize, and the further spread of static caravan sites has been stopped by refusing planning permission, and their quality improved by imposing tougher conditions on landscaping and facilities.

Today, in the latter part of the 1980s, British society is increasingly polarized between the haves and the have nots. On the one hand there are the increasingly affluent executives, professionals, the better-paid office or industrial workers and the better-off retired enjoying higher incomes and paying less in taxes than they did before 1979. They want better accommodation and can take two or more holidays or 'breaks' a year. On the other hand, figures published by the Department of Health and Social Security in July

1986 showed that the numbers living in poverty had increased from 11.5 million in 1979 to 16.3 million in 1983, and must be even higher today. These include the four million unemployed and their families, the low paid, the single-parent families and the elderly who have to live on their pensions, many of whom cannot afford a holiday at all. Some of the second group live on the edge of open country, in such places as West Cumberland or Teesside for example, but many more live in the inner cities of the great conurbations where the open country is a world away. The gap in our social services identified by the Tourist Board and the TUC in 1974 has widened, and the case for subsidized holidays as part of a social welfare programme is overwhelming. It would also provide a secure source of income for modestly priced accommodation, unaffected by rates of exchange or fears of terrorism.

The policies of the national park authorities are evolving in two directions simultaneously, corresponding to the social divisions we have described. Much the strongest force at work is pushing them into co-operation with the tourist industry and going 'up market' to attract more affluent visitors. But there is also a trend, although a much weaker one, to encourage the provision of cheap accommodation for back-packers and campers, and to encourage farm tourism and bed and breakfast accommodation. The Peak, the Yorkshire Dales, and the North York Moors have all experimented with converting the numerous redundant field barns of northern England into 'stone tents' or 'bunk barns' with help from the Countryside Commission. The Peak Board already operates a booking service for this popular form of camping. But the reality is that there is too little cash to bring these ideas to fruition, and only a glimmering of a policy for making the parks available to large numbers of young people who lack the means to get there and to enjoy them. For the top end of the market the sky seems to be the financial limit.

The most controversial example of the upward trend is the time-share and leisure complex. At the Langdale centre in the Lake District, two-bed lodges were on offer in 1985 for one week a year at from £6900 to £7950 plus a £95 a week management fee. The development includes an hotel, pub and restaurant and a leisure centre which offers squash, a gym, swimming pool, sauna and indoor games. Of course Langdale also offers the beauty of the Lakes and the opportunity to walk, sail, water-ski, windsurf, canoe and enjoy the open air. But is it really in the spirit of the national park to be offering 'a holiday in the Caribbean, a tropical dream come true' where you can 'sip your drinks under the palm trees'? And what about the 'private lake frontage with four acres of land on the shores of nearby Coniston Water' in a park where the public has very limited access to the lake sides, and it is the policy of the park authority to try to increase it?

THE BUSINESS OF TOURISM

All the park authorities seem to be very conscious of the dangers of encouraging tourism in forms that are incompatible with the natural beauty and sense of freedom that draw people to the national parks year after year. But they are under strong pressure both from the tourist operators, some of whom are feeling the pinch, and from the government and the Tourist Boards which offer money and marketing as a bait and seem to be preoccupied with promoting particular areas less for their real qualities than for commercial gimmicks, such as Lorna Doone in Exmoor. The government's enterprise supremo, Lord Young, sees tourism as the main growth area to replace Britain's lost jobs in industry. The policy document *Pleasure, leisure and jobs* (1985), sub-titled *The business of tourism*, sees the government's role as being to sweep away all 'unnecessary obstacles'. It ignores the fact that the new jobs will mainly be seasonal, low paid, part-time women's work while the major benefits accrue to large enterprises.

Some parks, such as Exmoor, are trying to restore the fortunes of a tourist industry that is in serious decline. Others such as the Yorkshire Dales, which have never had a strong network of hotels or guest houses, now want to establish themselves as holiday areas. But the Lake District, at the opposite extreme, is so packed with visitors that it is opposed to the provision of any more holiday accommodation. It wants to concentrate on enhancing the qualities of scenery and quiet that led the Consumers' Association to rate it in 1982 as the best part of the country for scenery and walking. Yet the same survey showed that the Lake District had the highest proportion of visitors complaining about 'touristy commercialization or crowds' – the clearest possible sign that people go to the national parks to escape the traps of the commercial tourism that has destroyed the peace and beauty of so many once-tranquil places.

The price to be paid, if large numbers are to be catered for at the popular places, should be a degree of management and constraint, not the degradation of natural beauty by the superficial attractions of souvenir shops, ice-cream vans and other devices for parting visitors from their money. In towns and settlements visitors should find most of the things they need, but they should be able to experience the natural world (as Olmsted advised at Niagara Falls a century ago) with the minimum of intrusive management, carefully planned essential facilities and a complete absence of commercial exploitation. Olmsted's answer to those who said that the commercialization of Niagara Falls was giving the public what it wanted, was to say that commerce gave the public no choice but to take what it offered. The fact that they accepted the arrangements was no evidence of their approval. Today, the fact that people will buy an ice-cream or a Coke wherever an enterprising operator spots a big enough crowd to make a profitable pitch, does not mean that the majority of visitors prefer it that way, or that vans should be allowed to intrude wherever the operator finds it profitable to go.

Several national parks are taking part in Tourist Development Action Programmes (TDAPs) sponsored by the English Tourist Board and the Development Commission. The prototype is the TDAP for Exmoor and the adjoining holiday resorts in which at least half the accommodation is provided by Butlins, now a subsidiary of Ranks, in its vast Somerwest World holiday complex at Minehead. We see nothing wrong with a tourist programme that is carefully designed to benefit the local economy, provided it is clear about the kind of leisure activities that are appropriate to a national park and tries to promote its quiet enjoyment by people who want simple and cheap holidays or trips. There is unquestionably a need to attract more visitors to some of the parks, and there is room in all of them for more walkers.

The Tourist Boards, the Development Commission, the agricultural departments, the farmers' unions and every rural organization have now latched on to farm tourism as one of the main ways – in some cases the only way – in which farmers can diversify. But we question the current orthodoxy which holds that grants for farm tourism will automatically increase farm incomes, create jobs for farmers' wives and daughters, strengthen the local economy and teach visitors the facts of farming life. The truth is more complicated. Bouquet and Winter's studies of farm tourism in the South-West in the early 1980s showed that the existing accommodation is seriously under-used, and that farm tourism provided less than 5% of farm income. The main reason for developing farm tourism was to develop property that had been made redundant by shedding labour, amalgamating farms and erecting new farm buildings. Those who benefitted most were the larger, expanding farmers with redundant farm buildings and substantial incomes, who could pick up the grants, find the capital for the development and set their costs against tax. But their ultimate purpose in many cases was not so much to develop farm tourism, except temporarily, as to provide a home for the farmer on retirement or for the son or daughter who could later join the business.

The small farmer, in most cases, will have neither the redundant buildings nor the capital to take up the grants. Furthermore, the Tourist Boards' insistence on higher standards as a condition of grant aggravates this problem. If tourist grants are to play a positive socio-economic role they must be firmly directed at two objectives: increasing the incomes of those farmers whose farms cannot yield an adequate income, and increasing the enjoyment of visitors who need good but inexpensive accommodation.

Chapter Eight

A Walkers' Charter

WALKERS AND THEIR NEEDS

Repeated surveys by the Countryside Commission and others have demonstrated the increasing popularity of countryside walks. More and more town-dwellers want to experience the natural world direct, as well as through the booming TV nature series. The most popular types of walk are paths through farmed land and woods, which reflects the importance of the local countryside for people living in towns. Although the majority of country walks are not taken on the moors and fells, it has to be remembered that seven of the national parks – Northumberland, the Lake District, the Yorkshire Dales, the Peak District, North York Moors, the Brecon Beacons and Dartmoor – provide magnificent local countryside for millions of people living in the northern conurbations and the cities of South Wales and south-west England. Furthermore, the diversity of landscapes to be found in the ten parks offers people opportunities for every kind of walk – field and woodland, lake and riverside, beach and cliff-top as well as the moorland and mountain with which perhaps the parks are usually associated.

The path and access systems, which are the primary recreational resource for both the energetic and the less active visitors, actually deteriorated over wide areas before 1974 through a mixture of increasing use and neglect, despite waymarking and the opening up of some new areas by the Forestry Commission, the National Trust and some park authorities. The expansion in the number of walkers was not matched by a corresponding increase in resources until the Countryside Commission sponsored the first Upland Management Experiment (UMEX) in Snowdonia and the Lake District in 1969. Virtually nothing was done to create a footpath network to meet walkers' needs or to create a bridleway network for riders. Since 1974 there has been a considerable improvement in the management of footpaths and access arrangements, and in providing guided walks and leaflets. But it would be entirely wrong to suppose that the systems are now satisfactory. There are fundamental defects in the law governing rights of way and access that have been amply documented for years and, in spite of the Wildlife and Countryside Act 1981, seem not much nearer to solution.

FOOTPATHS

The law surrounding footpaths and rights of way, enshrined in the National Parks Act of 1949 and subsequent legislation, is Byzantine in its complexity and only intelligible to specialists. Footpaths, bridleways and RUPPs (Roads Used as Public Paths) are a highway responsibility, but the highway authorities are obsessed with roads and motor traffic and still do not take their footpath responsibilities seriously. In national parks the park authorities have no statutory role, even for their upkeep, unless the county councils delegate footpath functions to them, as they now nearly all do. It is only in the Lake District and the Peak that the two boards have the statutory power to create, divert or close rights of way, but even they are not the highway authorities statutorily responsible for the upkeep of rights of way. The 1981 Wildlife and Countryside Act introduced a useful but minor change by making the highway authorities responsible for reviewing the definitive maps of rights of way continuously, instead of at 5-year intervals. But responsibility remained with the highway authorities. Footpath officers who have been appointed in the national parks have had to spend their time fighting their way through an administrative and legal jungle, instead of being able to get on with the job of exending and maintaining a first class network of rights of way, not only as maps but on the ground.

The Ramblers' Association, which was commissioned by the Countryside Commission to monitor the progress of the review, has reported that few national park authorities allocated extra staff to deal with the extra work, and several said that funds could only be obtained by cutting back even further on the maintenance of rights of way. Even so the authorities welcome the new procedure because it has broken a logjam and could, if given the necessary financial support, remove many question marks from the definitive maps.

The backlog of work on the footpaths themselves is formidable in several of the parks. A survey made by the Peak Board in 1985 revealed 1300 obstructions, 2200 roadside signposts missing, 510 wet, eroded or overgrown sections and 90 bridges in need of major repair or replacement (or even missing) on 4000 miles of footpath. Dartmoor, to take the opposite case, claims to have no great footpath problems. But even the Snowdonia National Park Committee, which with grant aid from several agencies had by 1986 nearly completed a major programme to repair the footpaths leading to Snowdon's summit at a cost of £1 500 000, is the first to admit that it has no comparable resources to tackle the pressing problems elsewhere. Because it is not the highway authority 'it cannot introduce improved and effective management and maintenance of the public rights of way network'. Massive problems remain on over-used walks everywhere: on Dartmoor's Ten Tors, the Lake District fells, the Three Peaks of the Yorkshire Dales, the Lyke Wake walk in the North York Moors and in many parts of Snowdonia, to cite the better known cases.

The Three Peaks area, which the national park plan calls the heartland of the Dales, is so seriously eroded as to make 'much of this internationally important landscape a virtual disaster area' (in the words of a member of the national park staff). A survey by the national park authority completed late in 1985 showed that 80% of the paths were very badly eroded, creating 'an almost irretrievable' situation. Not surprisingly, the erosion is worst along the route of the Three Peaks Challenge walk, undertaken by at least 15 000 people each year. The route suffers additionally from an annual fell race and cycle cross. The area is crossed by the Pennine Way. Add to these the facts that 150 000 people climb Pen-y-Ghent every year, 50 000 walk over Whernside and 50 000 more walk over Ingleborough, and the scale of the problem can be understood. But it is not simply one of footpath maintenance. Half the area has been designated an SSSI and is outstanding for its limestone pavements and other geological features and its botanical riches.

The park authority has agreed to a full rehabilitation scheme, the cost of which is estimated at £770 000 or more. The Countryside Commission was so pessimistic about the prospects of getting money on this scale from the government that it even toyed, for a time, with the idea that the park authority should launch a national appeal. The Commission has, in fact, decided to contribute £200 000 to the rehabilitation programme, and the park authority took a firm view (supported by the Commission and the Council for National Parks) that the responsibility lies with central government. It bid for an extra 5% in Government grant for its share of the cost of the first year's work in 1987-8. The Government gave the park authority the 5% it asked for with one hand but took it away with the other, by taking it off the increase in grant for other purposes. The authority decided to close the financial gap by drawing on its last reserves.

The resources available for footpath maintenance vary enormously from one park to another, and bear little relation to the scale of the problems. The Yorkshire Dales Committee, which is responsible for 1076 miles of footpaths, already spends nearly £200 000 a year on them, while the Lake District spends £250 000 on a far larger and more heavily used system. The Brecon Beacons spend a mere £14 000 a year. The North York Moors authority has no programme to maintain the network. It responds *ad hoc* to complaints and problems and concentrates on the most-used footpaths. The Peak Board is alone in stating the simple truth that the footpath network is the park's principle recreational asset, although its expenditure is at a modest level of around £90 000 for 1986–7. The Peak does, however, supplement its own staff through the work of the Peak Park Conservation Volunteers organized by two full-time staff, whose contribution is expected to double from 3000 to 7000 man-days between 1986 and 1991.

All the parks have come to rely on voluntary labour and Manpower Services Commission teams of unemployed workers, without whose help (worth many hundreds of thousands of pounds) many lengths of footpath would be unwalkable. But even with MSC help and volunteers, the park authorities see no firm prospect of bringing their entire footpath network into a good state of repair, let alone extending it on any scale.

ACCESS AND A PLAN
FOR WALKERS

The official view in central and local government that the present system of '*de facto* access', in which the public's presence is tolerated by landowners, covers most needs is shockingly complacent. The truth is that definitive rights of way are scarce in many parts of the hill country. In the Yorkshire Dales, for example, the only well known fells whose summits can be reached by definitive rights of way are Ingleborough and Shunner Fell. The definitive path maps, now subject to review, are severely defective because they were compiled by parish councils, with the result that footpaths and bridleways stop at parish boundaries, or are omitted altogether. Many walkers are reluctant to risk trespassing by leaving a definitive path. Notices (see Plate 24) may tell the walker that a permissive path, on which he walks at the landowner's pleasure, has been provided, or they may warn him not to trespass off the right of way. But they never tell him that *de facto* access to open land is permitted. Such consent can, moreover, be withdrawn at any time, and the public is usually ignorant of where access is tolerated and where it is not. The present state of the law inhibits access to many areas even in national parks.

Paradoxically, access is one of the few policy areas where the park authorities are equipped with the powers they need. They can make access orders and they have powers to buy land compulsorily if need be wherever the public is denied access to open country. But with the exception of the Peak Board the park authorities are unwilling to use these powers and, out of deference to farmers and landowners, tend to equivocate even on the desirability of the public having the *right* of fresh air and exercise in open country.

The Peak Board's clear policy is to enable the public to wander at will over the park's 174 square miles of open moorland, except where some restriction is necessary in the interests of nature conservation. The knowledge that the Board will exercise its powers to make access orders or to buy land compulsorily has made it possible for the Board to negotiate formal or informal agreements to make 55% of the park's open country accessible. It was undoubtedly the knowledge that the Board would use these powers that persuaded two farmers, who had bought the Roaches and were obstructing public access to its rock climbs, to sell to the Board in 1979. In securing access to the remaining third of the park's moorland, some 56 square miles, the Board faces (as it said in 1978) the reluctance of landowners to allow public access to the most valuable grouse moors. Some of this reluctance has been overcome since then, but by no means all. Even though Snailsden Moor has been included by the Ramblers' Association in those areas (identified in *Forbidden Britain*) to which it is demanding public rights of access, we are confident that in time the Peak will achieve its objective.

In marked contrast to the Peak Board, the Snowdonia park authority has no policy for using its powers to secure public access to all the open country in the park. It believes that access agreements should be used to resolve problems in enclosed farmland and to provide access to popular beauty spots. It makes no secret of the fact that it is not convinced of the need for a legal right of access even to all common land. In this respect its position is opposed to that of the Brecon Beacons, which favours such a right and has bought large tracts of land to ensure it, and of Dartmoor which has secured it by promoting the Dartmoor Commons Act. But Snowdonia is far from alone in adopting a negative approach to access. The equivocations of the Yorkshire Dales and the North York Moors park committees are written plainly into their park plan reviews; they express sympathy with the public's right to roam, but are clearly disinclined to make an issue of it with the landowners. Indeed, the policy documents of most of the park authorities betray what the

Lake District is frank enough to call 'the opportunistic approach'. That is, they are willing to buy land and enter into agreements to secure access as and when opportunities occur, but they have no access strategy or programme. This attitude is more defensible in the Lake District, where the public already has very extensive rights of access over common land and over land owned by the Lakes Board or the National Trust, than it is elsewhere.

The view that the quieter and remoter areas cannot absorb more visitors without a fatal loss of character, implicit in policies to be found in most park plans, does not always stand up on examination. There are some quiet and remote areas of which this is true and the case for retaining a very low level of use so as to protect fragile environments and habitats from excessive human interference makes sense. But there is much good walking country in nearly all national parks where, with a very modest input of management, more walkers could be accommodated without doing any harm to farmers' interests or causing any lasting damage or detriment to the distinctive natural character. The Snowdonia Plan was explicit in giving lack of resources as the reason for concentrating management on Snowdon, the Glyders and Cadair Idris and for not encouraging people to walk on the Arans and other little-used hill and mountain areas that constitute the greater part of the open country in the national park. In 1984, after years of argument with intransigent farmers, the Snowdonia National Park Committee negotiated 'a courtesy path' along the ridge of the Arans, a superb range of mountains in the south of Snowdonia. But the public are confined to three access points, they have no right to stray from the path, they cannot break off the walk at any intermediate points, and camping is forbidden.

One of the main omissions from the national park plans and their recent reviews is a strategy or a plan for walkers, riders and cyclists – one might call it a Walkers' Charter. Nowhere has the full potential of a national park for these activities been assessed and developed into a costed plan and programme, although the elements of such a plan are to be found in every park. Opening up the Arans and similar areas would call for a whole package of measures. An upland management service would have to be introduced on a modest scale, legal rights of access extended to commons and to open country and rights of way extended to form a comprehensive network related to car parks, bus services, cheap accommodation and tent sites. The need to start and finish a walk from the same car park severely circumscribes walkers' opportunities. The absence of public transport in the Arans, for example, rules out the most exciting linear walks for all but the most athletic. The public needs comprehensive bus and rail timetables, of the kind pioneered in the Peak and the Dales, and maps similar to A. W. Wainwright's *Walker's guides*, or Stile Publications' admirable walkers' maps for the Yorkshire Dales, designed by Arthur Gemmell. Above all, perhaps the national park authorities, whether boards or committees, should be highway authorities for footpaths and rights of way for walkers, riders and cyclists, with all the powers and resources required to establish and maintain a comprehensive network.

COMMON LAND:
a breakthrough?

Since 1979 the House of Commons has rejected three private bills presented by back-bench Labour MPs to give the public a legal right of access to open country and to common land. It is true that the public does have legal rights of access to what are technically 'urban commons', which paradoxically include large tracts of fell in the Lake District, but there are no public rights of access to the million acres (404 800 ha) or so of non-urban commons in the uplands. Long established habits of access are being whittled away in the absence of the legislation recommended as far back as 1959 by the Royal Commission on Common Land to secure public access for fresh air and exercise. The Brecon Beacons Committee's purchase in 1985 of eight commons, formerly part of the Tredegar estate and extending to nearly 9 000 ha, from the Eagle Star Insurance Co. at the bargain price of £30 000 was intended among other things to secure public access that was under challenge. The Dartmoor Commons Act, 1985, secured rights of access for walkers and riders, and made the national park responsible for recreational management.

The chances of early legislation to secure the public's legal rights of access to common land have been enhanced by the agreement achieved by the Common Land Forum set up by the Countryside Commission in 1983. After 39 meetings spread over two and a half years, 20 of the 21 organizations represented on the Forum – landowners, commoners, farmers, local authorities and amenity and recreation bodies – reached agreement. Only the Farmers' Union of Wales held out, mainly because it objected to the Forum's agreement that existing rights of public access to commons should not be disturbed. The main question now is whether government will introduce legislation to implement its implied promise to translate the main recommendations of the Forum into law. Only when a new Act has come into force will the loss of commons through deregistration be stopped and the technical deficiencies in the 1965 Commons Registration Act be put right. Once the legislation has been passed, management associations must be set up for all commons and they must prepare management schemes, which have to be approved by the county councils (which can delegate the function to national park committees) or by national park boards.

The management scheme must include a right of public access to all commons 'on foot for quiet enjoyment' and on horseback where riding has been customary or is agreed to by the association, subject to reasonable conditions. To prevent commoners dragging the proceedings out and postponing the public's rights, the Forum has recommended that the Secretary of State should make a statutory order under which the public's rights would come into force within five years at the most, whether or not a management scheme had been approved. The benefits to walkers and to the national parks should be substantial, particularly in those parks where very little of the open country is classified as urban commons. However, considerable efforts will have to be made by the conservation and recreation interests, both to overcome departmental timidity and lethargy, and to clarify some ambiguities and to remove some weaknesses in the Forum's report. The legislation should require the county councils to delegate their commons functions to national park committees, and ensure that the park authorities and conservation interests are well represented on the commons management associations. The public must have access to information and the right to raise issues of general concern.

The suggested duties of the management associations include promoting the conservation and enhancement of natural beauty and good standards of livestock husbandry. But the Forum evaded the crucial ecological issues raised by the overstocking with sheep and cattle that is encouraged by the hill farming support system (see Ch. 14). Another serious weakness in the report is that, although the Forum agreed that management schemes would exclude commercial afforestation, it also agreed that the Secretary of State should have the right to allow it. This could have damaging effects on access, wildlife and landscape, as will be seen in Chapter 15. Nevertheless, although the Department of the Environment will have to be hustled into speedy and effective action, the Forum report has rightly been hailed by the Open Spaces Society as a milestone in the long history of common land.

TRANSPORT FOR WALKERS

The ubiquitous private car and the ever-increasing demands for more road space, car parking and facilities for car-borne visitors have tended to obscure the valuable experiments pioneered by the national park authorities in recreational transport. It is too easy to overlook the probability that in the twenty-first century the wasteful use of energy inherent in the present pattern of private transport will not be tolerable, once Britain's natural oil and gas have been seriously diminished. The ability of town-dwellers to get to the countryside will then become more dependent on shared or public transport systems.

The outstanding leader in this field has been the Peak Board which has pursued three aims in giving financial support to recreation transport services: helping the 7 million people without private transport, who live within 75 miles of the park, to visit it more often; retaining bus services for local people; and persuading car owners to leave their cars behind when visiting the park. It can be said that progress towards the first two objectives has been achieved. By 1985 no recreation area of the park was without a bus service during the summer season. The Board sponsored some services itself and 30 more were supported jointly with the county councils and the passenger transport executives (PTEs) of the adjoining metropolitan counties, which were abolished in 1986. The introduction of 'go-anywhere' tickets by the various public transport bodies and companies transformed independent bus and rail services into an integrated network, which is linked to waymarked footpaths.

The Wayfarer services were developed as part of the Wayfarer Project initiated by the Countryside Commission in 1981 as an experiment in the promotion of public transport for countryside recreation. But the critical factor was the involvement of the metropolitan counties whose extensive bus networks reached far into the surrounding countryside. The object of the experiment was to market existing services, not only to secure social and environmental ends, but to improve the commercial viability of public transport by increasing its use at off-peak times. For example, a single ticket sold in advance allowed unlimited use of bus and rail services in Greater Manchester and parts of Cheshire, Derbyshire and Staffordshire. Following the success of the Peak scheme a similar 'go-anywhere' ticket was introduced in 1984 by the West Yorkshire PTE in co-operation with the National Bus Company and British Rail, bringing the Yorkshire Dales National Park within reach of Leeds, Bradford and the rest of the West Yorkshire conurbation.

The North York Moors National Park Committee has also shown considerable initiative in promoting public transport to improve access to open country. It has contributed to the cost of the Moorsbus service which has taken people at subsidized fares to the moors from Scarborough and other centres of population since 1981. It has co-operated with Cleveland County Council in organizing coach trips to the moors for handicapped and financially disadvantaged people. The reopening of the Historical Railway from Pickering to Grosmont in the heart of the park now gives access to forest trails and to the park authority's Levisham Estate from a specially constructed halt at Newtondale. The Committee has used its influence to keep open the British Rail Esk Valley Line to Whitby, and to enable walkers to enjoy valley walks of exceptional interest.

One of the greatest success stories of recreation transport must surely be the Dales Rail service on the Settle–Carlisle railway over the Pennines, of which Colin Speakman gives a lively account in his stimulating book *Walking in the Yorkshire Dales*. Built in the 1870s as part of the Midland Railway's main line to Scotland, the Settle–Carlisle link runs from Ribblesdale to the Eden Valley through the Yorkshire Dales National Park. With its huge viaducts and tunnels it is a monument to the skill of its engineers and builders, and its splendid panoramic views give the traveller the most spectacular railway trip in England. Dales Rail kills two transport birds with one stone, opening up a weekend service to the cities from remote upland stations previously closed by British Rail, and, with connecting buses, enabling the people of towns and cities in Yorkshire, Lancashire and Cumbria to walk in the Yorkshire Dales and Lake District national parks. The Ramblers' Association made the first move in 1974 when, on a summer weekend, it opened stations and brought hundreds of walkers to the Dales on a chartered train. In 1975 Dales Rail became an official experiment with the support of the Yorkshire Dales National Park Committee, British Rail and the Countryside Commission. Then the West Yorkshire PTE came in, which made it possible to extend the service with connecting buses, and to improve Dales Rail's financial viability. But as we write, the survival of Dales Rail hangs in the balance.

The most serious threat comes from British Rail's renewed intention to close the line, on account of the high capital cost (estimated at over £18 million in 1984) of rehabilitating the structures and track that BR has wantonly neglected for years.

Characteristically, BR's decision is based on narrow financial calcu-
lations of profit and loss. But consultants appointed by the national
park and other authorities found that when social factors are taken
into account the economic benefits of closure only marginally
exceed the costs of retention. A further study of the line's 'heritage
potential' for the Countryside Commission concluded that in these
terms the line was 'a national asset', with considerable potential for
education, in addition to its value for recreation and as a local
service. The hearing on the closure in April 1986 revealed an
astonishing degree of support for the line from more than 22 000
objectors and one dog! Paradoxically, while pressing for the line to
be closed, British Rail announced plans for an expanded service to
be run from May 1987. But the last word rests with the Minister of
Transport who is committed to a competitive public transport
free-for-all. The deregulating Transport Act of 1985 and the
abolition of the metropolitan counties in 1986 threaten to destroy
much of what has been achieved in pioneering public transport in
the national parks.

PART THREE

The national park system – running the show

Chapter Nine

Ministers and quangos

AGRICULTURAL DOMINANCE

National parks in England and Wales are a national asset run by local government. The system established in 1949, as we explained in Chapter 2, was a compromise between the central government and the county councils. It was supposed to produce the 'right' balance between the national interest in conservation and recreation, and the local interest in jobs and incomes – particularly those of farmers and landowners. Theory, however, is one thing and practice another. The purpose of this part of the book is to examine the way the system really works and to establish where effective power lies, and how the balance between competing interests is struck.

The formal heads of the system are the Secretary of State for the Environment for England, who takes the lead, and the Secretary of State for Wales. Until recently, the Secretary of State in England delegated the job to a junior minister, the Under Secretary for Sport and Recreation, whose very title betrayed the low priority given to conservation. The job was upgraded in 1985 when William Waldegrave was appointed Minister of State for the Countryside, Sport and Recreation, to give the Government a greener image. These ministers and their departments promote legislation, determine the national park budgets within limits set by the Treasury and pay the National Park Supplementary Grant. They decide major planning applications and have to approve the planning policies laid down in the structure plans of the local planning authorities. They appoint a third of the members of the national park authorities, and all the members of the two conservation agencies, the Countryside Commission and the Nature Conservancy Council.

The root problem is that government departments and statutory undertakers are not committed to national park objectives and policies, which are still seen more as obstacles to be got round, or in some cases ignored, than as constraints to be accepted. Moreover, the department nominally responsible for the countryside, i.e. the Department of the Environment, does not take the main policy decisions. Some 95% of the land in national parks is used for agriculture, woodland or forest. Farming and forestry operations enjoy an exceptional degree of immunity from development or other control, except in SSSIs. The European Commission, the Minister for Agriculture, Fisheries and Food (MAFF) and the Secretary of State for Wales (as ministers for farming and forestry), and the Forestry Commission all wield far more influence on land use and management decisions than does the Department of the Environment. Traditionally the DoE has played second fiddle to MAFF, but since Mr Waldegrave's promotion it has appeared to some observers to be bidding for the leading role in countryside matters.

The Treasury, through its concessions on capital transfer tax, capital gains tax and income tax, has enormous influence in determining whether rural land is afforested, or bought or sold, and whether it can be acquired by bodies dedicated to conservation, such as the National Trust or the national park authorities. Substantial areas of 'heritage land' have been exempted from CTT in national parks, and so brought within the scope of conservation management. The Countryside Commission plays a crucial role in advising the Treasury whether or not to grant exemption, and in agreeing the management plan. The landowner benefits by passing on the land to the heirs without having to pay CTT. The Department of Trade and Industry (which promotes mining and quarrying), the Department of Transport, the Ministry of Defence and the Central Electricity Generating Board exercise more power over the land they own or influence than do either the DoE or the national park authorities. None of them pay much more than lip service to the conservation of the national parks. They will, of course, make concessions where this can be done without damage to what they believe to be their primary interests, particularly if it enhances their image in the public's eyes, but this does not change the reality. A particularly crude example of the way in which a minister can drive, not a coach and horses but 24 000 vehicles a day, through a particularly sensitive part of a national park was the Bill to route Okehampton bypass through Dartmoor National Park which was forced through Parliament in 1985. We discuss a number of these 'explosive issues', including nuclear power, military training, quarrying, as well as the Okehampton bypass, in Chapter 13. Although there have been some improvements in the attitude of the Forestry Commission and of some water authorities towards the national parks in recent years the broad impression we formed in 1977–80 remains unchanged.

LANDOWNERSHIP:
public and private

Several facts stand out in the statistics of landownership in the national parks (Fig. 15). Some 74% of the land is privately owned, and the greater part of the land in public ownership is held by bodies that are not committed to the objectives or policies of the national parks. But there is, nevertheless, a large area in public or semi-public ownership in most of the parks with immense potential for implementing national park policies. In the Lake District around 40% of the land is now in some form of public or semi-public ownership, and in Dartmoor the proportion is about 45%. The Duchy of Cornwall, the Ministry of Defence and the Forestry Commission own most of the hill country in Dartmoor. The Forestry Commission owns more than a fifth of the Northumberland National Park and nearly as big a proportion of the North York Moors. The water authorities own one-seventh of the Peak District. The Ministry of Defence owns another fifth of Northumberland National Park and one of the most sensitive stretches of the Pembrokeshire Coast. The Central Electricity Generating Board and the Forestry Commission hold key areas in Snowdonia. Some national park authorities (e.g. the Yorkshire Dales) own so little land that their estates are barely visible at the scale of Figure 15.

The National Trust, whose purposes are almost identical with those of the national parks, is overtaking the Forestry Commission as the largest landowner in the national parks. We regard it as neither a public nor a private landowner, but as a semi-public body. It is private in the sense that it is independent of Government and nominally responsible to its million or more members. It is public in the sense that it holds its land and property for conservation purposes under Acts of Parliament. The Trust is by far the largest landowner in the Lake District, where it owns or manages about a fifth of the land. It is also a substantial owner of land in Snowdonia, the Peak District, Exmoor and the Brecon Beacons. Altogether it owns over six times as much land as the national park authorities. But these immense estates do not pay their way and their maintenance has suffered in consequence. The Trust needs £7.5 million to clear up the backlog of work in the ten valleys in the Lake District where it owns property, and is launching an appeal for £500 000 a year for the foreseeable future. It gets another £500 000 a year in cash or labour from the Manpower Services Commission and the Countryside Commission, but it needs in all £2.5 million every year

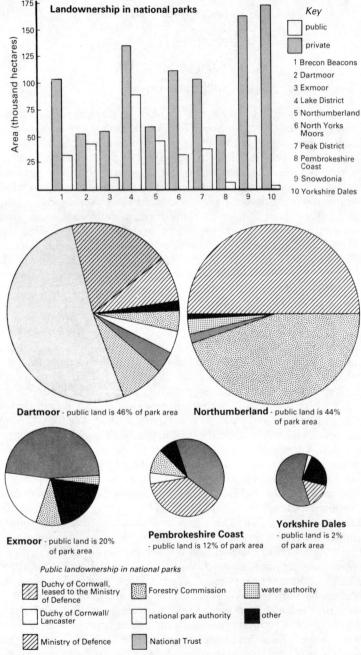

Figure 15 Landownership in national parks. The bar charts (top left) show how much of the total land area is in private and public ownership; the circles show how much land is owned by each public agency or body.

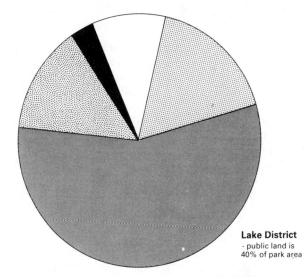

Lake District
- public land is
40% of park area

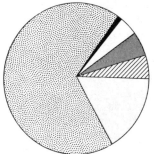

North Yorks Moors - public land is
22% of park area

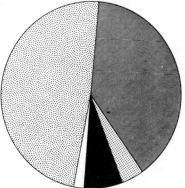

Snowdonia - public land is 23% of park area

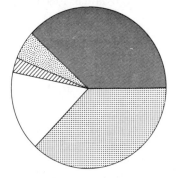

Peak District - public land is 26%
of park area

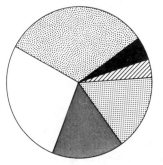

Brecon Beacons - public land is 24%
of park area

to maintain its Lake District property at the high standard it deems essential. The Trust is now more co-operative and consults the park authorities over the management plans for its estates, as does the Duchy of Cornwall which owns almost one-third of Dartmoor National Park.

The Countryside Act of 1968 laid a duty on all public bodies 'to have regard to the desirability of conserving the natural beauty and amenity of the countryside'. But this feeble injunction had no effect whatsoever on the behaviour of the public holders of land. Another approach was initiated in 1977 when the DoE issued a circular asking government departments and agencies holding land in national parks to make a comprehensive review of their national park land, and to consult the park authorities at an early stage on any substantial management action or physical development. Initially this circular was, for all practical purposes, ignored. The circular did not invite the authorities concerned to agree to anything that would prejudice their primary responsibilities. It has resulted in some carefully worded statements by these bodies being inserted, to take one example, as an appendix in the revised *Dartmoor National Park plan* of 1983. It remains to be seen how big a shift in their policies will be brought about by the rather more positive duties towards conservation and recreation imposed on the agricultural ministers, the water authorities, the Forestry Commission and the agricultural ministers by recent legislation which is discussed in later chapters.

The sad reality is that, at the very moment when the public authorities are beginning to take their conservation and recreation responsibilities more seriously, the Tory government is bent on selling much of the public land to the highest bidders, without even imposing any conditions to safeguard public access or conservation. The obligation imposed on the Forestry Commission in 1980 to sell 'surplus' land was part of a general policy designed to force the water and all other public authorities to do the same. As we write, the North West Water Authority is considering the disposal of its land at Thirlmere and Haweswater in the Lake District. Even if the Government does not push through its decision to privatize the water authorities much of their estates totalling more than 50 000 ha in national parks could be put into private hands. Early in 1986 a leak to *The Economist* revealed ministerial discussions on the possibility of selling the entire Forestry Commission estate of 1.2 million ha (over 100 000 ha in national parks). The buyers would often be private forestry companies which invest city money in afforestation to make tax-free capital gains for wealthy investors (see Ch. 15). It is true that the Forestry Commission and water authorities give national park authorities and the Nature Conservancy Council an opportunity to buy land they put on the market, if it is of high conservation value, at market price. But neither the authorities nor the NCC have a fraction of the resources to compete in the market with the City, which can now buy hill land by offering prices two and three times its agricultural value.

It seems, moreover, that the government's obsession with selling off public assets could even extend to the national park authorities' land. The Department of the Environment stated government policy in Circular 27 of 1985: 'national park authorities should, as far as possible, pursue their responsibilities without holding land themselves, though Ministers have recognised that acquisition by agreement, with possible lease-back or resale with appropriate restrictions, may be preferred in certain circumstances'. Far from being pressurized into land sales or denied the money to make essential purchases of land, the park authorities should be given a statutory power, already possessed by the National Trust, to declare their land 'inalienable' unless Parliament consents. Public land holdings in the national parks should be seen as a land bank, to be used to advance national park purposes (including social and economic purposes).

THE COUNTRYSIDE COMMISSION

The job of the national park authorities is assisted and complicated by the need to work with and through a great many government departments and agencies, the number of which has been estimated by the Snowdonia National Park Authority at no less than 25. The two of most immediate concern to the national parks are the Countryside Commission – the successor to the National Parks Commission – and the Nature Conservancy Council. Since 1982 the Commission has enjoyed the same autonomous status outside the civil service as the NCC, but it is wrong to regard either of them as being completely independent of Government or, for that matter, mere lackeys of ministers or their departments. But all their members are appointed by government, and the membership now reflects the political complexion of the hard right government that has been in power since 1979. They are wholly dependent on government for their funds. Philip Lowe and Jane Goyder have argued, in *Environmental groups in politics*, that one of the functions of these agencies is to hold the environmental pressure groups at arm's length and to act as a 'negative filter' between them and the government, which only consults the agencies or takes their advice when it wants to.

The Countryside Commission is the agency responsible for advising the Government on the conservation of natural beauty and on recreation throughout England and Wales. In recent years it has tended to interpret its remit more widely. It has been responsible for advising the national park authorities since its formation in 1968. It submits to Government the names of people it thinks suitable for appointment to the national park authorities, and acts as middle men between the authorities and the government. It advises the authorities on their bids for government grant, and then advises the government on how much of the bids it should meet. It has powers to designate new national parks subject to the confirmation of the Secretary of State, whose hostility to new national parks had been clear for many years until he agreed to give The Broads the status, if not the name, in 1986. The Commission has also embarked on a review of the boundaries of the existing parks, which it was empowered to do by the Wildlife and Countryside Act 1981. This has proved to be a far bigger exercise than was originally foreseen. It could open a Pandora's box of pressures to reduce the area of the parks or to weaken their defences, when the original intention of the review was to sort out some obvious anomalies in the drawing of the boundaries.

The government that finally conceded autonomy to the Commission in 1981 simultaneously cut down its grant and reduced its staff to less than 100. Its grant was subsequently raised again from £11.4 million in 1982–3 to £19.5 million in 1987–8 – an increase of 20% in real terms – and its staff raised to 115. But the Commission's basic problem is that it is inherently a weak agency, standing between those who exercise political power – Government and local government – and those who own and manage the land. Since it became autonomous it has been the policy of the Commission, led by its chairman Sir Derek Barber, to make a virtue out of necessity by adopting the voluntary approach to conservation favoured by the Government.

Its programme, adopted in 1982, summed up both its limitations and its role: 'we do not own any land. We do not have a field staff. We cannot instruct anyone what to do or what not to do . . . But we can advise and persuade'. Sir Derek firmly believes that confrontation solves nothing. His ideal world is inhabited almost entirely by people of good will who resolve conflicts through discussion, oiled by compensation where appropriate. Belligerent conservationists are 'yesterday's men and women', and the bother caused by hideous buildings or 'the odd cascade of Sitka spruce on the wrong mountainside' are inevitable, mere 'hiccups' in a well ordered countryside. But Sir Derek has been persuaded by experience to see the need for some controls, and is clearly alarmed by the extreme views of the farming and forestry lobbies which we discuss in later chapters. He has become a firm advocate of developing the Environmentally Sensitive Area concept (see Chs 12 & 14) into a nationwide policy for promoting more traditional, lower-input farming.

Within the limits of this philosophy, which we will examine in later chapters, the Commission has a creditable record. Its perspective is far broader than that of the NCC, as can be shown by listing only some of the issues it has dealt with in recent years. It has given unstinted and generous support to the Broads Authority, without which it would not have achieved national park status and special legislation to give it powers that other national parks have not yet achieved (see Ch. 17). It has designated AONBs (sometimes in the teeth of strong opposition from hostile interests), brought heritage coasts into being, fostered country parks and demonstration farms, and conducted experiments in land management and integrated transport serving city and country, and studies of the economy and landscape of the uplands. It has supported the national park authorities at public inquiries into mineral developments and, albeit slowly, promoted long-distance footpaths.

The new knowledge it has obtained has enabled it to channel its grants more effectively. Experience has forced it to move, however gingerly, to ask government to give the park and other authorities some powers of last resort to control afforestation and to protect valued countryside features. But the very range and constant shifts in the Commission's interests and the muted tone of its policy recommendations, betray the difficulty it experiences in finding a clear role for itself. It tries to steer a tricky path between central government and the local authorities, presenting itself at one moment as a partner in the conservation lobby and at another acting as an arm of Government itself.

The Commission has tended to blow hot and cold over national parks. It disbanded its national parks section in 1974. But it took advantage of an officially inspired review of the economic efficiency of national parks (see Ch. 10) to appoint two officers to be responsible for national park affairs in 1985. In the same year it launched a campaign to 'Watch Over the National Parks', designed to arouse greater understanding of national parks and more support for them. The need for such a campaign is clear from the Commission's own survey, which revealed that half the people questioned thought that the National Trust ran the national parks. The Commission now sees its principal role in the national parks as the creation of a climate of opinion in support of national parks and, in particular, of a higher level of financial support for them. At a national level the campaign was initially ignored by the media, because a politically timid Commission had nothing to say beyond advancing the passive concept of 'watching over' the national parks. A vigorous campaign to expose the immense gap between the needs of the park authorities and the meagre resources the Government provides could have obtained wide coverage. The Commission does indeed want the parks to have more money, but not so much more as to embarrass its political masters. Its financial recommendations are governed by political calculation rather than by a professional assessment of the parks' real needs. Its recommendation to the authorities to bid for a cash increase of between 12 and 18% for 1987–8 corresponded very closely to what the Government agreed to, but would not satisfy real needs. The national parks campaign has, nevertheless, been useful to the park authorities at the local level, by focussing their efforts on the best ways of improving their relations with the local communities, the crucial (and sometimes critical) audience that they have to convince.

THE NATURE CONSERVANCY COUNCIL

The Nature Conservancy Council is responsible for giving advice to government and all public bodies on nature conservation. It designates National Nature Reserves (NNRs) and Sites of Special Scientific Interest. Its strength lies in the fact that, despite the transfer of much of its scientific function to the Institute of Terrestrial Ecology in 1973, it remains a scientific body, staffed by scientists and basing its advice on scientific criteria. In theory, once the NCC has established the special scientific interest of a site it must designate it as an SSSI whatever the political consequences. In practice, of course, natural science is not so precise as the theory suggests. But the respect in which science, with its supposedly objective and neutral criteria, is held gives the NCC an authority denied to the Countryside Commission.

The NCC has other advantages. It does not rely exclusively on persuasion. It achieves its results in the main by buying or leasing NNRs (most of which it manages) and by negotiating management agreements with the owners or tenants of SSSIs. Its authority extends to Scotland and it has a substantial field staff. Its regional and Welsh offices, through which it deals with the national parks, have greater resources than the Commission's, but also a heavy burden of field work. The NCC has some powers, (albeit limited and rarely used) to delay potentially damaging operations and to

Plate 8 (*above*) Rievaulx Abbey, Ryedale, in the North Yorkshire Moors. **Plate 9** (*below*) Hadrian's Wall, near Housesteads in the Northumberland National Park.

Plate 10 (*above*) The long, narrow, curving limestone walls around Chelmorton in the White Peak reveal the mediaeval field pattern. **Plate 11** (*below*) A sponsored walk in Littondale: note the field barns, characteristic of the Yorkshire Dales.

Passive and active recreation:
Plate 12 (*above*) relaxing at Dartmeet, a 'honeypot' much improved by the Dartmoor National Park Authority; **Plate 13** (*right*) a climber on Stanage Edge, one of the many gritstone cliffs in the Peak District.

Two faces of the Lake District: **Plate 14** (*above*) the peace of Ullswater, with Helvellyn in the background; and **Plate 15** (*below*) Bellman Launching, one of the three crowded and inadequate public launching sites on Lake Windermere.

Plate 16 The causeway carrying the 'miners' track' up Snowdon, recently repaired in the Snowdon Management Project.

Management: **Plate 17** (*above*) volunteers on a conservation project in the Yorkshire Dales repair a footpath at Dowber Gill, Great Whernside; **Plate 18** (*below*) a drystone waller in Longnor, scene of the Peak District Integrated Development Project.

Management: **Plate 19** (*above*) the traditional craft of coppicing revived in the Yorkshire Dales National Park Authority's wood at Carperby; **Plate 20** (*below*) broadleaved trees being planted on private land, with a subsidy from the same authority.

Plate 21 (*above*) 'The best known eyesore in the Peak', Eldon Hill Quarry. In 1987 the government rejected an appeal by Thos. W. Ward (Roadstone) Ltd against the park authority's decision to refuse a large extension. **Plate 22** (*below*) proposed pressurized water reactor at Trawsfynydd in the Snowdonia National Park: photo montage published by the Central Electricity Generating Board.

Plate 23 Visitors to Dartmoor's northern wilderness are warned of the dangers from artillery or rifle fire, when the ranges are in use, and from unexploded ammunition when they are not. Cranmere Pool is in the heart of Dartmoor.

Plate 24 Visitors to Tarr Steps, one of the most popular places in Exmoor, are reminded that they have no legal right to walk along a 'permissive' path.

Alternative land uses in the national parks: **Plate 25** (*above*) hill farmers gather their flocks on Shap Fell in the Lake District; **Plate 26** (*below*) Forestry Commission conifer plantations blanket the North York Moors.

Plate 27 (*above*) The graziers' Broadland: Halvergate marshes, where traditional grazing is now subsidized through an Environmentally Sensitive Areas scheme, to avoid conversion to arable farming. **Plate 28** (*below*) The visitors' Broadland: a river cruiser, Hickling Broad.

Plate 29 The magic of Broadland: Cockshoot Dyke, leading into Cockshoot Broad; their waters, once clouded and lifeless from pollution, have been restored to life by one of the Broads Authority's earliest conservation projects.

buy land compulsorily, if it can find the money and if the 'national interest' in the site can be established.

Since 1982 the NCC has been almost totally preoccupied with the daunting task, imposed by the 1981 Wildlife and Countryside Act, of notifying some 40 000 owners and tenants of 4000 SSSIs of their precise boundaries and of the potentially damaging operations to which the NCC would object. The government's grant to the NCC was increased to £36.5 million for 1987–8, but this leaves the NCC with very limited resources for the wider countryside. Its involvement in national parks is primarily in the notification and renotification of SSSIs, and in responding to farmers who have notified it of operations in an SSSI for which a grant is to be sought. The park authorities prefer, as a rule, to leave such proposals to the NCC, partly because the authorities are happier if the NCC meets the cost of any management agreement, and partly because the NCC has powers that the authorities do not have. The NCC's advice is also sought by the park authorities on the nature conservation value of sites outside SSSIs.

At its best the NCC can exert a strong influence. Its report on *Nature conservation and agriculture* in 1977 placed its scientific authority behind the criticisms of modern farming made by less prestigious critics. Its policy statement *Nature conservation in Britain* (1984), which embraced the principles of the World Conservation Strategy, expressed alarm at the impact of economic forces and policies, and published devastating figures of habitat losses to show that no further compromises were acceptable. Its language has sometimes been tougher than that of the Commission. But like the Commission, it avoids any direct challenge to government, and it is susceptible to political pressure. And problems can arise, as happened recently in joint appraisals of potential Environmentally Sensitive Areas, if each agency approaches a problem from its own standpoint.

If one takes the ecological view, that scenery is the visual expression of the living landscape, the 'great divide' between the Nature Conservancy Council and the Countryside Commission seems distinctly odd. Whatever justification there was for this division in 1949, the argument today surely favours their merger into a single conservation agency. The NCC stated in evidence to the House of Lords in 1976 that the differences between itself and the Commission were 'fundamental and inevitable'. This opinion, which contradicted other NCC statements to the effect that scenic beauty, wildlife and landforms 'are inter-related and indivisible', reflected the NCC's scientific preoccupations. But its 1984 policy statement *Nature conservation in Britain* redefined the purpose of conserving nature as being 'primarily cultural', for its 'scientific, educational, recreational, aesthetic and inspirational values'. In short, it has widened its scope until it is indistinguishable from that of the Countryside Commission.

In our view, the existence of two agencies, one run by scientists and the other by generalists or planners, has institutionalized the differences between two sets of professionals, each of which would be encouraged by closer association to broaden and illuminate what is too often a restricted point of view. Unification would enable the united agency to develop a strong regional presence, where the Commission is very weak indeed and the NCC preoccupied with detailed tasks such as renotifying SSSIs. Both are increasingly concerned with an ever-growing area of common interest. Dr Bryn Green, a former Regional Director of the Nature Conservancy and now a Countryside Commissioner, has argued that 'a united organisation structure is essential if amenity land planning and management is to be effective'. The Labour Party has argued for a united conservation agency. There are difficulties in effecting a merger of this kind, not the least of which is the resistance from the professionals on either side. It would be essential to prevent the NCC swamping the Commission, which has the broader outlook but only one-fifth of the staff. It might be necessary to detach the NCC's direct land-management functions, which take up most of its time and energy, from its policy-making, advisory and funding functions. The government considered a merger in 1979–80, but characteristically it did so as an economy device not as a means of bringing nature and landscape together. We return to this theme in Chapter 16.

THE VOLUNTARY BODIES

The split between the conservation agencies is mirrored by the divisions between the 50 or so amenity, conservation and recreation groups that make up the conservation lobby or lobbies. The Countryside Commission co-ordinates its relations with 13 national organizations through Countryside Link, and the NCC co-ordinates its relations with 33 national and international organizations through Wildlife Link. But whereas the NCC spends most of its money directly on its own projects and organization, the Countryside Commission directly subsidizes a large number of voluntary groups and projects. Several of these have become heavily dependent on Countryside Commission funding, which was essential to give the Farming and Wildlife Advisory Group a national presence and to develop the Council for National Parks into a remarkably effective organization. The benefits to these organizations are obvious, but it remains to be seen whether dependence on government money will, in the long run, make it more difficult for voluntary groups to criticize and to oppose government policy. For a fuller account of the voluntary bodies and their relations with the government and its agencies readers should consult *Countryside conflicts* by Lowe, MacEwen & others, and *Agriculture: people and policies* by Cox, Lowe & Winter.

The total membership of these voluntary bodies runs into millions, with a good deal of overlap between them, but the diversity of their interests and the split between nature and landscape conservation have made it difficult for them to get their act together. This was painfully obvious during the passage of the Wildlife and Countryside Bill in 1980–1, when the landscape conservation interests were able to form a common front much earlier than the nature conservation lobby, and the NCC and the Countryside Commission were never able to harmonize their positions. The divided counsels in the conservation camp played into the government's hands and contrasted painfully with the united front consistently presented by the National Farmers' Union (which virtually drafted the government's conservation policy) and the Country Landowners' Association. They have the overwhelming advantage that the NFU, in particular, has enjoyed an intimate relationship with Ministers and civil servants that has no parallel in British government. Agriculture is the only industry with its own minister in the Cabinet (in Tory cabinets almost invariably a 'gentleman' farmer), although the relationship became strained in 1986–7.

The agricultural departments have carefully avoided forming any regular links with the conservation lobbies. The one significant exception is the Farming and Wildlife Advisory Group (FWAG), which MAFF helped to establish and has supported strongly with premises, staff and some money. MAFF associates with and works through FWAG and its money-raising arm, the Farming and Wildlife Trust, because FWAG is debarred by its constitution from exerting any pressure for changes in law or policy. It shares MAFF's basic position that modern, profitable farming is not incompatible with conservation, and avoids any discussion of the need for changes in policy or the introduction of controls. 'FWAGGERY', as one national park officer calls it, tends to be favoured by bigger farmers (often those who have already intensified their units and have money to spare), and to concentrate on keeping or creating some wild places. It does not challenge farming interests.

Nevertheless, the bankruptcy of the Common Agricultural

Policy has forced the agricultural departments onto the defensive and enabled the voluntary amenity, conservation and recreation bodies, despite their divisions, to exercise increasing influence from 1980 onwards. The national parks owe their existence and their progress very largely to the relentless pressures exerted by the Councils for the Protection of Rural England and Wales, the Royal Society for the Protection of Birds, the Open Spaces Society, the Ramblers' Association and the Council for National Parks, to name but a few. Without the active intervention of the local societies, such as the Friends of the Lake District, the Dartmoor Preservation Society, the Sheffield and District branch of the CPRE and the Exmoor Society, and their ability to influence national organizations, many a battle to protect the national parks would never have been fought. New local societies have recently been formed in the Yorkshire Dales and the North York Moors. Their relations with the park authorities are mixed, and are never as intimate as those between the park authorities and the farmers and landowners. But their influence is growing, and their future role could be of decisive importance.

The crisis in farming has, for the first time, begun to bring the conservation and the farming interests together at local level. A conference organized by the Exmoor Society in 1982 to discuss our book *National parks: conservation or cosmetics?* was banned by the NFU. It forbade its county secretary for Cumbria, who had accepted an invitation to speak at the conference, to take part. But in 1985 every farming and landowning group was represented at a successful and crowded conference organized by the same society on the theme of farming and conservation. The success of the Commons Forum in reaching an agreement in 1982, which we described in Chapter 8, also suggests a greater readiness for the different interests to have a constructive dialogue with each other, even if very basic differences remain.

Chapter Ten

The national park
authorities

WHERE POWER LIES

The term 'national park authority' is a courtesy title. It is never used
in the legislation which, as we explained in Chapter 2, entrusts the
administration of the national parks to the county councils or, in the
cases of the Peak District and the Lakes, to the two planning boards.
'National park authority' is a convenient term to describe national
park boards and committees, but it attributes a good deal more
authority to the latter than they actually possess.

The boards are autonomous local planning authorities. They
combine the power to make policies in the structure plans with the
power to control development. They settle their own budgets and
levy a rate by precepting on the constituent councils. The boards
appoint and employ their own staff and are free to use or not to use
the services of county council officials, or to engage outside consultants. They can buy land or conclude management agreements on
their own authority. They are responsible for the conservation of
historic buildings or areas. They make their own standing orders
about procedure and administration. They can only be controlled by
the county council if, as has happened in the Lakes, the majority
party can muster a majority on the board. But the multiplicity of
authorities in the Peak gives its board an exceptional degree of
independence of the county councils, although currently a majority
of members support Labour. In both cases the boards are beyond the
reach of the county council chief executive and his management
'team' of chief officers.

The committees have far less autonomy. The county councils,
through their planning committees, frame the planning policies of
their respective counties (including the national parks) in the county

structure plans, although the national park committees are responsible, by law, for development control. County councils may also
delegate to national park committees such functions as the preparation of local plans, the conservation of areas of historic or archi-
tectural interest, the making of tree preservation orders, advertisement control, the review and modification of public rights of
way, footpath maintenance and the conclusion of management
agreements with landowners. But not all county councils delegate
all these functions, so that the actual powers of a national park
committee vary from park to park according to the tolerance of the
county council concerned.

It would be wrong to create the impression that the national park
committees are mere tools of the county councils. They have all
built up effective departments with skilled staff, and they enjoy real
autonomy in the exercise of the planning control, conservation and
recreation functions allocated to them. But the county councils do
impede or prevent the progress of their national park departments
(as they call them) in varying degrees. They impose strict controls
on current and capital expenditure and staffing. They appoint all the
staff (apart from the national park officer), and they compel the
national park officer to waste a lot of time and money pushing his
financial and staff requirements through county council committees. (We say 'his' because there has never been a woman national
park officer or assistant NPO, and the proportion of women in the
senior positions is scandalously small.) It took the Snowdonia
National Park Officer two years and 17 meetings of various
Gwynedd County Council committees and sub-committees, not to
mention meetings and discussions with county council officers, to
secure agreement to the appointment of one additional officer in
1985.

The county councils use their standing orders to regulate the
administration of the national park committee and department, and
to limit the roles that can be played by government-appointed
members. Standing orders also require the national park committee
to get legal, technical and other professional advice from other
county council departments. As the councils are understaffed, the
parks often have to take their place in a queue and suffer long delays,
and they have to pay for the service at rates laid down by the county
council. It was for this reason that the Pembrokeshire Coast
National Park Committee, wearied of the endless tussles with
Dyfed County Council, prefaced its bid for government grant in
1985 by advising the Countryside Commission and the government
that if it were reconstituted as a board it could improve its
effectiveness and bid for the money it needs.

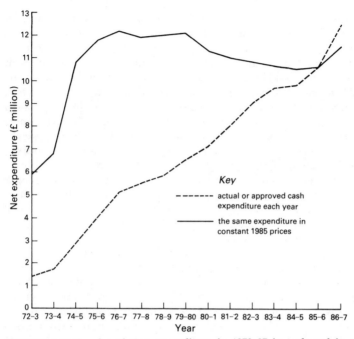

Figure 16 National park net expenditure in 1972–87 in cash and in real terms 1972–4 values estimated. Values from 1974–5 onwards are actual expenditure net of income, and from 1984–5 are net approved expenditure of which the Department pays 75% to the county councils and national park planning boards through the National Park Supplementary Grant. The figures given in Figures 17 and 18 are, in contrast, gross inclusive of income (source: Council for National Parks).

The government's consultation paper on *The future of development plans* (September 1986) says that the responsibilities of the county councils and the two national park planning boards would remain 'as now', should its proposal to abolish county structure plans be carried out. In fact the proposal has serious implications for mineral and other developments that are discussed in Chapter 13.

THE FINANCIAL LOTTERY

The 1974 Finance Act introduced the National Park Supplementary Grant (NPSG) as part of the government's support to local authorities. No rate was fixed by law, but it is calculated at around 75% of the net expenditure of the local authorities on national parks after allowing for receipts from other sources – but only up to a limit approved by government. This left the county councils to find the other 25%, although they did not have to do so. The 75% grant was a key element in the 'new deal' that followed the Sandford Report, which had recommended that in real terms the expenditure of the two boards should be doubled and that of the committees trebled by 1978–9, and that expenditure should continue to rise thereafter. Figure 16 shows what really happened. The lower line shows the 'approved' expenditure in cash terms soaring upwards in an almost unbroken line from 1972–3 (Sandford's base year) to the present time. But the upper line shows that expenditure in real terms peaked in 1976–7 at double the 1972–3 figure, and fell thereafter. Sandford's initial target, which he regarded as the rock-bottom minimum was never achieved. The increase in grant in 1986–7 only took expenditure back to 1974–5 in real terms, and in the meantime the national park authorities had been obliged to take on many more duties.

By 1982, when national park expenditure was dropping fast in real terms, stories were circulating in government circles about the 'inefficiency' of the park authorities. Tales about staff clock-watching and typists knitting were spread by some politicians. So in 1983 the Government decided to subject the national park system to a review of its 'economic efficiency', which was conducted by a firm of management consultants, Arthur Young McLelland Moores and Co. Their report, which was published by the Countryside Commission in 1984, was only mildly critical of the 'economic efficiency' of the authorities and on the whole its recommendations were helpful even if coloured by a narrow managerial approach. The review clearly found as a matter of fact that the boards were getting more efficient legal and other services, and getting them more cheaply. It was critical of the excessive paper work generated by county council administration, and found that the output of the boards' staff was substantially greater than that of the committees. It criticized overcharging by the counties, and recommended that county councils should impose no restrictions either on the staffing or the expenditure of the committees. The county councils have shown a marked reluctance to implement this recommendation however, and have been supported by the Association of County Councils which asserted unambiguously that the county councils, and not the committees, are legally the national park authorities.

The economic efficiency review conceded that the parks should be spending more money on conservation, but said that no case had been made for an overall increase in resources because the park authorities had failed to show how much money they needed to implement the national park plans. Accordingly, a new procedure recommended by the review was introduced in 1985 for the authorities' bid for national park grants for 1986–7. Each bid had to be accompanied by 'functional strategies'. This unlovely bureaucratic term concealed some good sense. For the authorities were required to break down their objectives, policies, work programmes and needs for money and staff (their 'strategies') under six main 'functions' – conservation, town and country planning, interpretation and information, recreation, support to the local community and administration. The new system could have generated immensely larger bids for grant and exposed the gulf between the needs of the park authorities and the resources at their disposal. But the opportunity was largely missed. The reason was the depressing influence of the government's financial squeeze on local authorities (which would have to pay 25% of the net cost of any increase), and the resulting timidity of the park authorities, the county councils and the Countryside Commission, which discouraged 'politically unrealistic' bids.

The result was a series of bids ranging from a request for 40% more cash from the Yorkshire Dales down to less than 5% more (a standstill in real terms) from Brecon Beacons. The final outcome was an overall increase of 10% in cash or 5% in spending power which met the lower bids in full, and cut down the higher bids with varying degrees of severity and equity. The winners proved to be Dartmoor and Exmoor, both of which got more than the average increase. The big losers were the North Yorkshire Moors and the Yorkshire Dales which bid for 31% and 40% respectively, but only got 10% and 9%. For technical reasons, intelligible only to those who understand the Mad Hatter's arrangements for controlling local government expenditure, for the North York Moors this represented a cut of 3% in their *actual* expenditure and of 9% in real terms. The result was to leave the park committee desperately short of cash for a whole series of imaginative conservation and other programmes it had initiated.

This process, instead of being the cool appraisal of needs that the authorities had been led to expect, was a carve-up, or a lottery. The outcome was not, of course, entirely negative. The new procedure holds out great promise for the future if the local authorities permit, and the Countryside Commission encourages, bids designed to meet real needs and if the government puts up real money to meet them. Preparing the bids and strategies forced the park authorities to rethink their policies and to reassess their needs, and to submit bids for a 24% increase in grant for 1987–8.

The efficiency review also exposed the high bureaucratic 'dual control' over national park finance. There are, in fact, not two but three levels of control. The park authorities' budgets have first to be approved by the county councils, except in the Lake District and the Peak. They are then submitted to the Countryside Commission which forwards them with recommendations to the Welsh Office and the Department of the Environment. When, after months of non-communication, the government then informs the Commission of the approved level of expenditure, the Commission has to haggle in a few hectic days with the departments over the division of the money between the park authorities – which are not consulted. The result was that in 1985 the county councils and the boards submitted net bids totalling £12.6 million, which were reduced by the Commission's recommendations to £11.8 million, and further reduced by government to £11.5 million on which it paid grant of £8.6 million. In the event, despite their financial problems, the county councils responded positively. In Devon and Somerset the new Alliance groups with Labour support made good most of the shortfall in Dartmoor and Exmoor by raising their contribution to an unprecedented 34%. The Countryside Commission took a firmer line for 1987–8, by supporting bids for net expenditure totalling £14.3 million. In the final settlement the Government approved net expenditure of £13.05 million, on which it pays grant of £9.8 million – an increase of £1.4 million or 13.4%.

HOW THE MONEY IS SPENT

Figures 17 and 18 show us how the park authorities' money is spent on the various 'functions' to which expenditure is allocated in the 'functional strategies' – conservation 21%, recreation and visitor services 49%, administration 26%, town and country planning 8% and support to the local community a mere 2% (see Ch. 4). These categories are distinctly arbitrary (two authorities put litter collection under conservation) and many activities (the ranger service for example) serve several functions. Figure 18 points out the enormous differences in the resources available to each park, reflecting not only the extent of the park and the severity of the pressures exerted on it, but also the failure of the system to distribute the money according to real needs. Figure 18 also shows up very marked differences in the priorities that parks give to the several functions, which again reflects particular pressures and political attitudes. The Peak, for example, has to spend far more money on development control because it regularly faces the high costs of public inquiries into quarrying and mineral development.

There is a strong case for government paying grant at a higher rate than 75% to park authorities where needs are high and rateable

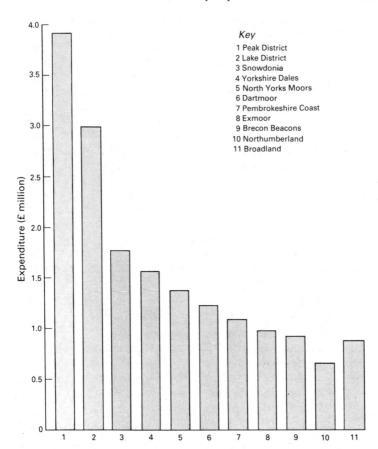

Key

1 Peak District
2 Lake District
3 Snowdonia
4 Yorkshire Dales
5 North Yorks Moors
6 Dartmoor
7 Pembrokeshire Coast
8 Exmoor
9 Brecon Beacons
10 Northumberland
11 Broadland

Figure 17   Where the money goes: national park expenditure for 1986–7   The estimated park expenditure for 1986–7 by the ten national park authorities (£16.6 million) and the Broads Authority (£0.88 million). The expenditure by each authority is largely determined by historical accidents, and by the degree to which each authority is free to bid for, or to spend, the money it needs. The two autonomous boards, in the Peak District and the Lakes are far ahead.

values low. But the county councils fear that if they contribute less than 25% of the net expenditure their case for political control will be undermined. So instead of pressing for a fairer system that would greatly increase the grant to the poorer counties, they tend to keep down the expenditure. The national parks have in fact done very much better than other local government services during the relentless squeeze exerted by central government since 1979, that has cut local services to the bone and compelled members and

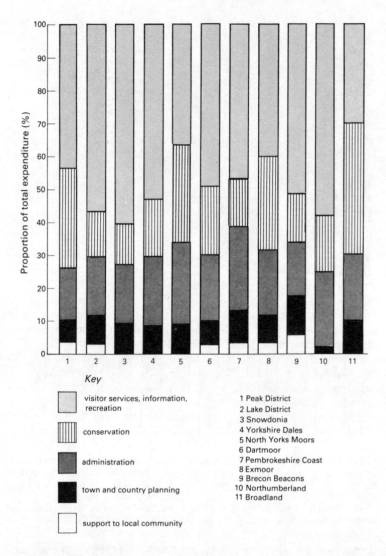

Key

visitor services, information, recreation	1 Peak District
	2 Lake District
	3 Snowdonia
conservation	4 Yorkshire Dales
	5 North Yorks Moors
	6 Dartmoor
administration	7 Pembrokeshire Coast
	8 Exmoor
	9 Brecon Beacons
town and country planning	10 Northumberland
	11 Broadland

support to local community

Figure 18 Where the money goes: how each park authority spends its money How the estimated expenditure by the ten national park authorities (£16.6 million) and the Broads Authority (£0.88 million) for 1986–7 is divided between their different functions. Visitor services (average 49%) get the largest share, but conservation (22%) is rising in relation to it. Support to the local community (2%) is negligible: Snowdonia, Yorkshire Dales and North York Moors spend £10 000 a year or less, too little to be shown on the scale of this chart (for further details of spending on the community see Ch. 4).

officers alike to make appallingly difficult decisions. The Rate Support Grant for England was cut from 65% to 46% of net expenditure between 1974 and 1986 (although in Wales it is 66%), while the National Park Supplementary Grant has remained at 75% and in real terms has regained the level of 1974–5.

The crude techniques introduced by government in recent years to control local government expenditure are baffling in their complexity, defy common sense and concentrate local decision-making in the hands of ministers and their civil servants. Government authorizes higher spending on national parks with one hand, and penalizes the county councils for spending it on the other. It approves budgets that include essential items of capital expenditure, and gives the national park authorities the money to do the works. But it then compels the county councils to make a corresponding cut in the capital they spend on their environmental services, such as libraries, fire stations or museums. It advises the park authorities to turn for help on capital items, such as buying land, to the National Heritage Memorial Fund, and then cuts the Fund's grant for 1986–7 by 2% in real terms. Its budget of £13.5 million is an absurdly small sum with which to protect the entire cultural heritage of buildings, works of art and landscapes of the United Kingdom, at a time when a single painting can cost £8 million – or as much as the government spent on ten national parks in 1986–7.

It would be entirely wrong to depict the park authorities as money-guzzling, local government bureaucracies. They are inspired to an exceptional degree by a commitment to, and enthusiasm for the cause they serve. By increasing efficiency, cutting down capital expenditure, and tapping additional sources of money and labour they were able to avoid the most damaging consequences of the cuts, and even to increase their staff from 625 to 675 between 1979 and 1986 while extending the range of their professional skills. They have made use of help from the rural development agencies, the tourist boards, English Heritage and its Welsh equivalent for ancient monuments (CADW) and the Countryside Commission for one-off projects. They have entered into cost-sharing partnerships with bodies like the National Trust and the water authorities. Nearly all the parks have made considerable use of voluntary and part-time labour, particularly for their ranger and warden services and for footpath and conservation work.

The major source of additional labour has been the community service schemes of the Manpower Services Commission, which give temporary jobs to the longer-term unemployed. Without them the national parks would have been totally unable to tackle the backlog of work on footpath maintenance, woodland management, information programmes and scientific surveys on which, at a rough, unofficial estimate, 405 people had MSC 'places' (not full-time jobs) in 1985. Exmoor alone valued its MSC teams for 1986–7 at £182 000, equivalent to an extra 18% on its total expenditure. However, as a study by the Dartington Institute showed in 1985, the MSC schemes are a very mixed blessing. The administration is highly bureaucratic and, as the MSC does not recognize the park authorities (except the two boards) as its agents, the park authorities have to get allocations of MSC labour from the county councils. Organization and supervision place a big strain on the permanent staff. No sooner have the unemployed acquired skills and motivation than they have to be dismissed.

The MSC rejected the idea put to it by one park authority that the park authority or some other single agency could bring together would-be trainees and farmers or contractors who would train them on the job. Young people would acquire more skill and do better work if directly responsible to skilled people. But the MSC prefers to organize mobile gangs with their own vehicle under a supervisor who is chosen because he or she is on the jobless register. The MSC's aim is not to provide real jobs but to massage the statistics so as to reduce the numbers of long-term unemployed on the register. The result is that the numbers of MSC schemes in individual parks go up and down like Yo-Yos. The Dartington study showed that national park officers were unanimous in saying that the work could be better done and more easily supervised if they could offer permanent jobs for which people could be appropriately trained. Because the MSC keep no separate statistics for work in the national parks MSC expenditure is not included in national park statistics.

Although it is commonly believed that the government and the local authorities split all the costs of the national park between them in the ratio of 75 : 25, the cost to the authorities is reduced by the substantial sums paid by the public for visitors services, information, rents, planning applications and other services. Moreover, the Rate Support Grant reduces the ratepayers' contribution, nominally 25%, by nearly half. Figure 19 shows that the taxpayer paid 60% of the gross expenditure in 1986–7, the public 24%, the ratepayer 12% and reserves and other grants provided 4%.

The county councils have good reasons, from their point of view, for restraining national park expenditure on current or capital account. Nevertheless, the 'burden' on the taxpayer is not measurable and that on the individual ratepayer trifling. The average ratepayer in Somerset, for example, pays three pence a month for the Exmoor National Park. But the system is grossly unfair for the poorer rural authorities. The average ratepayer in Gwynedd pays

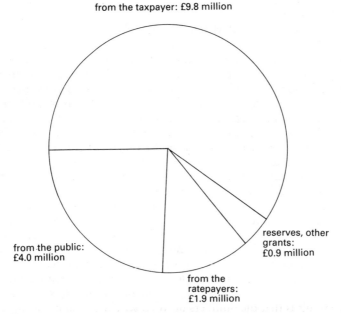

from the taxpayer: £9.8 million

from the public:
£4.0 million

reserves, other
grants:
£0.9 million

from the
ratepayers:
£1.9 million

Figure 19 Where the money comes from: national park income 1986–7 The ten national park authorities get the money to pay their estimated expenditure of £16.6 million for 1986–7 from four sources: from the taxpayer (National Park Supplementary Grant £8.6 million, Rate Support Grant £1.0 million, other grants £0.2 million), from the public (payment for information, parking, visitor centres, planning fees, rents, etc.), from the ratepayers and from reserves, balances, etc. (Estimated by the authors from information supplied by the national parks authorities and the Countryside Commission.)

about 15 times as much for the Snowdonia National Park as the averge ratepayer in Derbyshire, Staffordshire, Barnsley, Oldham or Sheffield pays for the Peak, although Snowdonia's resources are far smaller. The government could easily eliminate the inequalities, since the cost of the national parks in 1986–7 was a mere 0.005% of local government expenditure. The government spends more on the Covent Garden Opera House than it does to maintain ten national parks which cover 9% of the surface of England and Wales and are enjoyed by 50 million people or more every year.

MEMBERS AND OFFICERS

There has been very little discussion about the members who
constitute the national park authorities. The elected members are by
definition local politicians. They may be county or district councillors, although county councillors often represent parts of the county
that are remote from the national park. Of the 15 county councillors
on the Peak Board in 1986–7 only two lived in the Park. The
councillors' dominant concerns are local, above all to provide jobs
and to keep down the rates. Some elected members are committed
to national park purposes, and most of them become more committed after a spell on the board or committee. But they tend to be
drawn from a very limited sector of rural society, overwhelmingly
from those who have the time and the money (the retired or the
better off) to be able to devote much of their time to council affairs.
Councillors are busy people, who have to serve on many committees and sub-committees. The national park committee is, therefore, only one among many, and rarely as important in members'
eyes as the education or policy and finance committees where the
real power lies. Councillors tend to give less time to national park
affairs than do the appointed members.

   If a reasonable balance is to be struck between 'national' and 'local'
interests it is essential that ministerially appointed members should
understand and be committed to policies that will promote conservation and recreation. Unfortunately the statutes lay down no
criteria to govern ministers' appointments. They can and do make
the crudest political appointments, whether they are Tory or
Labour. A study made by Ian Brotherton for the Council for
National Parks of the appointments to national park authorities
between 1972 and 1982 showed that after 1979 ministers systematic-
ally packed the authorities with Tories, often farmers and landowners, to the exclusion of people who had some special skill,
experience or knowledge relevant to the national parks. The study
showed that nearly 400 people who served as ministerial appointees
since 1951 had been drawn almost exclusively from the higher
socio-economic groups, with a heavy bias towards farmers and
landowners. This confirmed a survey we made of the membership
in 1978, which showed, in addition, that women are grossly
under-represented (although the proportion rose from 12% in 1978
to 16% in 1985), as are the small farmers and manual workers. There
are no farm workers on any park authority. Local people often
complain that they are not sufficiently represented, but they are

better represented than the people of the towns, cities and conurbations who form the great majority of the parks' users.

Mark Blacksell of Exeter University, who was for some years an appointed member of the Dartmoor National Park Committee, has drawn attention to the fact that appointees cannot take part in any of the county council meetings where the main policy and financial decisions are taken. Because they are not members of any organized political group or caucus, they are almost invariably excluded from the discussions by telephone or otherwise that fix decisions before the park authority meets. On appointment they are not given much guidance or briefing on the 'national interest' they are supposed to promote, and they tend to become spokesmen for specific local groups, such as farmers, landowners or conservationists.

Dr Blacksell has attempted to measure the power wielded by different elements in the national park system, and has concluded that chairs and vice-chairs are in a very dominating and powerful position. Standing orders and custom combine in some county councils to exclude ministerially appointed members from the chair and, in some committees, from the vice-chair. It is customary in both the boards to have an appointee as vice-chair, but some county council standing orders prevent appointees from serving in the chair even of a sub-committee. Dr Blacksell puts the influence of the national park officer and his staff below that of the chair and vice-chair, but well above that of county or district councillors. And he puts the ministerial appointees at the bottom of his scale of influence or power. There are, of course, exceptions to every rule. Some ministerial appointees with outstanding skills and commitment have been very influential particularly where, as in the Peak, the council representatives are often divided. But Dr Blacksell is right to say that the ministerial appointees are second-class members. We question, however, his view that the national park officer exercises less power than the chair and vice-chair.

The 'functional strategies' raised fundamental political and strategic questions – precisely those that the members and not the officers should answer. But the Exmoor National Park Officer was almost alone in submitting his 1986–7 functional strategies and bid for grant to the members for debate. In most parks they never went beyond the chair and the vice-chair. This tells us a great deal about where power in the national park authority really lies. The government determines the size of the national park cake and the slice that each park gets. But one has to probe the inner workings of local politics to discover precisely how that slice is subdivided by the park authority.

CONCLUSION

What all this boils down to is that the national park system is too weak at every level to realize its great potential for comprehensive countryside management. The park authorities do not have enough money and people or enough powers to do the job properly. Furthermore, they often show excessive concern for the interests of farmers and landowners, who are strongly represented on the authorities. Government departments lack commitment to national park objectives, and so do several of their agencies. Government is still pursuing policies that sharply contradict the green sentiments that ministers now express with growing emphasis. The Association of County Councils and many councillors seem to be more interested in defending their dominant role than in helping effective, responsible and sensitive national park authorities to emerge. But the strongest impression we have formed is that despite the weaknesses we have identified, and the weight of political inertia to be overcome, the national park authorities have a great potential. If the need for a radical reform of local government, to promote among other things the integration of conservation and recreation with social and economic development, is placed on the political agenda much could be learned from the national park system. The opportunities that were missed, or only partly grasped, in 1949, 1968, 1972 and 1981 should be seized in the new climate that is more favourable to the comprehensive land management that the national park authorities have been trying out.

Chapter Eleven

Management –
or getting things done

UPLAND MANAGEMENT

The management of land is to take decisions as to what is done or not done. Reg Hookway, as Director of the Countryside Commission after 1968, pushed the concept of 'management' in a conscious attempt to move the emphasis of national park authorities away from controlling development and towards getting things done. National park management plans were a key element in the reorganization of 1972–4 that we described in Chapter 2. They took a comprehensive view of the parks' problems, and listed appropriate policies quite literally by the hundred. But where they lacked specific powers their policies tended to be very general: to be in favour of this, or to press for that or to encourage the other. To get things done is, however, quite another matter. The management plan, whether for a national park or a much smaller area, was only one element in the new 'management' doctrine. The other two, which we will now examine, were the management agreement and the upland management project, both of which have proved useful, but neither of which has been found to have the capabilities or the potential originally attributed to them.

In 1969 the Countryside Commission, in collaboration with the Ministry of Agriculture, launched the first Upland Management Experiment, which it called UMEX 1, in a few parishes in the Lake District, and in 1970 in Snowdonia. The objective was 'to test a method of reconciling the interests of farmers and visitors in the uplands by offering financial encouragement to farmers to carry out small schemes which improve the appearance of the landscape and enhance the recreational opportunities of the area', and to assess what effect this had on farmers' attitudes towards landscape and recreation. The key to the success of UMEX proved to be the appointment of a project officer, who was given a wide discretion to take practical steps to solve the problems he had identified. For the first time in the history of the national parks, an officer appeared on the scene offering farmers help, jobs and money. The Ministry of Agriculture dropped out when James Prior killed the Ministry's newborn Rural Development Boards in 1970. But the first stage was sufficiently successful in the Lake District to be extended into a wider area for a second stage (UMEX 2) with a full-time officer, independent of the Ministry. Upland management passed beyond the experimental stage in 1976 when it became an integral part of the national park administration in the Lake District with a budget in 1985–6 of £184 000. The experiment was unsuccessful in Snowdonia, largely because the National Park Authority failed to provide money or staff on the scale required, or failed to secure the necessary funding from government.

Today the Upland Management Service, UMAS as it is known in the Lake District, is responsible for the network of footpaths and other rights of way, and much of its work involves repair and maintenance jobs that are done in other parks by rangers and ground staff. About two-thirds of its budget is spent on footpaths and access, and the rest goes on repairing stone walls, planting broadleaved trees and other conservation projects on farmers' land.

The success of upland management has been considerable in terms of minor works such as erecting stiles, bridges and gates, repairing walls and fences and repairing or diverting paths. It has provided some much needed part-time jobs, for the Lakes Board makes a point of employing farmers and others in addition to its own full-time staff. UMAS has changed the attitudes of many farmers from resentment towards a remote bureaucracy into something approaching enthusiasm for a service that knows them, helps them and employs some of them. Every Lakeland farmer the authors have met has spoken highly of UMAS and some of this popularity has even rubbed off onto the board itself. Although the term Upland Management Service is not generally used, most national parks have adopted this approach in one form or another. The concept of the area project run by a project officer has been extended on a modest scale to heritage coasts, to a few AONBs and to some areas on the fringes of large cities or conurbations. In all of them it has proved to be a successful technique for getting minor recreational works done and easing the friction between farmers and visitors.

UMAS has every right to claim that it has been successful on its own terms. But it is also necessary to recognize the limits of these schemes which have been spelt out clearly by the Countryside Commission itself in its reports on the Lake District and Snowdonia experiments in 1976: 'it was evident during the course of Stage 1 that it would . . . only scratch the surface of the real social and economic problems faced by the farming community . . . with less and less indigenous help to keep the fabric of the area intact there was every chance of the dereliction accelerating'. The irrelevance of upland management to the solution of deep-seated economic and social problems, led the Commission and the Lakes Board to commission a study of the Hartsop Valley by Gerald Wibberley and others. The report, published in 1976, presented a vivid picture of an ageing, declining community living on the margin of survival, whose farmers had neither the time, the labour, the economic incentives nor the capital to maintain landscape features that brought no financial benefit to them. Its main conclusion was that neither the Lakes Board nor the local authorities could solve the problems: 'it is imperative that the government should provide financial and legislative backing for measures aimed at attacking rural housing shortages, assisting hill farmers and maintaining a national asset'. It is a message that, as we will see in later chapters, has not yet got through to government. Upland management does many useful things, but comprehensive countryside management is not one of them.

It was precisely because upland management could not even attempt to reconcile countryside policies or reshape hill farming that the Lakes Board urged major changes in agricultural policy and initiated a third experiment in 1980 – UMEX 3 – which attempted to integrate tourist development and landscape and nature conservation on 25 farms with Ministry of Agriculture grant-aided farm development plans. But the experiment failed because farm development plans concentrated almost exclusively (as they had to do at that time) on increasing food production and labour productivity, and were found to be incompatible with the Board's wider objectives. The scheme was quietly dropped.

MANAGEMENT AGREEMENTS

It is highly instructive to trace the course by which management agreements came to be regarded by the government as the key device by which the 'voluntary' approach to countryside conflicts could be made to work. The Countryside Commission began to push management agreements as the sovereign remedy for resolving conflicts between farmers or foresters and conservation interests in the early 1970s. By management agreements they meant formal, written contracts between a public authority and landowners, tenants or occupiers of land, by which the latter agreed to manage their land in a specified manner, and were usually paid to do so. But further thought and experience soon demonstrated the limitations of this approach. A report to the Commission in 1978 by one of its officers, Michael Feist, spelt them out. Management agreements, he said, could not remedy incompatible policies in central government which are the main cause of conflict. They could not tackle such basic problems as the inability of the small hill farmer to survive in an adverse economic climate, or shortage of money to pay the cost of conservation practices. Subsequent experience has also shown that where they are used to resolve conflicts of interest, both parties resort to expensive professional advisers, including lawyers and surveyors, with the result that negotiations are inordinately costly and long drawn out. Where the authority has no legal power to control whatever the farmer or landowner wants to do, and an agreement is made for a period of years, a management agreement does no more than provide short-term protection to a site, very often at a high price, and defers the ultimate decision on its fate. And, as the public authority negotiates from weakness it is forced to pay 'over the odds', as the Somerset County Valuer once put it, to secure the agreement.

In situations where there is no serious conflict of interest, mutual respect and goodwill often create a climate in which it is possible to achieve results, usually on a small scale. The multitude of informal agreements made under the Upland Management Service in the Lake District, or by similar means elsewhere, show that large dividends of goodwill and co-operation can be earned by small investments of money and manpower on minor works. The management agreement at Upton Castle in Pembrokeshire Coast National Park illustrates the case where the owner of a stately home who cannot afford to keep up the grounds is relieved of the cost of doing so, in return for opening them to the public. At Deeper Marsh on the River Dart, Dartmoor National Park Committee has agreed a management plan with the landowner, the commoners and the South-West Regional Water Authority to improve parking, protect grazing areas and restore the river banks to the mutual benefit of all concerned. But where there is a basic conflict of interest and large sums of money are at stake intractable problems can arise.

All the park authorities can show examples of formal or informal agreements for tree planting, or the leasing or purchase of land for this purpose. The Brecon Beacons have shown what a poor but enterprising authority can do in a short time. By using Forestry Commission grants for tree planting schemes of more than 0.25 ha and getting free labour from the Manpower Services Commission to supplement its staff resources, it was able by 1986 to enter into 48 management agreements covering 200 ha and carried out over 400 smaller schemes ranging from 1 or 2 to 200 trees. By 1985–6, it was planting 16 ha a year. The cost to public funds has been only £26 000 a year. On average, owners had to meet only 20% of the cost. 'Management' worked because there were no serious conflicts of interest, the park authority offered favourable terms and the schemes made only small demands on the pockets or the energies of the farmers or owners. The limitations of this particular enterprise are obvious. The 'best guess' that the authority can make is that although more trees are now being planted than felled in the national park the rate of planting is about one-third of the rate at which woodland is being lost from felling, overgrazing and non-management.

The most extensive management agreement in any national park is the result of the Treasury's agreement to exempt 6235 ha of the Bransdale Moors on the Nawton Tower Estate in the North York Moors National Park from capital transfer tax (CTT). Since the 1976 Finance Act, land of outstanding scenic, historic and scientific interest can be exempted from CTT provided that the character of the land is protected and public access secured. The Estate secured the exemption in 1978 by entering into a management agreement (on terms approved by the Countryside Commission) with the park authority by which the Estate will be managed for sheep, grouse and informal recreation. An agreement that might have cost £30 000 a year, index linked against inflation on the terms negotiated in Exmoor, costs the NPA nothing. The true cost is hidden, being met by the Treasury foregoing large sums of CTT once in every generation.

THE EXMOOR SAGA

The management agreement concept was taken up very strongly by the National Farmers' Union and the Country Landowners' Association in the mid-1970s when the reclamation of moorland in Exmoor had become a public scandal and a national issue (for a full account of the Exmoor story and the Wildlife and Countryside Act see *National parks: conservation or cosmetics*, A. & M. MacEwen 1982, Ch. 8; and *Countryside conflicts*, P. Lowe *et al.* 1986, Chs 6–8). Exmoor and Dartmoor are the two largest areas of more or less open country in southern England. Exmoor's moorland is less than half as extensive as Dartmoor's. It is a fragile, precious resource, and was the major factor in Exmoor's designation as a national park in 1954. The mild climate, the lowish altitudes, the flattish tops of the moorland plateau, some relatively good soils and the lowest rainfall of the western national parks provided favourable technical conditions for reclamation. Exmoor is within the agriculturally Less Favoured Areas and qualified for the generous subsidies on offer until 1984 for land reclamation, together with the payments on the additional stock that could be carried on the 'improved' land. From the 1950s, the Ministry of Agriculture encouraged farmers to maximize their profits and land values by reclaiming the moorland. The result is that, whereas in 1954 the moorland was about a third of the park's area, today it is about a quarter, and is so fragmented (as can be seen from Fig. 20) that any further loss to agriculture or forestry would destroy the sense of limitless open country that is already largely a visual illusion.

Exmoor became a test case between the NFU and the CLA and the conservationists, represented by the Exmoor Society and nationally by the Council for National Parks and the Council for the Protection of Rural England. The Society commissioned an expert study in 1966 from Geoffrey Sinclair, who showed that in the nine years up to 1966 3700 ha of moorland had been lost to agriculture or afforestation. The response of the NFU and CLA was to assert 'the right and duty' of farmers 'to expand their enterprises and to improve their productive capacity to a maximum'. They ruled out any compromise or agreement about conservation. The Devon and Somerset County Councils, whose committees administered the park, tried but failed to persuade the Labour government to give them powers to control moorland reclamation in the 1968 Countryside Act. All the government would concede was a section enabling the park authority to make orders requiring farmers in specified areas to give six months notice of their intention to convert moor or heath. The obvious next step was for the park authorities to make an order applying to the whole of the 'critical amenity moorland' map that was being prepared. To avoid compulsory notification the NFU and CLA suggested a 'gentleman's agreement', which was concluded in 1969, by which their members agreed voluntarily to notify any proposals to convert moorland within the 'critical amenity' area. Nineteen proposals were notified between 1969 and 1973, but not a single agreement was negotiated. The NFU and CLA were not prepared to accept any serious restrictions on farmers' rights, and the park authority was unwilling to pay compensation on the terms demanded by the farmers. After negotiating for two years with one farmer, who was also an appointed member of the committee, the park authority declined to pay.

The issue was brought to a head, in 1976, when the vice-chairman of the park committee, Ben Halliday, who was also an appointed member and the owner of the Glenthorne Estate, notified a proposal to convert 101 ha at Yenworthy and North Common, two of the last remaining stretches of heather moorland on the coastal ridge. At about the same time one of his neighbours notified a proposal to convert 142 ha of heather moorland at Stowey Allotment, in the very heart of Exmoor. These proposals precipitated a crisis, not least because the park committee adopted a highly equivocal attitude. It approved the Stowey Allotment proposal by a majority, after rejecting an offer by the Countryside Commission to pay £9000 to the owner to delay the conversion for a year to enable some other solution to be worked out. The Commission submitted an adverse report on the committee's handling of the issue to the Secretary of State for the Environment, who intervened and, jointly with the Minister of Agriculture, set up an enquiry by Lord Porchester to investigate 'land use in Exmoor'.

The Porchester report, published in December 1977, confirmed all the facts about moorland loss and the threats to the remaining moorland that had so long been denied by the NFU and CLA. Lord Porchester did not blame the farmers for taking advantage of the grants offered by the Ministry of Agriculture, but he severely criticized the Ministry for its negative attitude to conservation. He blamed the Ministry above all for the serious inroads that had been made into a fragile moorland landscape, and advocated a virtually rigid regime of conservation for the heartland of Exmoor, the coastal heaths and other moorland of primary importance – in fact, as it turned out when the maps he recommended were drawn, for more than 80% of the moor. He recommended that the park authority should be given the power to make Moorland Conservation Orders, binding in perpetuity, for which compensation would take the form of a lump sum equal to the decline in land value resulting from the order. But he also suggested that farmers should be encouraged to conclude voluntary conservation agreements, under which they could be paid for positive conservation work.

The National Park Committee accepted all the Porchester recommendations except the one on compensation. But at the very meeting at which it endorsed the Porchester report it also agreed to negotiate a management agreement that allowed Ben Halliday to plough up 40 ha at Yenworthy Common, and compensated him with annual payments equal to the profit foregone for agreeing to conserve the remainder of the moorland on the Glenthorne estate. This agreement established the principle, for which the NFU and the CLA had pressed at the Porchester inquiry, that a farmer should be compensated for the hypothetical loss of profit generated by agricultural subsidies. It paved the way for the compensation provisions of the 1981 Wildlife and Countryside Act.

Had the Labour government's 1978 Countryside Bill become law it would have implemented the Porchester recommendations although, in deference to the NFU and CLA, it also placed considerable reliance on voluntary management agreements. The government had no majority, and the Tory Party opposed the Bill because it objected both to the lump-sum compensation provisions and to the power to make Moorland Conservation Orders. The Bill fell with the fall of the Labour government, and the general election of May 1979 brought in a Tory government that had no intention either of imposing controls on farmers or of withdrawing the subsidies that were the generators of insidious landscape change. The Thatcher government was so blind to the 'green' issues at that time that its anxiety, according to a Cabinet paper leaked to the *Sunday Times* in 1979, was 'to reduce oversensitivity to environmental considerations'. Between August and October 1979 the Government published consultation papers, drafted in collaboration with the NFU and the CLA, for a new Wildlife and Countryside Bill. Its provisions for national parks and nature conservation relied almost entirely on voluntary co-operation to secure conservation objectives.

THE EXMOOR SETTLEMENT

This was the green light for which the NFU and CLA were waiting. In November 1979 the Exmoor National Park Committe, the CLA and the NFU began highly significant negotiations, to which the Department of the Environment, the Ministry of Agriculture and the Countryside Commission sent observers. Their purpose was to draw up financial guidelines for management agreements. Whereas Porchester had proposed a once-and-for-all compensation equal to the loss in land value, the NFU and CLA insisted that farmers and landowners should have the right to choose to be compensated either by a lump sum or by annual payments related to the loss of grant and profit. The guidelines were finally signed on these terms on 7 April 1981, at the time of the Wildlife and Countryside Bill's second reading in the Commons. They incorporated an agreement that farmers would voluntarily give up to 12 months notice of all potentially damaging operations within the total area of 19 5000 ha of moor and heath shown on what had come to be known as Porchester Map 1. At the same time the park authority adopted the

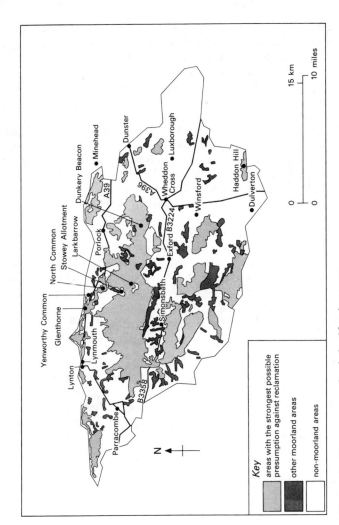

Figure 20 Exmoor moorland classification map

Key

areas with the strongest possible presumption against reclamation

other moorland areas

non-moorland areas

N

Yenworthy Common
Glenthorne
North Common
Stowey Allotment
Larkbarrow
Dunkery Beacon

Parracombe
Lynton
Lynmouth
Porlock
Minehead
Dunster

Simonsbath
Exford B3224
Wheddon Cross
Luxborough

A39
A396
B3358

Winsford
Haddon Hill
Dulverton

0   15 km
0   10 miles

strongest possible presumption in favour of conserving the moorland vegetation by traditional farming on 16 000 ha of critical
moorland, about 82% of the total, i.e. within Porchester Map 2.
Both maps are reproduced in Figure 20.

The success of the Exmoor negotiations was important for the
Government; its speakers in the second reading debates in both
Houses referred to them as indicating a new spirit of compromise
which confounded Porchester's worst fears and vindicated the
voluntary approach. The NFU and the CLA, meanwhile, viewed
the Exmoor agreement as providing a model for similar agreements
elsewhere and in their parliamentary briefings made many references to the Exmoor solution as indicating the soundness of a
voluntary approach. That such arguments were effective is indicated by the statutory guidelines for compensation relating to
management agreements drawn up following the passage of the Act
which do, indeed, follow the principles established in the Exmoor
agreement.

The Porchester report can now be seen as marking a clear
watershed. The process of moorland conversion, or destruction, has
virtually been halted. Only 88 ha have been 'improved' since 1979,
all of them outside the critical moorland of Map 2, and all with the
approval of the national park committee. By April 1986, 13 agreements had been signed or approved, under which compensation is
being paid to protect 821 ha, nearly all moorland, for 20 years at an
annual cost of £53 700. However, 1157 ha have been protected by
purchase over the same period, including two large, key moorland
areas at Warren Farm and Larkbarrow bought from the Fortescue
Estate in 1981 and 1983. Whenever the park authority has been
given the opportunity to buy land it has done so, because in the long
run it provides lasting protection at a far lower price. In the case of
Warren Farm the National Heritage Memorial Fund (which had
grant-aided the purchase) got most of its money back when the park
authority sold the farm subject to agreements that secured its
conservation and recreation objectives. The park committee
retained ownership of the moorland.

The relative success of the management agreements in Exmoor
can be attributed to three factors that are peculiar to Exmoor. The
first is that the Exmoor farmer knows from the start, without
haggling, that he will be compensated for a 20-year agreement to
forego reclamation at a standard sum per hectare if he observes the
conditions laid down in the agreement. The 'standard sum' is
determined every year by the Agricultural Economics Department
of Exeter University, on a formula that makes a generous assessment of the average rate of profit of an Exmoor sheep farm. The

standard sum has fluctuated violently between £24 a hectare in 1979 £118 a hectare in 1986–7. It is not surprising that so far every Exmoor farmer has elected to take an annuity rather than a lump sum, because he can claim it regardless of the rate of profit he actually makes. He can get more than the standard sum if he can prove his case from his books. But in most cases it is fair to assume that the rate of compensation exceeds the profit that would have been made – and the compensation is earned without the risk and without the work of reclamation. The farmer cannot lose.

The second factor peculiar to Exmoor is that the Government relieves the park authority and county councils of any financial misgivings by paying a 90% moorland conservation grant (compared with the normal 75% grant in national parks) on the pretext that Exmoor is a 'special case'. The truth is that Exmoor was only special because the conservation lobby succeeded in turning into a national scandal what research into moorland loss by Parry and others at Birmingham University showed to be a typical situation. The third factor peculiar to Exmoor is that for over 20 years it has been the scene of a running conflict, that has provoked one major enquiry, three attempts at legislation and intervention by the Countryside Commission and the government. Even Tory Ministers have made it clear to Exmoor farmers that unless the voluntary system is made to work, there will be no alternative to the controls that the NFU and CLA have opposed for so long. The Porchester inquiry finally convinced the farmers and landowners in Exmoor, apart from one or two mavericks, to accept conservation and to concentrate their efforts on extracting the highest price for it. But the government, in taking the Exmoor model as the prototype for the Wildlife and Countryside Act, paid scant regard to the special circumstances that existed there or the inherent limitations in the method.

Other national parks had to face similar problems without the benefits that the Exmoor National Park Authority enjoyed. And the situation in Exmoor has changed since the grants for moorland reclamation (although not for pasture improvement) were withdrawn in 1984. The high guaranteed price of cereals even persuaded a farmer at Long Holcombe in Exmoor to notify the park authority of a proposal to convert 180 ha of moorland above 1000 ft to cereal production without a grant. He rejected the 'standard' compensation sums, based on the profitability of sheep farming, as far too low, and the park authority had to buy him out in 1986 by paying £180 000, or £1000 a hectare. The park authority was only able to pay such a price – inflated by the guaranteed price of cereals – because it got grants from the Countryside Commission, the NCC and the National Heritage Memorial Fund. It remains to be seen whether proposals to grow cereals on Exmoor are seen as a new device for milking the taxpayer, or the dying kick of the frenzy for reclamation that so nearly destroyed Exmoor. Falling hill farming profits could in future make compensation for 'profit foregone' less attractive than payments for conservation management.

Chapter Twelve

The Wildlife and Countryside Act –

a false dawn

NATURE CONSERVATION

The feebleness of the Wildlife and Countryside Bill in the form in which it was presented to Parliament in 1980 provoked a flood of criticism. Part 1 of the Bill, which was concerned with the protection of species, engendered much debate but not much heat as its provisions had been drafted in consultation with the Royal Society for the Protection of Birds to implement an international convention. Part 3, which concerned public rights of way, has been discussed already (see Ch. 8) and controversy focussed mainly on the Government's foolish decision to allow beef (but not dairy) bulls to be grazed on rights of way. Part 2 of the Bill, which dealt with nature conservation and national parks, had been drafted in consultation with the NFU and CLA. Neither the Countryside Commission nor the Nature Conservancy Council was consulted until the basic policies had been agreed with the farmers and landowners. As a result the Bill conceded next to nothing to conservation. It offered a modicum of protection to a handful of 'super SSSIs', by giving ministers powers to make orders requiring landlords and tenants to give up to 12 months notice of any potentially damaging operation. But this was intended to protect only a mere 40 or so out of some 4000 Sites of Special Scientific Interest. A similar reserve power enabled ministers to make orders requiring 12 months notice to be given of proposals to convert moor and heath in national parks, but ministers also announced that they had no intention of making any orders. The power given to park authorities in 1968 to make such orders was repealed. One clause removed a legal doubt about management agreements, by making it possible to enforce their provisions not only against the original signatories but also against their heirs or successors in title. But apart from these items Part 2 of the Bill was, from the standpoint of conservation, as empty as a drum.

The outcry was so great and the lobbying so intense that 2300 amendments were put down for debate, and the Bill only scraped home in the end by two votes in the House of Lords on the last possible day of the 1980–1 Parliamentary session. The government stuck unwaveringly to its 'voluntary' approach, but had to make concessions that marginally improved the Bill and compromised the principle. The government was compelled, above all, to extend a real measure of protection to every SSSI by introducing an arrangement called 'reciprocal notification'. The Act as finally passed requires the NCC to renotify owners and occupiers of every existing SSSI of its boundaries, and of any operations it regards as potentially damaging to its scientific interest. Any new SSSIs have to be notified in the same way. In return, to enable the NCC to negotiate management agreements, the period of notice for potentially damaging operations can be extended to 12 months by a ministerial order but only, according to a recent legal decision, if the site is of 'national' significance. These clauses were so badly drafted that farmers were able to damage or destroy proposed SSSIs before the Secretary of State could make orders, or before the notification of a new SSSI could take effect. These loopholes were closed by an amending Act in 1985, but the loopholes were in fact characteristic of the bureaucratic nightmare that the Act created.

The protection given by the Act is far from complete. Even now the NCC has no power at the end of the day to stop a damaging operation once the delaying period has expired, unless it has the money to buy the land compulsorily, and the government agrees to compulsory purchase. Not only had the NCC to renotify 40 000 owners and occupiers of existing SSSIs, but it had to approach each of them individually to establish good personal relations and to reappraise every site scientifically. The NCC was understaffed, and this gigantic task diverted it from many other important jobs; it was forced, to take a minor example, to withdraw from giving advice to the Peak National Park Board in whose offices it had installed an ecologist. By March 1985 the NCC had renotified 1420 of the 4000 SSSIs in the UK and notified 486 new ones. It estimated that about a third of the SSSIs would need management agreements at an ultimate cost of about £15 million a year. By the end of March 1986 the NCC had negotiated only 362 management agreements for SSSIs, at an annual cost of nearly £2 million, with continuing and inflating obligations on much the same scale.

FARMING AND CONSERVATION

Other changes in the Bill were forced on the Government by an unexpected defeat in the House of Lords on an amendment that would have transformed the role of the agricultural ministers in national parks. It was moved by Lord Sandford, the former Tory Minister and chairman of the Sandford Committee on national parks (see Ch. 2). It would have empowered the agricultural ministers to give financial support in national parks (and possibly elsewhere) to farmers' schemes to promote conservation, to maintain the rural population or to diversify the economy. The Sandford amendment was anathema to the Ministry of Agriculture. The government's response, therefore, was to accept 'the spirit of Sandford' while emasculating his amendment. The outcome was two new clauses, now Sections 32 and 41 of the Act, which placed obligations on the agricultural ministers to give advice (but not money) to farmers for Sandford's purposes, and to 'further conservation' when grant-aiding farmers in national parks or SSSIs – but only so far as might be consistent with the agricultural purposes of the scheme! The overriding purpose of any agricultural grant had still to be to promote profitability and productivity, with conservation tagged on as a frill or an afterthought. The government's amendments also turned the Exmoor precedent into a new legal principle: that if a minister withheld a farm grant on conservation grounds in a national park or an SSSI the farmer *had* to be offered compensation for the loss of the grant. Before the Act came into force no compensation was payable if a minister exercised his discretion not to pay a farm capital grant. In the Brecon Beacons, for example, no compensation was payable when the Secretary of State for Wales withheld a grant for reseeding 150 ha of bilberry, heath and bracken at Fan Vrynich in 1981 just before the Act came into force. But Sections 32 and 41 require the NCC or a national park authority to reward the farmer or landowner whose environmentally damaging proposals have been denied grant by offering a management agreement with compensation. The guidelines issued under the Act spell out the obligation to base the compensation on the assumption that the grant would have been paid. They also extend the same principle to afforestation, by agreement with the NCC, although the Act does not in fact apply to afforestation.

The Act thereby transformed a 'voluntary' system of management agreements into a hybrid system. It is obligatory on the NCC and the national park authorities, but voluntary for the farmer or landowner. In SSSIs, it is true, the NCC does have some real powers. But in the national parks the farmers and landowners still hold all the cards. Their only real obligation is to notify the NCC or the national park authority under the 1980 Farm Grant Notification Scheme (see Ch. 2) if they intend to claim agricultural grant on their operations. They can accept or refuse an agreement. They can accept or refuse the compensation offered. If, as the guidelines provide, the compensation terms are taken to arbitration in disputed cases the farmers or landowners are not bound by the result. They can be awarded more, but not less. The authority remains bound by its original offer. And, at the end of the day, the farmer or landowner is free to go ahead with the damaging operation, albeit without grant. The 'voluntary' approach had become the 'pay through the nose' approach.

Ministers, it is true, have the power of last resort under Section 42 to make temporary stop orders requiring farmers to give up to 12 months notice of their intention to reclaim moor or heath in national parks. The Snowdonia National Park Committee took the logical view, having identified in their Section 43 Map (described in Ch. 6) those areas of moor and heath it thought 'particularly important to conserve', that all such areas should be protected by a Section 42 order. The Secretary of State for Wales ignored the request. Ministers have also rejected requests by the national park authorities in Exmoor, North York Moors and Pembrokeshire Coast for orders to impose a 12-month stop on individual farmers who had declined to enter into management agreements. The park authorities find themselves in what we call the 'catch-42' situation. Ministers say that they will only make an order if the notification system has broken down and the authority is unaware of the farmers' proposals. But the authority cannot see the need for an order unless it knows of the proposals – in which case (catch-42) it cannot get one! As ministers refuse to make blanket orders, it is difficult to see how on this crazy interpretation of the Act orders will ever be made. In fact Section 42 is drafted both to ensure that notice is given and to enable the park authority to stop the operation for up to 12 months – a fact ignored by ministers whose priority seems to be to avoid controls at (almost) any cost.

ABUSING THE ACT

It is now obvious, after nearly five years' experience, that Part 2 of the Wildlife and Countryside Act was fundamentally mis-conceived. Even in the one area of SSSIs where it has improved the situation, it has failed to provide a sound or lasting or economic solution. Every national park officer deplores the com-plexity and the antagonism inherent in the negotiation of agree-ments. Even if they are entirely 'voluntary', the farmer knows that he can extract money from the park authority, which knows that it can be made to pay. Until the Act was passed it had been relatively easy to negotiate informal agreements with some farmers who had notified an unacceptable proposal to the park authority, even if the authority had to concede more than was desirable on occasions. But once the Act was passed farmers knew that the park authorities and the NCC could be forced to offer compensation for hypothetical profits foregone. In a paper given to the Agricultural Economics Society in March 1983 the Exmoor National Park Officer warned that 'trivial and spurious claims' might abuse the goodwill on which the Exmoor scheme depended. The authorities had to go through what the Brecon Beacons Committee has called the 'complex and burdensome' procedure for negotiating compensation which, it said, 'would not necessarily give adequate protection to the site concerned in the long run'. Farmers called in their unions, and the negotiations were turned into a bean-feast for lawyers, valuers and land agents.

In the latter part of 1985, Laurence Gould and Partners, a leading firm of environmental consultants, presented a report commis-sioned by the Department of the Environment on the working of the Wildlife and Countryside Act. Ministers sat on it for many months, and only released it surreptitiously by placing a copy in the House of Commons Library after its contents had been leaked in June 1986 by the Friends of the Earth. It had clearly been suppressed to prevent it having any influence on the Agriculture Bill as it went through its committee stages. It found that the process of renotify-ing SSSIs triggered off demands for compensation in one-third of the cases, and it expects the publication of 'section 3' maps of open country to have the same effect: 'Potentially the 1981 Act together with the Financial Guidelines place a price on virtually all the destructible features of scientific or landscape interest, which the owner or occupier may claim on threat of destroying it ... It is impossible to test the genuineness of an individual's intention without putting the site at risk'. Moreover, Gould said 'most management agreements prepared to date demand no positive contribution on the part of the claimant towards the management of the site'. The Gould report estimated that compensation costs may rise to about £18.4 million in 1989–90. If administrative costs are included the total could go as high as £31 million annually in compensation payments, plus £52 million in lump-sum payments. The government estimated the cost of the Wildlife and Countryside Bill, when it was published, at £700–800 000 a year at the most.

Land agents now advertise their skills and services in negotiating management agreements on behalf of farmers and landowners. One national park officer, who confesses that land agents have become his '*bête noire*', describes the attitude adopted by land agents since the Wildlife and Countryside Act was passed:

> 'they all know that their fees will be paid by the authorities, so that doesn't worry their client. The higher the compensation they get the higher the fee will be, and both the farmer and the park authority wilt under the pressure of such people. I am having to engage a land agent at this moment in order to have an officer right in the system to combat the others of his own profession, and carry the whole thing through. I have done deals, leaning on a gate, with which the farmer has been content, and then the agents have locked antlers for another 12 months, costing the public purse considerably more money as a rule'.

The Gould report confirms that the Act will 'exacerbate the complexity and increase the amount of professional time involved'.

SUCCESS STORY –
or irrelevance?

In the countryside at large, where the Countryside Commission only offers a 50% grant, compared to 90% in Exmoor and 75% in other national parks, management agreements are almost a total failure. By April 1986 three county councils had signed four agreements to protect less than 60 ha. Even in the national parks the results are unimpressive. The 14 Exmoor agreements are all based on the voluntary system agreed with the NFU and CLA and, as we have seen, the area protected by them is far smaller than the area protected over the same period by purchase. By April 1986 58 agreements had been signed by the ten national park authorities protecting about 1550 ha for periods averaging about 18 years, at a cost of £337 000 in lump sums and an initial annual commitment of about £80 000. Only three agreements protect land in perpetuity –

200 ha to be precise. A further 44 agreements to protect another 1200 ha were under negotiation in April 1986, but if all are concluded successfully (which is unlikely) the total protected area will still be less than 0.2% of the land area of the national parks – four-fifths of this small area being in Exmoor and Dartmoor. It is significant, however, that Dartmoor has been very reluctant to enter into the open-ended financial commitments of the Exmoor type, by which the conservation balloon is kept aloft by continuously burning money. Of Dartmoor's 24 agreements 16 have been bought by paying lump sums, and the authority's annual commitment is only £10 000.

The only other authority to have concluded more than two agreements is the Peak, which had negotiated 11 agreements by April 1986, nearly all for woodland but including one to protect the mediaeval wall system at Chelmorton. The Peak's use of management agreements can be put in perspective by comparing the total area of 30 ha protected by this method with the acquisition, over much the same period, of four major properties (the Eastern Moors, the Roaches, North Lees and the Harpur Crewe Estate) totalling 5391 ha. Acquisition has enabled the Peak Board to protect this land in perpetuity, and to invest in substantial programmes to conserve and restore natural and man-made features.

The complacent government view is that the Act and the Farm Grant Notification Scheme can be seen as a great success story. They are, of course, two elements in a single package, for the notification of an operation for which the farmer intends to claim grant is the main trigger for negotiations over a management agreement. Each park authority handles on average about 500 farm grant applications a year, and the proportion to which objections are raised is only about 5%. This is primarily due to the fact that the vast majority of proposals for grant-aided developments are unobjectionable, modest developments. But until 1985 the agricultural departments paid grants even to those farmers, believed to be about one in five, who had gone ahead with the work without notifying the park authorities. How much damage was done by these unauthorized developments it is impossible to estimate. There is also some evidence that park authorities failed to challenge some schemes that were damaging to the environment, either because farmer-dominated committees were tolerant of such operations as fertilizing rough grazings, or because they did not wish to be saddled with open-ended compensation obligations, or because they believed that the agricultural ministers would not support them if they pressed their objections. Such a belief is warranted by the fact that in five of the first eight cases referred to ministers they over-ruled the national park authorities.

The ink was hardly dry on the Act before demands were being raised on all sides for major changes to be made. The government gave somewhat grudging support to the Amending Bill, promoted by David Clark and enacted in 1985, to close the loopholes that allowed farmers to damage SSSIs. The Government refused to allow the Bill to be used to make more far-reaching changes, but the message that came through insistently at every level in 1983–5 was that fundamental changes were needed, above all in the agricultural policies that were the main generators of conflict and environmental loss. At the sharp end, so to speak, the North York Moors National Park Committee expressed its disenchantment with the Act after five of the first seven farmers to whom it offered management agreements went ahead with their damaging operations. It passed a resolution on 5 September 1984 that it was faced with an 'impossible task without proper powers and safeguards when seeking to protect moorland and other valuable habitats from damaging operations'. It concluded that 'management agreements are not the answer'. At the national level the NCC's strategic statement *Nature conservation in Great Britain* (June 1984) underlined 'the overwhelming impact' of modern farming on wildlife and its habitat in Britain. The Countryside Commission published a report in the same year on 'new agricultural landscapes' which showed that over the previous decade 'there has been a continuing erosion of features of landscape, wildlife and historical interest principally because of the demands of modern agriculture'.

Throughout 1983 and 1984 the House of Lords committee that examined the draft EEC farm structures regulations was inundated by evidence from both the conservation agencies and many voluntary bodies demanding radical changes in farm policies. The commitee's report, published in 1984, berated the Ministry of Agriculture for being 'backward looking' and too 'production-oriented', and criticized the Department of the Environment for meekly tagging along at Agriculture's heels. An equally critical report on agricultural research and the environment was published in the same year, by the House of Lords Committee on Science and Technology. The House of Commons Environment Committee that investigated Part 2 of the Wildlife and Countryside Act gave its blessing to the 'voluntary approach', but nevertheless recommended that the park authorities should be able to apply for landscape conservation orders (LCOs) to protect threatened sites. The committee, with a Tory majority, took the lead from the environmental minister, William Waldegrave, who referred in his evidence to the agricultural incentives on offer as 'the engine of destruction'. This led the committee to express its 'underlying concern' that without fundamental changes in agricultural policies 'conservation will be set in weak opposition to the forces of intensive and, paradoxically, frequently unwanted production'. It was, however, the failure of the voluntary approach to resolve the conflict in the Broads over the Halvergate marshes in 1984–5 (see Ch. 17) that finally spelt out the bankruptcy of Part 2 of the Wildlife and Countryside Act, which becomes increasingly irrelevant in a rapidly changing situation.

ENVIRONMENTALLY SENSITIVE AREAS

The crisis in the Broads coincided with the financial crisis in the Common Agricultural Policy, that forced the agricultural ministers to introduce milk quotas almost overnight in the spring of 1984. They coincided, too, with the hammering that the Ministry of Agriculture was getting in the proceedings of the House of Lords committees. The Ministry's first reaction, motivated primarily by a desire to save money, was to eliminate or to reduce the more damaging farm capital grants (including those for moorland reclamation) which it did in 1984, and to introduce in 1985 a new grant scheme more biased towards conservation and the smaller farmer, which we discuss in Chapter 14. But the new grant scheme was irrelevant to the Broads. There farmers wanted to change the use of the marshes from traditional grazing to cereal cropping, to pick up the inflated EEC guaranteed prices, by using their control of the Land Drainage Boards to lower the water table. The Council for National Parks, the CPRE and others suggested that instead of subsidizing land drainage or offering costly management agreements the Ministry should use its own money to support traditional grazing. But the response of the Ministry (itself held back by the Treasury) was to drag its feet at every stage. First it argued that to do so would be in breach of the Treaty of Rome. When proved wrong, the Ministry approached the EEC with extreme reluctance, in the belief that the EEC would turn the idea down. In fact the British initiative secured the inclusion in the 1985 EEC Farm Structures Directive of a new article, no. 19. This allows member states to use their own (although not yet the EEC's) money to support the incomes of farmers in environmentally sensitive areas (ESAs) who agree to farm in ways that will conserve the landscape and natural habitats.

Having secured the EEC's agreement the Ministry's primary

considerations were to designate the smallest possible total area, at the lowest possible cost. The Countryside Commission and the NCC, when asked to advise the Ministry on possible sites for ESAs, began with an initial list of no less than 140. They whittled this down to a firm list of 46 which included the whole or a large part of every national park. They then reduced this to a priority list of 14, including some of the Yorkshire Dales and the northern part of the Peak, but omitting all the other national parks. The national park authorities felt aggrieved by their omission from the final list. But the overriding priority of the Treasury (whose consent is required for each ESA individually) and of the agricultural departments was to devise a voluntary scheme that would be simple and cheap to administer. As this book went to press, the government had decided to designate initially only a handful of ESAs in the United Kingdom at a cost of £6 million a year. These are the Broads, the Somerset Levels, West Penwith in Cornwall, two sections of the Cambrian Mountains in Wales, one, or possibly two, ESAs in Scotland and some dales (but no moorland) in the North Pennines. These include Swaledale and other dales in the north of the Yorkshire Dales National Park.

Experience in Exmoor, where a range of standard compensation sums is on offer, has shown that to devise appropriate management regimes with agreed stocking levels in a diverse landscape still requires detailed negotiations. But farmers in the ESAs will only have to accept a simple prescription for land management in return for annual payments, the rates of which had not been announced as this book went to press. As farmers remain free to stay out of the scheme, all the existing financial supports are still available. To induce them to 'opt in' the ESA standard sum must offer the more prosperous farmers at least as much as they get from headage payments, and ministers have conceded that farmers would not have to reduce the 1985–6 stocking levels, however excessive. Consultants have estimated that if 75% of farmers in an ESA 'opt in' (an optimistic figure) substantially *more* money will be required in subsidies than at present. It seems unlikely that anything like 75% of the farmers will opt for the ESA payments, unless the Ministry of Agriculture can offer more money than the £60 per hectare it first mentioned to the farmers' unions for the Pennine Dales. But the Treasury's limit of £6 million – a trifling sum compared to £2.2 billion spent on the production of surplus food – has dictated both the small number of ESAs and the levels of compensation on offer. The Government proposed in February 1987 to raise the number of ESAs to 18 as part of an ill-considered policy package for rural areas. We look at the potential for ESAs in Chapter 14.

PART FOUR

The influence of government

Chapter Thirteen

Explosive issues

The toadstool towers infest the shore:
Stink-horns that propagate and spore
　　Wherever the wind blows.
Scafell looks down from the bracken band,
And sees hell in a grain of sand,
　　And feels the canker itch between his toes.

This is a land where dirt is clean,
And poison pasture, quick and green,
　　And storm sky, bright and bare;
Where sewers flow with milk, and meat
Is carved up for the fire to eat,
　　And children suffocate in God's fresh air.

'Windscale', by Norman Nicholson,
Selected poems 1940–82.

THE NUCLEAR TIME BOMB

National park authorities have been relatively successful in controlling small-scale developments, but they have failed more often than
not in their efforts to resist massive developments sponsored or
supported by central government. In this chapter we will look at the
most 'explosive issues': the literally explosive issues of nuclear
power, military training and the extraction of rocks and minerals,
and the politically or metaphorically explosive issue of road
construction.

　　Experience teaches us that no development is too grotesque for
government to advance the argument of overriding 'national interest' to justify its location in the national park. Those who think that
such a proposition is absurd, or exaggerated, should consider the

decision taken in 1959 to build a nuclear power station at Trawsfy-nydd in Snowdonia. When we wrote our original book on national parks in 1980–1 Trawsfynydd was no longer a live issue. We contented ourselves with recalling that the inspector who held the inquiry, Colin Buchanan, recommended the Minister to reject the proposal despite the enthusiastic support given to it by a professor of town and country planning who advised the Snowdonia National Park Joint Advisory Committee. Buchanan summarized the pro-fessor's view as being that 'no national park is really complete without a nuclear power station'. Ironically the very remoteness of Snowdonia from centres of population, which had led to its designation as a national park only five years before, was advanced as the reason for siting a nuclear power station in it. In reality one of the drawbacks of nuclear power is that the heat from remotely sited power stations cannot be used for industrial purposes or to heat buildings. More than 60% of Trawsfynydd's primary energy is used to warm the lake in which excess heat is dissipated.

When we visited Trawsfynydd in February 1986 the CEGB had listed it as one of six sites in England and Wales where, subject to technical investigations, it was considering the construction of a 1250 megawatt (MW) pressurized water reactor (PWR) (Plate 22). It would have nearly three times the power of the existing 475 MW Magnox Reactor which will reach the end of its life around 1996. The Snowdonia National Park Committee was saying nothing until the investigations were complete, but members to whom we spoke were clearly reluctant to oppose the PWR, arguing that the visual damage had already been done and that hundreds of jobs were at stake. In fact, the PWR would employ only two-thirds of the 600 who work at Trawsfynydd now. Some 3000 people (most of them from outside the area) would be employed to build the PWR, which from one point of view represents job opportunities but from another means that every 25–30 years this part of Snowdonia has to be subject to massive physical and social upheaval.

However, this was two months before Chernobyl. The simple truth is that the decision to build a nuclear reactor at Trawsfynydd and to send high-voltage transmission lines radiating over the national park was wrong for two reasons. If nuclear power is safe, there is no need to site it in a 'remote' national park; and if it is so dangerous that it must be remote, it is questionable whether there are any safe sites in the British Isles or Europe, or even in the world. The existing Magnox station at Trawsfynydd could still be the death of Snowdonia, if events turns out badly.

The Lake District lives under the shadow not only of the reactors at Heysham but also of the vast Sellafield military and civil nuclear processing plant on the Cumbrian coast. The risk of child leukaemia in the area is abnormally high, as it is near Dounreay. The Lakes Board has become uncomfortably aware of the threat that fear of Sellafield poses to the tourist business, and of the pollution that Sellafield has caused in the national park itself. The House of Commons all-party Environment Committee's damning report on Sellafield, which was published in March 1986, found that the Irish Sea, which washes the beaches of the Lake District National Park, is one of the most radioactive seas in the world. It called, among other things, for improved safety measures on waste disposal at the dump at Drigg, on the very edge of the national park.

The solution to these problems lies, we suggest, in a non-nuclear future in which the vast sums spent on nuclear research and development are diverted into alternative sources of energy, the clean use of fossil fuels, and the conservation of the immense quantities of energy we now waste. The argument that nuclear energy is the cheapest source of power is an empty one: the ultimate cost of nuclear power is unknown and unknowable. The 'costs' quoted by the CEGB do not cover the costs of research, waste disposal, or reactor closure – let alone contingency sums for another or a bigger Chernobyl. Hill farmers in Snowdonia and the Lake District, still forbidden to sell their lambs months after Chernobyl and facing losses beyond those the government will meet, have learned the hard way the unpredictable and immeasurable consequences of nuclear accidents. They have become more wary of Sellafield and Trawsfynydd, and forced to understand that hill country with high rainfall is exposed both to nuclear fall-out from a nuclear accident anywhere in Europe, and to acid rain.

QUARRYING AND MINING

The changed character of the demand for minerals and the concentration of production in fewer, larger, more capital-intensive plants, have sharpened the conflicts of interest inherent in mineral extraction. Modern earth-moving equipment can literally move mountains. This revolution has not affected the vastly reduced Welsh slate industry, nor has it been felt strongly in the Lake District, where the green Westmorland slates are still quarried. But it can be devastating in the limestone quarrying areas or the china clay workings. It is hard to conceive of anything more destructive of a rural landscape than such limestone quarries as Eldon Hill (Plate 21) or Tunstead in the Peak or the Swinden or Ribblesdale quarries in the Yorkshire Dales, with working faces up to a mile long, periodical blasting, large noisy industrial processing plants, heavy traffic congesting the roads and dust polluting the villages and countryside for miles around. The china clay workings at Lee Moor in Dartmoor and the vast waste tips are incongruous, although recent attempts at landscaping have led to the removal of some tips and the establishment of vegetation.

New threats emerge from time to time. Prospecting for oil and gas is now taking place – the whole of the North York Moors are covered by exploration licences – and an anthracite coal seam runs across the Pembrokeshire Coast National Park. The short-term commercial interests of the mineral companies conflict with the long-term national interests in conserving landscape and nature, and husbanding precious, finite resources by thriftiness in use. Local people want jobs, but they also have an interest in protecting their health and the environment in which they live – and on which the tourist industry depends. Large-scale capital-intensive production means that fewer people are employed, unless the area of operations is greatly extended. Moreover, once a multinational company has sunk large capital sums in a mine or a processing plant it tends to demand extensions. A classic instance of this occurred in the Peak District in 1985 when Laporte Industries successfully applied to sink a new mine at Hucklow Edge to work the largest remaining untapped reserve of fluorspar in the UK – primarily to ensure continued output and employment at the Cavendish processing mill nearby. In granting the application the Peak Board was strongly influenced, despite the impact of dust and noise on a nearby village, by the prospect of keeping 190 jobs. It did, however, impose numerous conditions.

Bullying tactics seem to characterize the big multinational companies, and smaller companies are vulnerable to the unpredictable swings in the prices of minerals and the demand for them. Rio Tinto Zinc (RTZ) provoked an explosion of protest when it was discovered accidentally in 1969 that it had been stealthily buying up mineral rights for three years and drilling for copper ore in the Capel Hermon area of Snowdonia National Park without applying for planning permission. RTZ did not go ahead with an application to extract copper from Snowdonia, because copper prices fell. Changing market conditions also explain the decision of Consolidated Goldfields in 1979 to withdraw its application for a vast potash mining and refining complex that would have discharged 12–14 tonnes of sulphur and soot per day from an 80 metre chimney into the air near Whitby in the North York Moors National Park. Its decision made it easy for the Secretary of State to reject the scheme, while holding the door open for a less brutal project.

The uncertainties of mining speculations may also explain the tactics used by Mark Weinberg, the city financier who acquired the Gwynfynydd gold-mine in the beautiful and popular Coed y Brenin forest in Snowdonia. Within eight months of reaching agreement with the national park authority in 1985 on the level of production, he threatened to close the mine and sack its 23 workers unless, within three weeks, the authority agreed to allow him to treble production. He claimed that he had already invested £2 million in his speculation, and could not attract further capital from outside investors without the additional output. The authority, to its credit, refused to be stampeded by this (as it turned out) empty threat, or by the bait of an additional 12 jobs if permission were granted. But it did concede a more modest increase of production some months later, under fairly rigorous conditions.

Neither the scale nor the destructiveness of modern quarries nor the need to husband finite natural resources were fully anticipated when the national park legislation was passed in 1949. But Lewis Silkin, then the Minister of Town and Country Planning, spelt out three conditions – now known as the 'Silkin test' – that would have to be satisfied before new mineral workings would be allowed in a national park:

(a) it had to be demonstrated that the exploitation of these minerals was 'absolutely necessary' in the public interest;
(b) it had to be clear beyond all doubt that there was 'no possible alternative source of supply'; and
(c) if those two conditions were satisfied, permission was subject to the condition that restoration took place at the earliest possible opportunity.

The Silkin test laid the onus of displacing the presumption against mineral exploitation firmly on the developer. But the inspector's report in 1986 on the Topley Pike inquiry in the Peak District stated explicitly that the Silkin test was now only of historic interest, and that he must look for policies to the structure plans. Successive Labour and Tory ministers have modified the test in three fundamental ways. Ministers removed the presumption against new and extended mineral workings from the Peak District and North Yorkshire structure plans, and substituted a statement that these would 'normally' be resisted only if they constituted a 'major intrusion'. They shifted the onus of proof that the proposals were necessary in the public interest, and that there was no practicable alternative source of supply, onto the national park authorities. They also deleted policies designed to reserve the highest grade of chemical limestone for uses that require its unique chemical properties. Four-fifths of the 2½ million tonnes of high-grade chemical limestone extracted annually from the Yorkshire Dales are used for road construction.

The first test case was ICI's proposal to extend its quarry at Tunstead by driving a face one mile long more than half a mile into the Peak District National Park, so as nearly to double its output. Tunstead is an immense integrated plant which combines the production of high quality limestone products (its primary purpose) with the production of roadstone – both from the highest grade chemical limestone. The Peak Board rejected the application in 1974, ICI appealed and, after a protracted public inquiry in 1976, the inspector reported in favour of ICI in 1977. After litigation in the High Court, Michael Heseltine gave a decision in ICI's favour in 1980. Few cases illustrate more clearly the protracted, wasteful, costly and unfair nature of the gladiatorial contest as a device for making decisions on minerals applications and determining policy.

In the meantime, the 1976 report of the Stevens inquiry into planning control over mineral development had confirmed many of the difficulties experienced by park authorities and others. Its main recommendation, calling for a national survey of key minerals and a national strategy for their exploitation, has been ignored. Other elements of the report were enacted in the 1981 Town and Country Planning (Minerals) Act which enables planning authorities to insist on proper treatment of sites for up to five years after quarrying has ended, and to consider revoking or amending earlier conditions. But hardly was the ink dry on the Act than the House of Lords threw another spanner into the works by its decision in 1982 in the case of Hartshead quarry in the Peak, that to re-open a disused quarry is not 'development' – which means that several hundred disused quarries in the United Kingdom can be re-opened without planning permission.

One recent decision does hold out some hope that the quarry companies' claims may be subjected to more serious scrutiny in the future than they have been in the past. The Peak Board announced in May 1986 that for the first time in its history it had won a complete victory in a major quarrying appeal, when the Secretary of State rejected Tarmac Roadstone's application to extend its 32 ha limestone quarry at Topley Pike. The inspector upheld the board's objections on three grounds: that the extension would seriously damage the national park landscape and its wildlife in a beautiful part of the White Peak; that dust from the quarry would damage vegetation in the nearby SSSI; and that there was no clear need, nationally or locally, for the reserves to be worked because there were many alternative supplies of roadstone.

However, in the same month the Secretary of State announced an interim decision on the application by Eskett Quarries Ltd to extend their quarry at Coolscar in the highly sensitive Upper Wharfedale. Coolscar has been dragging on since 1981. The Yorkshire Dales National Park Committee refused the application, but then indicated its readiness to concede a smaller extension. There have been two public inquiries, in each of which the inspector recommended granting permission for the extensions. After the first inquiry he also recommended limiting extraction to 100 000 tonnes a year, as this would satisfy the demand for high-grade chemical limestone. In July 1984 the Secretary of State informed the participants in the inquiry that he was disposed to accept the inspector's views, but the company argued that to extract anything less than 250 000 tonnes a year would be 'uneconomic'. In January 1985 it began to extract limestone (largely for aggregates) at that rate from the extended area for which it had no planning permission. The Secretary of State's interim decision is an all too familiar compromise. He indicated in 1986 that he was prepared to grant permission for the smaller area, allowing the extraction of 175 000 tonnes a year with a time limit of ten years on the permission. The company is likely to get only part of what it wanted, but it also demonstrated that it could snap its fingers at the national park authority and the Secretary of State with impunity for 17 months. Mineral policies would be further undermined if, as the Government has proposed, they do not have to be submitted (as now) to the Environment Secretary for approval. The Peak Board won the Topley Pike inquiry largely because it rested its case on structure plan policies approved by Government. In 1985 T. W. Ward (Roadstone) Ltd tried to overturn an earlier Government decision to close Eldon Hill quarry by 1997. But in 1987 the Secretary of State ruled that quarrying must cease because its continuation would run "right to the heart of the reasons for designation of the national park".

Plans for the management of resources in the parks should be prepared within the framework of a national minerals policy. The frugal use of minerals and the conservation of the environment should be built into policies and plans at national and local level. But full control over exploitation and after-use is unlikely to be achieved unless mineral rights are publicly owned, and their exploitation governed by licences granted by the State and designed, to extend maximum protection to landscape and to nature.

SHELLING THE WILDERNESS

The use of national parks for artillery ranges and other forms of military training was established many years before the national parks were designated. The question that has to be faced is whether the designation of a 'national park' has any validity if such a manifestly destructive and incompatible use continues to be tolerated within it. The basic problem is that, as the Countryside Commission complained in its annual report for 1984–5, the Ministry of Defence takes the view that 'defence of the realm [operations] will override all other considerations'. In its report for 1985–6 the Commission said that the MoD did not seem to have excluded national parks or other protected areas from its search for another 20 000 ha of training land. The 'green tide', it observed, had certainly not found its way into the thinking of the MoD or, for that matter, the Department of Transport. When representatives of the Ministry met the Council for National Parks in October 1985 the MoD emphasized that decisions on the level of training were 'political', and not to be challenged. Thus, in marked contrast to minerals where each development has to be justified, the State insists that it does not have to produce any evidence to support its judgments of military necessity.

The Countryside Commission and the Council for National Parks, while recognizing the 'inherent conflict' between military training and national park objectives, agree that it is 'at present' unrealistic to expect military training in the parks to cease. The CNP demands (as does the Commission) an urgent review of the potential for releasing MoD land. The CNP also wants more public access to live-firing areas; the clearance of unexploded missiles from land available for access (as in the Otterburn range in Northumberland where the paths have been cleared but not the moorland); the preparation of comprehensive management plans and some alleviation of such widespread nuisances as low-flying aircraft. These demands, while useful as far as they go, do not in our opinion go far enough.

The extent of military use in national parks is well illustrated in Figure 21. It will be seen that the Ministry of Defence is permanently established in every national park except Exmoor. Its land holdings are concentrated in three main areas, in each of which it is one of the largest employers. In Northumberland the ranges and dry training areas occupy 22 878 ha, or about a fifth of the national park. In the Pembrokeshire Coast, the Castlemartin tank range of 2700 ha (the use of which by panzer units of the West German Army increased in 1986) occupies one of the most spectacular stretches of the coast and

	1	2	⚡ (live firing)	🧍 (dry/adventure)	🏰 (army camps)	✈ (low flying)	🪖 (restricted access)
Dartmoor	5.00	10.00	●	●	●	●	●
Exmoor	—	—		●		●	
Brecon Beacons	0.15	1.00		●	●	●	
Pembrokeshire Coast	4.40	—	●	●	●	●	●
Snowdonia	0.10	—	●	●		●	
Peak District	0.03	0.75	●	●		●	●
Yorkshire Dales	0.40	—		●		●	
North York Moors	0.80	0.50		●	●	●	●
Lake District	0.15	0.14		●	●	●	
Northumberland	21.60	0.20	●	●	●	●	●

Key

⚡ live firing

🧍 dry/adventure training

🏰 army camps and bases

✈ low flying aircraft

🪖 restricted public access

1 % of national park owned or leased by MOD

2 % of national park over which MOD has rights

Figure 21 Military use of national parks (courtesy of the Council for National Parks).

prevents the public use of the long-distance coastal path when firing is taking place. But Dartmoor, where the military own, lease or have rights over about 14256 ha, mainly for firing ranges, has for long been the scene of the greatest controversy and presents the conflicts generated by military use in the sharpest form.

Military training is dangerous, damaging, intimidating and obtrusive. The increasing range and fire power of new weapons continually require more space. The noise and disturbance caused by firing live ammunition are aggravated by the use of helicopters and low-flying aircraft. The ground is scarred by shell and mortar fire. In Dartmoor the widespread archaeological sites and tors are particularly vulnerable. The public is allowed access to the ranges when firing is not taking place, on a more generous scale in Dartmoor (where firing is suspended at holiday periods) than in Northumberland. But the ominous red lettered 'danger zone' markings on OS maps, the difficulty of knowing when firing will take place and the widely advertised existence of unexploded ammunition deter the walker. Controlling public access necessitates a vast apparatus of warning signs, flags, notices, huts and prominent observation points. Even 'dry training', in which no live ammunition is fired, can bring large numbers of men into quiet areas – firing blank ammunition, using pyrotechnics, supported by helicopters and vehicles, digging in and wiring. Military roads penetrate some of the remotest areas of both Northumberland and Dartmoor national parks. Low-flying aircraft continually shatter the peace of the remotest mountain summits and the quietest valleys. It can have come as no surprise when Lady Sharp concluded, in her report (1976) on military training in Dartmoor, that it was 'exceedingly damaging' and 'discordant, incongruous and inconsistent' in a national park.

The attitudes of the national park authorities tend to be ambivalent, particularly in Northumberland where recreational pressures on the Cheviot hills are relatively low and a tolerant park authority recently agreed to an extension of the Otterburn range. Established military bases provide jobs that would not easily be replaced, and there is some strong emotional and political support for the military presence. The Ministry of Defence is prepared to make marginal adjustments to its military training areas and programmes in the interests of public relations and has become positively keen about wildlife conservation. But it is determined to hang on to all its major training areas, including those in national parks, and to expand them. When the Harpur Crewe Estate was offered to the Peak Board in lieu of tax in 1985 the MoD used its power ruthlessly to consolidate its position. The Peak Board was only able to acquire the estate on terms that required it to accept continued military training on part of the land – an arrangement that the Board and the Countryside Commission publicly criticized.

The running controversy over the use of Dartmoor illustrates these tendencies very clearly. The MoD occupies over a quarter of the high moorland (Fig. 22). Its firing ranges occupy 78% of the 'wilderness' area that the park authority has identified in the northern moorland plateau, as well as the lovely upper Tavy and Cowsic valleys. The Duchy of Cornwall, which owns most of the high moorland, licenses the Okehampton and Merrivale ranges, extending to 10 000 ha, to the MoD. The public's complaints about Dartmoor were largely responsible for the setting up of the Nugent Committee's inquiry into military land in 1973. But his report led to only a token reduction of the military holdings. The Nugent report was followed by an inquiry by Lady Sharp into the continued military use of Dartmoor. Lady Sharp concluded that the MoD needed all its training areas in Dartmoor. A joint White Paper from the Defence and Environment departments followed, stating firmly that there was no possibility of making any significant reduction in

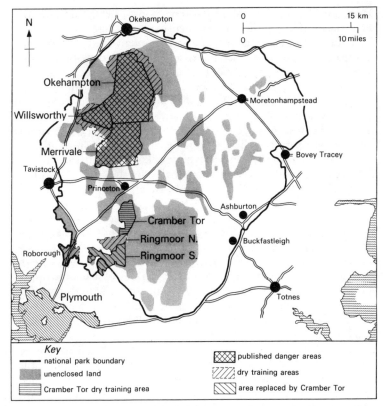

Figure 22 Military training areas in Dartmoor (Crown copyright reserved).

Dartmoor in the future. The MoD's determination to consolidate and extend its grip on Dartmoor is in opposition to the agreed policy of the Countryside Commission and the Dartmoor National Park Committee. This is now written into the revised national park plan which states:

> military training on Dartmoor as a National Park is inappropriate. The objective must be its ultimate withdrawal, and thus all decisions of the National Park Authority with regard to military matters must take this into account and seek to minimise the impact of training.

The Falklands war in 1982, Mrs Thatcher's election victory in 1983, and the increasing readiness to resort to military force in international disputes seem to have encouraged the MoD's intransigence. In August 1982 the MoD submitted proposals to modernize and extend the small arms ranges at Willsworthy and, as the

Dartmoor Committee had strong objections, referred them to the Secretary of State for the Environment under the agreed arbitration procedure. The Department of the Environment was not, however, an impartial arbiter, for it had issued a joint statement with the MoD in 1979 rejecting the transfer of the ranges to outside the park as 'not practicable'. The DoE's decision in favour of the MoD was a foregone conclusion. The Dartmoor Committee protested that, in addition to destroying natural beauty, the MoD was consolidating its hold on Dartmoor, and making it more difficult to phase out the military occupation. The National Park Officer reported on 6 December 1985 that 'the military now talk of much greater use [of Willsworthy] by all three forces from all over the country'. In 1987 an MOD spokesman said it was ready to buy more land that came into the market in Dartmoor.

The National Trust created an opportunity to prise the MoD out of its foothold in Dartmoor's southern moorland when it terminated the licence for dry training at Ringmoor in 1980. It did so because military use was inconsistent with the Trust's obligations to the public and incompatible with the purposes of a national park. But the South-West Water Authority came to the MoD's rescue by licensing some 500 ha at Cramber Tor, which is even deeper into the moorland. The park authority and the Countryside Commission accepted the situation as a temporary solution for three years. But in 1983 and 1984 the park authority accepted the licence for one year only, and in 1985 it formally objected to the licence being renewed, on the ground that it was not satisfied that the military had established a need for it. In fact Cramber Tor was only used for 39% of the available training days between 1981 and 1984. The park committee has produced figures to show that the use of the northern ranges for live firing and dry training falls far below their capacity. Even the Duchy of Cornwall, which feels bound in principle to accept government policy, has only renewed the licences for the Okehampton and Merrivale ranges on the condition that the need for live firing should be reviewed before they are due for renewal again in 1991.

The vast 'golf balls' of the Fylingdales missile radar stations on the North York Moors remind those who would get away from it all that there is no escape from nuclear war, of which Fylingdales would probably be a 'first strike' victim. Although nominally under British control, Fylingdales is run by the US military, primarily to give the US warning of Soviet missiles. In 1985 the North American Aerospace Defence Command in Colorado announced a proposal to replace the 'golf balls' by new installations, in the form of a huge, truncated pyramid that would treble their capacity. This appears to be a breach of the 1972 Soviet–American Anti-Ballistic Missile Treaty. The first the North York Moors National Park Committee heard of this American decision was from a report in the British press. The Council for National Parks and the North York Moors Association pointed out to William Waldegrave that a fundamental issue of principle was involved. For there appear to be no overwhelming technical reasons for siting the new installation in the national park, except the sheer convenience of using the existing site and the argument that its use involved no breach of the Treaty. The MoD investigated no alternatives. It assumed that it could use a national park as it (or rather the North American Aerospace Defence Command) pleased. The US's largest underwater surveillance station, monitoring Soviet submarine movements, is at Brawdy in the Pembrokeshire Coast National Park and, like Fylingdales, is a prime candidate for a nuclear strike aimed at disabling the US information network.

There are no easy solutions to the military use of national parks and no one solution has a universal application. But three possible approaches suggest themselves. One would be to exclude a military training area from the designated area of a national park on the ground that military training, and live firing in particular, totally negates national park purposes. This would consolidate the military presence, while amputating the vitals of at least three parks. Another would be to accept military training even in its most violent forms while using designation as a lever to extract some concessions from the military. Experience suggests that this guarantees the permanent presence of the military on whatever scale it chooses. A third strategy is to continue protective designations on the clear understanding that the MoD will progressively withdraw and terminate military training within a specific time. Every military claim would then be ruthlessly probed. But this strategy cannot succeed without a fundamental change in government policy, not only towards national parks but also towards military training and the use of violence as a means of settling international problems.

THE OKEHAMPTON BYPASS

In September 1983 the government dealt a double blow at Dartmoor National Park. Almost at the same time as the Ministry of Defence announced the improvement and modernization of the Willsworthy ranges the Transport Secretary announced his decision to route the Okehampton bypass through the national park. In both cases the Secretary of State for the Environment supported his political

colleagues. His endorsement of the southern route for the Okehampton bypass was particularly scandalous, because it was the first
case in which the policy governing new trunk roads in national
parks had been tested. Circular 4/1976, hailed in conservation circles
as putting a stop to damaging road construction and 'improvements' in national parks, was issued by the Department of the
Environment. It laid down the principle that 'no new route for long
distance traffic should be constructed through a national park unless
it has been demonstrated that there is a compelling need which
would not be met by any reasonable alternative means'. In 1980, in
deference to this policy, the Department of Transport (DoT) had
abandoned a project to build a new Manchester–Sheffield motorway through the Peak. The Okehampton decision raised the question whether the Government's proclaimed commitment to Circular 4/1976 had any real meaning.

Okehampton stands just outside the northern boundary of the
national park, and is bisected by the main London to Cornwall road,
the A30. Nobody denies the need for a bypass, as the town is a
bottleneck for holiday and goods traffic, which causes hazard, noise
and inconvenience to local people. In 1964 the DoT and Devon
County Council agreed on a northern route for a dual-carriageway
bypass, which remained in the county development plan for 12
years. Had the DoT stuck to it, the road would almost certainly
have been built by the early 1980s. It gives rise to no serious
objections, apart from complaints about the loss of farmland. But
the possible closure of British Rail's line to Meldon Quarry on the
hillside to the south of Okehampton led the DoT to present an
alternative route that would be a mile shorter, take 15 ha less
farmland and allegedly save an estimated £5 million. In the event,
the southern route turned out to be the more expensive!

Although British Rail's decision to keep the railway open destroyed the original rationale of siting new roads on abandoned
railways, the DoT committed itself to a southern route in 1976. It
deliberately chose conflict and delay, for five years earlier the
Dartmoor Preservation Association (DPA) had given warning that
the road was an 'environmental outrage', and would 'savagely
destroy the entire northern aspect of the national park'. There
followed technical investigations, a nine-month public inquiry
(which found for the southern route), an investigation by a joint
committee of both Houses of Parliament (which found the northern
route to be 'a reasonable alternative'), and a government Bill to
over-rule the joint committee. Nicholas Ridley, the Transport
Secretary, whose department was primarily responsible for more
than 15 years' delay, had the effrontery to argue at the end of the day

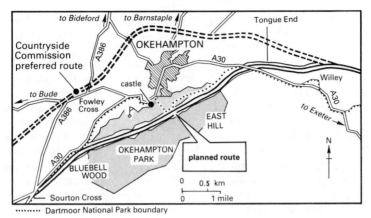

Figure 23   Okehampton bypass: the alternative routes   The 'planned route' to the south of Okehampton through the Dartmoor National Park is to be constructed (copyright *The Times*).

that to switch to the northern route would delay the bypass for up to nine years (a grotesque exaggeration) and bring 'economic disaster' to Cornwall!

In fact, thanks to an efficient management scheme, the traffic gets through Okehampton without long delays except on a few summer weekends. The DoT and Devon County Council, in their attempts to justify the southern route, have had to argue that, although within the boundaries of the national park, it does less damage to the landscape than the northern route. On the strength of the relative impact of the two routes as seen from a remote viewpoint, Ridley even told the House of Commons that the northern route would be an 'environmental disaster', although the farmland it traverses is no different from that traversed by the A30 all the way from Exeter.

As we found when we studied both routes, there is nothing unique about the enclosed farmed land to the north. It is pleasant and, at one point – Knowle Bridge – picturesque. It offers the people of Okehampton little in the way of recreation or visual stimulation. But to the south the semi-wild and wooded slopes of Dartmoor's borderland sweep down through Okehampton's ancient deer park to the edge of Okehampton itself. The park provides magical walks in the valleys of the East and West Okement and up the hillsides to the moors above, and contains the ruins of the Norman castle. It appeals to walkers, riders, naturalists, bird-watchers, picnickers and people of all ages. The ministers and their advisers who passed sentence of death on Okehampton Park did not understand the relative quality of the two landscapes.

They were able to get away with it because by 1985 every local authority affected by the bypass had joined the clamour for an early solution – and the earliest solution on offer was the southern route. The Dartmoor National Park Committee fought hard for the northern route at the public inquiry, but it gave up the struggle once the minister had made up his mind. Devon County Council, which had consistently backed the southern route when it had a Tory majority, came within four votes of opposing it in the autumn of 1985 when the Tories had lost control. It was the Dartmoor Preservation Society with the backing of nine other national and local amenity bodies and above all that indomitable octogenarian Lady Sayer, who took the fight to Westminster. They spent £50 000 – an enormous sum for a small voluntary society – to fight, and defeat, the DoT in Parliament. Little did they realize that the proceedings were a complete farce. An intransigent minister with the backing of the party whips was able to bring in a Bill to confirm the proposal that the Parliamentary committee had rejected. This was a serious abuse of the special procedure laid down for such cases, and can only deter people from petitioning Parliament in future.

But if the result in Parliament was bad, its sequel was worse. Within six months of forcing the Bill through Parliament, Nicholas Ridley was promoted to be Secretary of State for the Environment. What protection does Circular 4/1976 now offer, we wonder, if Mr Ridley takes a fancy to the Manchester–Sheffield motorway through the Peak District?

Chapter Fourteen

Hill farming at the crossroads

END OF AN ERA

The EEC's sudden decision in April 1984 to introduce milk quotas with the aim of limiting production and penalizing 'over-production', sent a shock-wave throughout the British countryside. It marked the turning of a tide in agricultural policy that had been running strongly for 40 years. The decision shattered farmers' confidence, for nobody believed that a policy of curtailing production could end with the milk quotas. On the contrary, they were seen as the beginning of a change to which no end could be seen. The National Farmers' Union proclaimed that it heralded 'the end of an era' – presumably the era of pouring billions into farming to promote higher productivity – but what the new era was to be remained obscure. In the absence of any clear government policy, apart from cutting public expenditure, the farming and landowning interests opened a debate on the alternatives.

Organic farming, hitherto derided as 'muck and mystery', suddenly became a respectable route to the growing of premium foods commanding higher prices. The National Farmers' Union, whose President Sir Richard Butler had denounced conservationists only three years before as 'braying do-gooders', suddenly discovered that conservation was not just a constraint on production but also a potential source of income. The EEC issued a Green Paper on the future of the Common Agricultural Policy which looked to lower prices to bring production and markets into balance, but also suggested 'setting aside' up to 10% of the Community's farmland by paying farmers not to produce on 'environmentally sensitive' land. In the UK there was talk of 'setting aside' anything from 1½ to 4 million hectares, and consultants employed by the NCC suggested

the 'release' of 2.6 million hectares of the least productive land by
the year 2000. A conference at the Centre for Agricultural Strategy
in April 1986 canvassed an immense range of alternatives such as
afforestation, and the growing of crops for energy or the biochemi-
cal industries, for medicine, flavouring or perfumes. No idea was
too improbable to be taken seriously. 'Diversification', both on and
off the farm, became the new catch-cry.

The debate necessarily takes a different form in the uplands,
where hill farmers are assured, by government and unofficial
sources alike, that whatever may happen to the producers of
unsaleable mountains of cereals, sugar or beef in the lowlands, the
supports the hill farmer has enjoyed since World War II are secure.
But, whatever ministers may say, if food is in surplus and land is to
be 'set aside' or switched to other crops or uses, the hill farmer is
highly vulnerable if the support he receives is justified, wholly or
mainly, by his production of food. A quick glance at the special
nature of hill farming and its recent history will make this clear. We
argued in Chapter 4 that the success of postwar hill farming policies
in creating fewer, larger, more technologically advanced units
employing fewer people was a major factor in pushing upland
communities to the verge of collapse. It becomes progressively
more difficult for the smaller hill farmers to survive because the
system discriminates against them. Hill farmers traditionally sell
'store' lambs and calves in the autumn for fattening by lowland
buyers. The store market, however, is a gamble in which the small
farmer particularly is at the mercy of the dealer who knows that the
farmer cannot afford either to take his stock home or to feed them if
he does. A succession of bad years culls the farmers who lack the
capital to survive as surely as it culls the weaker animals.

The dilemma has always been seen by the agricultural departments as an agricultural one, to be resolved by agricultural means.
Since World War II they have compensated farmers within the 'hill
line', for the natural handicaps from which they suffer by paying a
flat rate headage payment for livestock. Its overall aim was to
increase the scale and efficiency of the farm so that it could derive
an adequate income from agriculture alone and have sufficient
reserves to tide the farmer over the fluctuations of the market. The
advisory role of the Agricultural Development and Advisory
Service (ADAS) was crucial, for its officers won the confidence of
farmers by offering free advice in the farmers' best financial interest. ADAS fed through to the farming community the philosophy
of growth and expansion and advanced technology, as well as its
counterpart, the philosophy of the retirement or elimination of the
weaker.

FARM DEPOPULATION

When we wrote *National parks: conservation or cosmetics*? (to which we refer readers for a fuller account of the consequences of depopulation) we showed that headage payments had helped to conceal a wide range of social and environmental problems caused or aggravated by the acute shortage of labour on the farms. The consequences can be seen everywhere, in the neglect and removal of walls and hedges, the degeneration of small woodlands, the neglect and consequent overgrazing or undergrazing of commons and the spread of intrusive species such as gorse, rushes, rhododendron and bracken as labour is reduced and stock management adjusted accordingly. The Upland Management Service and similar work by the national park authorities and the National Trust have slowed down the rate of loss, but have only replaced a fraction of the labour that has been lost.

A study of five parishes in the upland plateau of the White Peak, by Rachel Berger in association with the authors, revealed a similar pattern. Between 1963 and 1976 the total number of holdings fell from 224 to 147, the decline being most rapid among the smallest holdings of below 10–12 ha. The number of holdings of 40 ha or more increased from 46 to 55. We concluded that by 1990 there would probably be no full-time farms of below 40 ha. Should milk continue to be in surplus in the EEC, all the smaller producers could well be forced to drop out or to move into livestock rearing on much larger farms with much less labour. When we contacted a number of the farmers in 1985, after the introduction of milk quotas, it was clear that the pressure on the smaller farmers had increased, although it was not possible to establish a complete statistical picture.

The farmers who are most likely to go to the wall include many of those who had succeeded in climbing up what one of them called 'the slippery slope' of continuous expansion by straining their physical and financial resources to the limit. Those we interviewed in the White Peak were neither lazy nor incompetent. Most of them cared deeply both for the land and the landscape. What they lacked was capital. What they regretted was their inability, with the labour at their disposal, to maintain the walls in as good a state of repair as they would like. Although the landscape of the White Peak shows few signs of deterioration on a superficial inspection, all the signs of long-term deterioration are there beneath the surface. The problems of the White Peak are structural and arise from agricultural policies which are powerfully reinforced by other social and economic trends.

ABUSES AND CONTRADICTIONS

It was precisely to counter the depopulation encouraged by earlier EEC policies on restructuring farms into larger units that the EEC Directive on farming in the agriculturally less favoured hill and mountain areas was introduced in 1975. Its aims were to sustain a minimum population, conserve the countryside, promote rural crafts and provide for leisure needs through farming. This Directive continued the old headage payments under the new name of Hill Livestock Compensatory Allowances (HLCAs). Grants for capital development are paid at a higher rate in the Less Favoured Areas (LFAs) under another Directive on farm modernization. Under a third Directive a socio-economic service is provided for the 'disadvantaged sectors' of the farming industry, of which clearly hill farming is one, and part-time or small farms are another. However, ADAS has always concentrated advice on what it calls 'viable farms', on the ground that the disadvantaged sector yields a low economic return. An expert from the Centre for Agricultural Strategy at Reading University said in 1981 that the needs of the small farmers had been very poorly served in terms of research and development. ADAS has only allocated token resources to socio-economic advice. The sharp reduction in its staff and the introduction of charging for its services from 1986 can only reduce still further the help given to those who need it most.

There is a fundamental contradiction between the aim of the EEC Less Favoured Area's Directive, to maintain the population and conserve the countryside, and the adoption of livestock headage payments as a means of achieving it. The Hill Livestock Compensatory Allowances (HLCAs) are paid on every breeding ewe and beef cow within the LFA, at half rate in the marginal areas added to the LFAs in 1984 and at the full rate elsewhere in England and Wales. Higher rates are paid for hardy breeds of sheep. The EEC pays 25% of the cost. But the system does not relate the level of payment to the severity of natural handicap, and places no effective limits on the stocking levels in open country. HLCAs, while providing a very useful cheque for the small farmer, encourage farmers to maximize production at the expense of the environment by pushing up stocking levels, reducing labour, and concentrating land in larger units.

Using data from the Upland Landscapes Study, Geoffrey Sinclair calculated that the help given to farmers in the Less Favoured Areas in 1979–80 was in inverse ratio to the degree of physical handicap they experienced or their social needs (see *New life for the hills*, M. MacEwen & G. Sinclair). One reason for this is that there are no upper limits on the number of livestock qualifying for headage payments, as there are in most other EEC countries. Sinclair found that in 1981–2 of some 20 500 farms in the LFAs of England and Wales the 11 000 smallest, with less than 50 cows or 300 sheep, averaged £590 each in grants and subsidies. But the 750 largest, with more than 300 cows or 1800 sheep, averged £13 200. In a nutshell, 30% of the money went to 6% of the farmers, benefitting the larger farms on the better land. There was found to be a similar bias in the provision of capital grants.

This situation was greatly aggravated by the EEC's sheepmeat regime, introduced in 1980. Its impact has been even more damaging than its ugly name implies, providing a bonanza for farmers on better land while discriminating sharply against those on the worst – a subsidy for those in the most favoured areas, 100% funded by the EEC! A fixed premium is paid for every breeding ewe, and a variable premium is paid on every fat lamb ready for the butcher. It is variable because it bridges the gap between the market price and the guaranteed price, which fluctuates throughout the year. There is also a beef cow subsidy funded by the EEC. The sheepmeat regime has encouraged farmers in the lowlands and on the better land and milder climates of the 'soft' uplands to move into the production of fat lambs. The experimental husbandry farms in Exmoor and in mid-Wales have led the way, and now sell the overwhelming majority of their lambs fat. With the help of capital grants farmers have invested in winter housing for sheep, intensified silage production, increased their flocks and put more sheep on the hills. By rearing fat lambs they qualify both for the hill farming subsidy, that compensates them for being unable to produce fat lambs, and for the fat lambs subsidy!

The farmers in the 'hard uplands', such as the fells of the Lake District, Snowdonia or the Scottish Highlands, cannot fatten their lambs. They have to sell them as 'stores', and have to survive as best they can on market prices with the help of the Less Favoured Area headage payments, which the Government has allowed to shrink in real value since 1980, on the ground that hill farmers generally have been prosperous. The result is not only to leave the farmers in the 'hard' uplands exposed to the vagaries of weather and the store markets, but to leave the farmers in the 'soft' uplands dangerously over-dependent on massive subsidies whose cost and inequity are indefensible.

THE UNACCEPTABLE PRICE
OF SUBSIDIES

This was precisely the warning given to hill farmers by Michael Haines, the professor of agricultural and food marketing at the University of Wales in Aberystwyth, in an article in *Farmers' Weekly* on 6 May 1986. He feared that the financial wave on which hill farmers were riding might be about to break. His analysis of hill farming and incomes for 1983–4 showed that something like 40% of the gross receipts of the farms in the Less Favoured Areas in Great Britain came from subsidies, and that on average the subsidies were about three times the farmer's net income. Using Professor Haines' figures we calculate that on a hypothetical hill farm with a gross income of £50 000 the British and European taxpayers are paying £19 500 in subsidies (three quarters of it from beef and sheep premiums) to provide the farmer with a net income of about £5 000 a year. Such a cost ineffective system is not sustainable. The implications for national parks are only too clear. For it has been estimated that about half the farmers in the Less Favoured Areas of England and Wales live in the national parks.

The irony is that these massive injections of public money, while inflating the profits of lowland farmers, have signally failed to achieve the increased incomes in Less Favoured Areas that, to farmers at least, was probably their main justification. In 1985 the net incomes of hill farmers fell to £1154 million, half the level of 1982. If one asks where the money has gone the answer must be that most of it has ended up in inflated land prices and in the hands of bankers, land agents, dealers, suppliers, manufacturers, contractors and builders – all those whose services the farmers have bought with their own and with borrowed money, but largely at the taxpayers' expense, to increase their output. Yet, because costs have risen faster than incomes, farmers have been left with smaller net margins than when they began, and a heavier burden of debt. This, above all, is what distresses the manager of a progressive hill farm in the south-west, with whom we discussed the problem early in 1986. For, in his view, the entire exercise has been counterproductive, both in social and in environmental terms. But if the regime is replaced by sheep quotas, as the bigger farmers seem to want, the hill farmers will face new difficulties.

Quotas for one product invariably push farmers into alternative crops. Milk quotas were the signal for lowland farmers to move rapidly into sheep farming, both to exploit the regime and to qualify for sheep quotas should they be introduced. This move by lowland farmers into sheep farming could pose a serious threat to hill farmers. The lowland farmer on better land in a softer climate can rear twice as many lambs per ewe. Each ewe has a longer life, and the lambs she produces have a better chance of survival. And the farmer can do this at less cost to the Treasury, because he does not get the headage payments available in the hills. Quotas would freeze the present pattern of production, and play into the hands of the larger, richer farmers, while shutting the door on the new entrant or the small farmer who can only survive through expansion.

Hill farmers are worried, some of them alarmed, by the dangers that they see looming ahead. There is a greater readiness than previously to look for alternative sources of income, and to take a kinder view of conservation both for its own sake and for the subsidies that it might possibly attract. But we question whether many hill farmers fully appreciate the fact that they have been lured into their present predicament by the entire agricultural establishment. The agricultural departments, the farmers' unions, the experimental farms, the advisory services, the Food and Agriculture Research Council, the agricultural colleges and university departments, the farming press and the salesmen of every relevant product have created a fake ethic of 'progress'. They have been the pushers of the drugs of higher inputs, ever higher outputs per man or per hectare and the dream of high profits on which too many farmers are now hooked. Getting them off the hook is bound to produce severe withdrawal systems that will have to be sensitively handled.

Some of the pushers of the drug of high-input farming have reformed, but others have merely adopted a green disguise. The real measure of the government's philistinism is demonstrated by its decision to slash the grant to the Soil Survey of England and Wales by three quarters. Maintaining soil fertility is one of the most basic conservation functions for human survival. Yet the Ministry of Agriculture has forced the Survey to curtail its research and cut its staff, and to turn to private sources for funding, at a time when research is showing soil erosion to be a far more serious problem in this country than complacent official statements have admitted. A report on *Soil erosion in Britain*, published by the Soil Association in 1986, concludes that 44% of our farmland is now at risk. In much the same way, the experimental husbandry farms are having to turn to petro-chemical and other companies for contracts to test their products, in the attempt to retain staff and continue research in the face of cuts in their grants. The Government has also rejected a proposal to establish an experimental unit in organic or low input farming, despite the public's readiness to pay higher prices for organic products. Consequently, its agricultural advisory service, already reduced in numbers, will in future have no experimental base from which to guide farmers towards alternative, lower-input techniques.

RECENT CHANGES

The changes in farm grants introduced in 1985 did, however, mark a shift towards conservation even if their primary motivation was to reduce the cost of agricultural support. The threshold of eligibility for capital grants was lowered to enable some part-time farmers to qualify for them. The payments to big farmers were reduced by lowering the maximum expenditure on which capital grant is payable over six years under a farm improvement plan from £130 000 to £56 000. The most destructive grants for land reclamation and improvement were eliminated, and land drainage grants reduced. A range of grants was introduced to encourage conservation or to reduce pollution, at 60% in the Less Favoured Areas, for the provision, replacement or improvement of hedges, walls, dikes, styles, footbridges, shelter belts and the handling of effluents or wastes. There are also 30% grants for managing or regenerating heather or controlling bracken. These grants are available without submitting a farm improvement plan, and those farmers who are receiving grant on the maximum capital expenditure of £56 000 can get conservation grants on an additional £24 000.

Grants for conservation purposes, useful as they are, yield no additional income, and require the farmer both to put up a percentage of the cost and then to manage his new asset. The new grants have already begun to improve the Exmoor landscape, where long neglected beech hedgerows are now being laid. But the grants only appeal to those who have spare capital and labour, as well as the necessary skills and enthusiasm. The inherent bias of the headage payments and livestock subsidies discriminates shamelessly in favour of the biggest farmers on the best land, and fosters exploitation of the environment. These changes fall far short of the 'revolution' that Professor Bateman, an agricultural economist at the University of Wales, Aberystwyth, has called for – one in which support is directed at a mixture of social and environmental objectives, and people are more important than livestock. The changes also fall short of the less radical, but nonetheless substantial moves towards conservation, integration and diversification, that have been advocated in 1985 and 1986 by an extraordinary diversity of pressure groups – extending from conservation and wildlife interests to Rural Voice (which represents a broad coalition of rural interests) and the more conservation-oriented landowners in the

Society for the Responsible Use of Resources in Agriculture and on the Land (RURAL).

The *Financial Times* (23 August 1986) reported that the Minister of Agriculture 'is trying to resist attempts ... to shift the balance of funding towards small farmers'. In *New life for the hills* Geoffrey Sinclair and Malcolm MacEwen have shown how to make headage payments both equitable and environmentally benign. It is essential to taper them to give proportionately more to the smaller and more handicapped farmers, and progressively less to those with larger units or on better land. There must be a cut-off point to stop the progressive growth of flocks and farms, and effective control of stocking numbers to prevent overgrazing and erosion. *New life for the hills*, suggested the introduction of a non-specific 'upland management grant', to be offered to farmers who prepare a comprehensive plan or negotiate a less formal agreement for the management of the total resources of a farm. It would not be money for nothing, or compensation for agreeing not to destroy an asset, but payment for constructive management. There are certainly other possible routes to the same ends.

ANOTHER WAY

Whatever new way is found to support comprehensive land management presupposes a major change in the climate of hill farming and of government itself. It calls for the integration of policies to achieve clearly defined objectives. Sir Derek Barber, the chairman of the Countryside Commission, has argued persuasively that the ESAs may contain the seeds of a desirable and practical restructuring of the Common Agricultural Policy. They could provide, he says, income support to farmers and curb food surpluses by funding environmentally benign, traditional management regimes (*Country Life* 26 June 1986). The prospects for ESAs have improved since the EEC let it be known in 1986 that it might contribute 25 or 30% of the costs out of EEC funds. But ESAs as currently conceived by the Ministry of Agriculture cannot possibly deliver the benefits claimed for them (except perhaps in the Broads and other small, relatively uniform areas) for the reasons given in Chapter 12.

The Labour Party's new environmental policy marks a total break (on paper at least) with the conventional, production-oriented policies pursued by earlier Labour and other governments. It proposes to shift agricultural spending from subsidizing production to enhancing and protecting the rural environment as part of an integrated policy for the countryside. It would shift support from the bigger, richer farmers to the poorer, smaller farmers, and create new jobs on the land. The Labour Party's proposals for annual grants to be paid for environmentally sensitive management, and giving priority to less intensive farming or broadleaved woodland in land that is surplus to farm production, are not unlike proposals made earlier in 1986 by the CPRE, the Council for National Parks, the RSPB and the Royal Society for Nature Conservation. They suggested three levels of management grants for ESAs for the conservation of moor and heath, permanent pasture, hay meadows, woodland and field boundaries, provided the farmer follows approved guidelines and submits a simple farm plan. The conservation groups' paper also suggested setting ceilings for Less Favoured Area headage payments related to approved stocking levels, and making all national parks and ESAs eligible for ESA payments.

There is no dearth of practical suggestions for a new support system that could guarantee the future of hill farming and the achievement of the wider purposes of the national parks. What is missing at the present time is the realization that hill farming is soon going to face the crisis that Professor Haines has predicted. Beef premiums are under threat in the EEC, and the cost of the sheepmeat regime cannot be sustained indefinitely. Sheepmeat may well be in surplus within a few years. Lamb production is rising fast (another half million lambs in 1986) while lamb consumption is dropping (it has halved in 25 years), in line with the wider trend away from eating red meat. The collapse of the sheepmeat regime could precipitate the collapse of hill farming. A senior civil servant in the Welsh Office was recently heard speculating on the possibility that Wales, having lost its coal and much of its steel might soon lose even its sheep to the lusher pastures of the lowlands. Even if the Less Favoured Area headage payments were retained, sheep quotas would leave the hill farmers to compete on unequal terms with lowland farmers. The losers would be the older farmers, the smaller full-time farmers on the margin of survival, expanding farmers trapped by indebtedness, the rural community, and the living landscape itself. The beneficiaries would be those larger or more aggressive farmers who could buy land cheap to ranch it with the minimum of labour, and the afforestation companies.

Chapter Fifteen

The woods and the trees

AFFORESTATION

The future of forestry in this new situation depends on many factors, not least among them being the policies of the EEC, the government and its agency, the Forestry Commission. The Commission has two separate but related functions. As the nationalized state forestry enterprise it is the largest landowner in the country, and in the national parks it owns almost as much land as the National Trust. As the national forest authority it advises the forestry ministers (the Secretaries of State for Scotland, Wales, and Northern Ireland and the Minister of Agriculture), promotes and finances private forestry and is responsible for forestry research. Its duties were extended by the Wildlife and Countryside Amendment Act of 1985, to achieve 'a proper balance' (whatever that may mean) between its primary duties of afforestation and timber production and the conservation and enhancement of natural beauty.

The Forestry Commission has begun to shed the single-minded obsession with planting monocultures of quick growing conifers for the sole purpose of sustaining the supply of softwood timber that dominated its outlook from its establishment in 1919. This policy was originally justified by a strategic need to replace the standing timber felled in two world wars. More recently the timber and forestry interests have sought to justify large-scale coniferous afforestation on other grounds. One is that Britain's forest area (10%) is one of the lowest in Europe. Another is Britain's dependence on imports for 90% of its timber. The Minister of Agriculture has tried to justify afforestation by the argument that it creates jobs, benefits the rural economy and enhances the environment – all false propositions if we are talking about coniferous afforestation on low-grade moorland, where forestry is on the same destructive capital-intensive, labour-shedding treadmill as modern agriculture.

At the time the Tory government was elected in 1979 the Forestry Commission had announced what it called a 'modest' programme nearly to double the rate of afforestation by planting an additional 1.5 million ha by 2025, some 43 000 ha a year, nearly all conifers in the uplands. The new government 'saw scope' for increasing the planting rate in the UK to about 35 000 ha a year but it wanted the greater part of the afforestation programme to be taken over by private forestry. The Commission was ordered to sell part of its estate, and by the end of 1985 it had sold 78 000 ha. Early in 1986 *The Economist* leaked a paper by Michael Jopling, the Minister of Agriculture (and of Forestry in England), suggesting the privatization of the Commission's entire estate of 1.18 million ha, and this remains a possibility for a third Thatcher government. Private forestry has increased its share of new planting to 83% of the 23 000 ha to be planted in 1986. The Commission's effort is increasingly focussed on planting the second rotation of trees in its earliest forests.

The Treasury requires the Commission to earn a 3% return on its plantations, even in national parks. In 1984 98% of the Commission's new planting was coniferous, usually on low-grade land that was often of high environmental interest. Although it claims that the second rotation creates the possibility of great improvements in species selection and design, the proportion of conifers on replanting is only marginally down. The Commission is now more accommodating in the design of sensitive areas, but it is obviously under strong pressure, as we were told in the North York Moors, to squeeze as much Sitka spruce and Lodgepole pine as possible onto the moorland plateau. The Commission still regards national park status as an obstacle to afforestation. It even joined with the private timber interests in 1985 in objecting (unsuccessfully) to the designation of the North Pennines Area of Outstanding Natural Beauty at the public inquiry on the ground that this might hinder afforestation.

The threat of insensitive coniferization in the uplands comes mainly from private forestry companies, which have made it clear that the recently improved grants for broadleaved planting hold no attractions for them. The private companies are city-based institutions, investing on behalf of rich people who are looking for a long-term tax-free capital gain. The attraction of afforestation to them lies in the planting grants, and even more in the concessions in income tax, capital transfer tax and capital gains tax that the forestry companies know how to manipulate on their behalf. The racket by which 'pop stars, snooker players and successful business men and women' are channelling £30–40 million a year into the coniferization of the uplands through these companies was exposed in detail in 1986 by Stephen Tomkins, in a pamphlet *The theft of the hills*, published by the Ramblers' Association. Mr Tomkins, a tax expert who worked for the Economic Forestry Group (EFG), was so disillusioned by the experience of finding ways of planting beautiful countryside that he resigned to work for conservation. EFG is the largest of the private forestry companies, and enjoys an intimate relationship with government. Michael Jopling told Prince Charles, ministers and other notables at the EFG Jubilee luncheon in 1986 that forestry offered 'the most promising alternative for land when no longer required for agricultural production'.

The Ministry has established a branch to promote the diversion of land producing food surpluses to other uses, notably forests and woodlands. EFG clearly has its sights on the uplands, whether national parks or common land, where common rights can often be bought out as hill farming declines. The Commons Forum report (see Ch. 8) if translated into legislation would block that loophole by creating 'statutory commons', but the Forestry Commission adopted an aggressive posture within the Forum on behalf of commercial forestry. As a result, although the model rules for managing commons would exclude commercial afforestation, the Secretary of State would have the power to allow it. In its current brochure EFG publishes a map of the Less Favoured Areas as 'hill land suitable for planting, whose "barren" state is man-made, and where only constant grazing by sheep keeps trees from returning'.

The Forestry Commission's own studies published in 1978 showed that of the 1.2 million ha of 'technically plantable' land in England and Wales, 570 000 ha were in national parks. The national park authorities are notified by the Commission of proposals for new plantations for which the owners intend to claim planting grants. But, although national park designation has restrained afforestation, national park plan policies have no legal force. The park authorities' afforestation maps are equally unenforceable and the Forestry Commission refuses to accept their status or their policy implications. The new landscape character and 'open country' maps (see Ch. 6) have a sounder approach to ecology, nature and landscape, but they have not been agreed with the timber interests and they, too, have no legal force. The park authorities have the right to express an opinion on private afforestation proposals to the Forestry Commission, or in the event of a dispute, to a Regional Advisory Committee (RAC) which is appointed by the Commission. If there is still no agreement the issue is referred to the forestry minister. There is, strange as it may seem, no formal machinery by which any private person or public authority can appeal to ministers against the Commission's own proposals to buy or plant land. The Commission has recently begun to set up informal consultation arrangements with some voluntary bodies at local levels.

The appeal procedure is confined to private proposals and is, in our view, authoritarian, secret and heavily biased towards afforestation. As we write, the Commission is considering some minor changes that would tilt the balance on the RAC towards people with farming and environmental interests, and put in the chair a person who would somehow be 'neutral' between farming, forestry and environmental interests – a kind of referee uncommitted to conservation in a conflict between opposing interests. In what the Commission regards as a concession, voluntary bodies would be allowed in future to submit written representations. But the entire proceedings would remain secret, and no opportunities would be given to objectors to cross-examine witnesses – or even to see the submissions made by the Forestry Commission to ministers at the final stage. The Lakes Board condemned this procedure in 1975 as 'a travesty of justice'. It objected to it again in 1985, because the Board had only been allowed to attend a site meeting with the minister and to see the Commission's submission to the minister 'by mistake' – which, the Forestry Commission said, would not be repeated in future!

One of the reasons why many national park and other local authorities want afforestation or replanting brought under planning control is that even if the minister or the Commission refuses a grant it may still be profitable for a private company to go ahead. The main incentive is not the grants, which are subject to conditions, but the unconditional tax incentives which can be worth very much more in the long run. Until 1982, if a forestry grant was refused no compensation was payable, and forestry companies rarely went ahead. But by bringing afforestation within the scope of the Wildlife and Countryside Act financial guidelines the Government guaranteed that every company refused a grant would claim compensation for the profit foregone – profit made up entirely of grants and tax concessions.

When Fountain Forestry proposed, in 1984, to plant 1100 ha of a superb SSSI at Creag Meagaidh in the Scottish Highlands, the Secretary of State for Scotland, then George Younger, refused to make a stop order under the Wildlife and Countryside Act, and he then approved grant for planting half the area – a classic Solomon-style 'compromise' of the type favoured by RACs. The NCC could only stop afforestation by buying the whole arrea for £430 000, a price that had been greatly inflated by Mr Younger's approval of grant. The national park authorities have only a fraction of the resources that would be needed to conclude management agreements or to buy land on these penal terms should there be a new wave of afforestation proposals.

FORESTRY AND 'SET ASIDE'

The concept of 'set aside', as opposed to reducing food surpluses by shifting to less intensive farming, has been taken up enthusiastically by the EEC, by the Ministry of Agriculture and the National Farmers' Union. Afforestation is far and away the most favoured alternative use. It provides a good example of the way in which the concept of 'integration' is abused by those whose primary interest is to promote their own sectoral interests. In the summer of 1986 the Nature Conservancy Council published a report on *Nature conservation and afforestation* which argued strongly for firm geographical limits to be set county by county to the expansion of afforestation in open country. This was challenged by the forestry interests and by John Bowman, the secretary of the National Environmental Research Council, on the ground that the NCC was claiming too much land for nature conservation. Both sides to the controversy seemed to regard conservation and afforestation as competing uses of land, to be 'integrated' by dividing the territory between them.

The integration of farming and forestry has been one of the Forestry Commission's stated objectives for many years, but it has been conceived, until very recently, as taking advantage of the forestry grants and tax concessions to enable farming and commercial afforestation to support one another. The poorer rough grazing land is afforested and the lost agricultural output made up by intensifying production on the remainder. Roads financed by agricultural and forestry grants and (until 1986) exempt from planning control in national parks have improved access to the plantations and to livestock grazing on the higher ground – and have inflicted enormous scars on the hillsides in recent years. It was not until the Forestry Commission's broadleaf policy was published in 1985 that existing broadleaved woodlands were seen to have any role in integrating farming with forestry. Even now, what passes for integration is still based on planting conifers, and the elimination of the semi-natural vegetation over both the afforested and the improved agricultural land.

The National Farmers' Union published a brochure in 1986 aptly entitled *Farming trees*, which advocated the 'setting aside' of

150 000 ha of farm land for commercial afforestation. It used the word 'integration', but by 'farming trees' it clearly meant applying modern farming techniques to growing trees. Its arguments were crudely economic. It emphasized that even in lowland areas farmers should concentrate on those tree species (notably conifers) and husbandry systems 'which are most economic in a farm business context'. It referred to conservation of wildlife and landscape not as ends in themselves, or integral elements in any scheme for planting trees, but as the price that could have to be paid to reconcile 'potential opposition'. It firmly rejected any control over afforestation because that would be 'a substantial disincentive'. In short, the NFU wants a free-for-all, in which land is allocated randomly by the market to highly subsidized afforestation. We are opposed to paying tree planting grants to any farmer except as part of a comprehensive land management plan that gives the first priority to looking after the trees, woods and hedges that are already there.

If the problem of surplus food production is approached in this haphazard way all grade 3 and 4 land would be at risk, including some of the best surviving mixed farming landscapes. The essential mixture of land uses and landscape types that provide essential habitats for birds and other species could be rudely disturbed. There would be no social control except over roads and buildings and over such individual features in national parks as might one day be protected by Landscape Conservation Orders. The European Commission has even suggested in its socio-structural proposals (1986) that additional annuities be paid to farmers aged over 50 who retire, or to their younger successors, if farms are afforested. The Countryside Commission observed, in scathing evidence to the House of Lords, that the abandonment of whole farms in this way, and the introduction of deliberately unproductive management (or the afforestation of random farms or parcels of land) seems to be 'the antithesis of the policy of integration that we have been pressing for for so long'. And the Council for National Parks and the CPRE observed in their evidence to the House of Lords that the EEC seemed to imagine that it was farmers rather than food that were in surplus.

Integrating conservation with development calls for land to be rationally allocated to afforestation or other uses, or to multiple uses, on a range of criteria that may conflict sharply with the short-term economic interests of the individual farmer. These criteria include the contribution that woodland can make to soil fertility, landscape, wildlife, recreation and local employment, and to the farm. Decisions should be taken within the framework of comprehensive area plans and coherent landscape designs, not farm-by-farm or field-by-field. The NFU prescription also disregards the irreversible character of afforestation, at least for a century or so. Integration has a time dimension. Land that may be needed for food when the energy glut and the food surpluses of the mid-1980s have disappeared should not be set aside for producing softwood, of which ample supplies will be available for centuries from the Soviet Union and other northern countries in exchange for our manufactured goods or services.

A THREAT –
or an opportunity?

The problem is not only how to avert the threat but also to seize the opportunity presented by the present crisis in rural land-use policy. The first aim in the uplands should be to shift afforestation away from windy sites on poor soils at high altitudes, where monotonous monocultures produce low-grade timber liable to windthrow and pests, with dubious long-term consequences for soil and wildlife. The corollary is to devise incentives for creating woodland (which is not the same thing as planting trees) on more sheltered land with high rainfall, a high water table and somewhat better soils that would grow better quality timber, broadleaved or coniferous, and provide more locally based jobs. New woods and forests, designed to take advantage of the valley profiles and contours and integrated with farming in a coherent land-use pattern, could play a positive role in rural communities, enhance the environment and remove the threat of coniferization from the hills. Incentives would be required, but instead of offering tax-free gains to rich people they should reflect the community's interest in, and need for, new woodlands in all their aspects. Some new woodland could be established by colonization, letting nature take its course with a little help from people, until a woodland climax is achieved.

Both new planting and restocking of old forests or woodlands should be brought under planning control or licensing, in national parks by the park authorities. Planting should be concentrated on ground with the least nature conservation interest, and should take the form of a skilfully designed mosaic, not blankets of uniform species. All new planting should conform to designs for the area concerned. No early cash returns should be expected by the Treasury, and support should be given not in the form of hidden tax concessions but by way of publicly accountable grants which would be taxable when the timber shows a profit. In return for its investment the public should have a right to enjoy the woods under reasonable conditions.

There is already substantial support for many of these proposals. National park authorities that see a serious threat of afforestation have long been calling for the power to control it. The most radical reform proposals have come from the Labour Party, which would cease to support afforestation through tax concessions, and would rely on grants and loans tied through management agreements to 'economic benefit, job creation and environmental enhancement'. There would be a presumption against coniferous plantations in national parks and 'other important areas', and a target of doubling the broadleaved area by the year 2015. Farmers would be offered annual payments to implement 'farm woodland schemes' in return for a share in the profit on the 'harvested crop' – a phrase that disturbs us. Sale of the Forestry Commission's land would stop, and the Commission's membership would include conservationists and forestry workers. New planting would be controlled. The statutory conservation agencies, in marked contrast, have weak positions. The Countryside Commission, which had abandoned its long-standing support for control over afforestation as 'out of tune with the times', revived it in 1984, albeit with exemptions up to 50 ha (since reduced to 20 ha). This would *encourage* private coniferous afforestation and undermine the present arrangements by which schemes can at least be challenged. But the Commission has resisted the Countryside Commission for Scotland's proposal, that the Forestry Commission should license afforestation and make grants and tax concessions dependent on observing the conditions of the licence. The Forestry Commission welcomed this proposal, and so did the NCC with the weak reservation that 'damaging' proposals to plant SSSIs could only be justified by 'a convincing case of national interest'. The NCC's 1986 report on *Nature conservation and afforestation* argues that afforestation should be 'foregone' on land of 'high quality for nature conservation', in nature reserves, national parks, AONBs and National Trust properties – provided the landowner is compensated for 'potential financial disadvantage'!

The government published a consultation paper on its proposals for Landscape Conservation Orders (LCOs) in December 1986, which would be confined to national parks, and the Broads. Afforestation was not one of the activities to be controlled. Even in national parks only some limited areas would be affected, and the government expected so little use to be made of LCOs that it saw no need for any more money or staff. LCOs fall far short of licensing or planning control, and notification of damaging operations would be voluntary. The authorities would be crippled by the obligation to pay compensation for hypothetical profits foregone, a requirement that has led to disenchantment with Tree Preservation Orders. Local authorities are reluctant to make TPOs because the owner is entitled to compensation. Until 1986 it was assumed that compensation was payable for the value of the timber; but a Lands Tribunal decision awarding a farmer compensation for the hypothetical profit (including agricultural grant) he could have made by converting the woodland to agriculture has sent a shudder of alarm through local authorities and the Nature Conservancy Council. This one case cost Canterbury District Council £46 000 in compensation for 39 acres, and £54 000 in costs. Introduction of LCOs will not stifle the demand for licensing or planning control over afforestation. Many Conservatives want control. The Association of County Councils consistently supported planning control over afforestation when the Tory Party was in control (until 1985).

BROADLEAVED WOODLANDS

The most urgent task is to save what is left of our once-extensive broadleaved woodlands, and to make the management of trees and woods a normal part of farm life, as it is in France and Germany. For this reason the U-turn made by the Forestry Commission in 1985 on the subject of broadleaved woodlands is a landmark in the history of forestry in this country. The Forestry Commission had presided for nearly 70 years over the depletion and degeneration of Britain's broadleaved woodlands. The Commission's secret and illegal plan to convert large areas of the New Forest from broadleaves to conifers led to the clear felling of close on 400 ha of broadleaved trees in the 1960s, and was only stopped when a public outcry forced the Government to suspend the felling. This incident, perhaps the greatest woodland crime of the century, is recalled here only to contrast the lengths to which professional foresters would go less than 20 years ago with the somewhat more enlightened attitudes they are adopting today. It was the need to make a response to the damning report of the House of Lords select committee on scientific aspects of forestry (1980) that forced the Forestry Commission to remove its blinkers five years later. The Committee called for a halt to any further clearing of broadleaved woodland for farming or for conversion to conifers, and recommended the establishment of long-term policies for Britain's woodlands.

The decline and degeneration of broadleaved woodlands and hedgerow trees is now much better documented than it was in 1980 (see Ch. 3) and there are even more grounds for alarm than there were then. The reasons for the loss of woodlands are complex, and have been clearly identified in studies by the Dartington Trust of small woods on farms. The switch from tenant farming to owner occupation means that 70% of the farmland of England and Wales is now managed by owner occupiers, very few of whom have any tradition, skill or desire to become foresters or to manage woodlands. Small farmers in particular are never able to look more than four or five years ahead at most, and cannot wait 30 years for a return on the capital invested in trees. They are not in the right tax bracket to benefit from tax reliefs on afforestation, and often lack the cash to invest even in grant-aided planting. Timber contractors are geared to large-scale harvesting, clear-felling or simple operations where they can be quickly in and out; they are not interested in the careful management and replanting of small woodlands. No arrangements exist for marketing the timber products of small farms, and the end result is that their woods are neglected or exploited for grazing and firewood because their owners see no other 'economic' use for them.

The policy for broadleaved woodland launched by the Forestry Commission in 1985, and the Ministry of Agriculture's paper of the same date on woodlands as a farm crop, have to be measured against their ability to solve these problems. Let us take the good points first. The Commission has imposed stricter controls on felling, reversing its original intention (announced in 1980) to relax these controls and thereby precipitate what we called 'a veritable massacre of small woods and copses'. The new policy is intended to maintain the area of broadleaved woodland by introducing higher rates of grant, up to £1200 a hectare, for planting and (for the first time) for the natural regeneration of pure broadleaved woodlands. The Commission now recognizes the unique value of ancient semi-natural woodlands, and the condition that grant will only be paid if timber production is the primary objective has been dropped, although it must be an objective. The Commission intends to encourage the maintenance and greater use of broadleaves in the uplands, particularly where they will improve the beauty of the landscape. Grant-aid is backed up by the publication of *Guidelines for the management of broadleaved woodlands* and by the offer of what must be a limited amount of advice from various sources.

The other side of the coin is less appealing. To maintain the present area of broadleaved woodland in such an underwooded country is an essential, but hardly ambitious target. Nor does the policy face up to the problems facing the owners of woodlands, many of which cannot yield the income that the Forestry Commission itself believes to be essential if they are to be managed. The policy provides no means of bridging the financial gap for the smaller farmer who cannot invest in afforestation as a device for passing on a large tax-free capital sum to his heirs, but has to find the money and labour to plant trees or to manage woods here and now out of his own pocket. It offers no compensation, as the Countryside Commission recommended in its uplands report, to the farmer who has to move his stock from woodland. And the Ministry of Agriculture's primary concern is to promote trees as an alternative crop.

Neither the Forestry Commission nor the Ministry of Agriculture seem to have grasped the basic fact that to make woodland management a normal part of farm management calls, as we said in the last chapter, for a revolutionary change in attitudes and skills, and will demand a major national effort spread over a generation or more. The Nature Conservancy Council gave a guarded welcome to the Commission's belated recognition of the value of ancient, semi-natural woodlands, but pointed out the defects of the scheme by asking for legal protection of these woods and a whole series of additional grants to meet the special needs of their owners. Tree Preservation Orders, as we have seen, are both ineffective and costly and do not, in any case, conserve woodland by ensuring lasting management. They only prevent felling. There seems to be a widespread opinion that the new grants will be taken up by the bigger and more enthusiastic farmers and landowners, and left alone by the great majority. A completely new approach is needed to save the small woods and enlist the enthusiasm of small as well as large farmers. The Dartington Trust has been successful in persuading the Forestry Commission and others to sponsor a hopeful experiment in the integration of woodland management with farming, Project Silvanus, which we will examine in the next chapter.

But the dominant trend in forestry policy is still to subsidize coniferous plantations by the private forestry companies. The decision of the Forestry Commission in October 1986 to pay EFG a grant to coniferize Ashtead Fell and Borrowdale – land every bit as beautiful as the neighbouring Lake District fells – was condemned by the CPRE as 'a slap in the face for the countryside'. The Government's rural policy package announced in February 1987, a derisory £25 million, left the incentives for commercial forestry untouched and afforestation uncontrolled. Moreover, it proposed to increase commercial afforestation by 7000 ha a year, and offered farmers £125 a hectare for new, mainly coniferous, plantations up to 20 ha. The package had little for small farmers, the rural economy or the countryside.

PART FIVE

The way ahead

Chapter Sixteen

The integrated approach

WORDS AND DEEDS

Since 1985 'integrated rural development' has become the new conventional wisdom of the rural establishment. It is generally understood to mean the harmonization of the policies of government departments and agencies, to prevent collisions between incompatible policies and to facilitate an integrated approach to decision making and problem solving at the local level. There is nothing easier than to adopt such approach in principle, but verbal endorsement of the concept of 'integration' is rarely accompanied by deeds that fully match the words. It is much easier to dress sectoral policies in the language of integration, and to claim that a balance has been struck at some acceptable point between competing interests, than to apply the spirit of integrating conservation with social and economic development. For the latter is not so much a matter of balancing one narrowly conceived sectoral policy against another as of ensuring that the principles of sustainable use and the conservation of nature, landscape and finite resources run like a thread through every policy.

The Countryside Commission's report *A better future for the uplands* (1984) stated the case for integration very clearly. It asked the Government to test the policies of all departments affecting the uplands against a set of unexceptional social, economic, environmental and recreational objectives. It was a notable advance for the Commission itself to take such a broad view of the inter-related upland problems. The evidence it had received in the year-long 'upland debate' had persuaded it of the need for significant changes in policy: the extension of planning controls to afforestation, farm roads and forest buildings, a switch in agricultural supports from maximizing productivity towards supporting conservation practices, and the need for positive programmes to satisfy such basic social needs as housing.

When the report shifted from broad conclusions to specific recommendations, however, it failed over and over again to carry its analysis through to its logical conclusions. The outstanding example was its recommendation that, although afforestation should be subject to planning control, plantations of less than 50 ha would be exempt. At almost every point, whether in proposals to help small farmers, to control overstocking of livestock, or to assist woodland management, the Commission's recommendations were timid. It asked the government for more money – but not much – by donating to conservation projects £5 million of the £90 million then being spent on agricultural support in the Less Favoured Areas of England and Wales, and putting £10 million–£15 million more into the development and tourist agencies. If measured by its own test against the social, economic, environmental and recreational needs of the uplands, its recommendations failed to pass.

However, the Commission went too far for the government. Mrs Thatcher summed up the government's policy in a parliamentary answer in 1986 as being 'to achieve the highest environmental standards that are cost effective and do not place unnecessary burdens on industry'. She could have said, more succinctly, 'the environment gets no priority'. Within this policy framework William Waldegrave responded to the uplands report in a bland, complacent letter to the Commission that accepted the broad policy objectives of the report but rejected virtually all the specific policy recommendations except the control of farm and forestry roads and buildings. Mr Waldegrave congratulated the government on its record over the entire range of rural issues, and awarded the government full marks for its 'first class' performance on country-side conservation – at least since the passing of the Wildlife and Countryside Act. He saw no need to control afforestation, and cited the livestock subsidies paid in the Less Favoured Areas as a success story. Mr Waldegrave went on to say that it was for the local authorities and other agencies to implement policies according to local needs, as they perceived them.

Nobody would imagine, from reading these honeyed words, that the government had precipitated a crisis in local government by slashing its resources, and resorting to unheard of penalties and restrictions to compel local authorities to toe central government's line. The county and structure plans which (according to the government) provide the 'ready-made framework' for local people to achieve integration at the local level, can control neither farming nor forestry operations and are more negative than positive. The government has also told local authorities in its White Paper *Lifting the burden* (1985) that structure plan policies should not be regarded as overriding, particularly if they stand in the way of economic growth. In September 1986 it proposed to abolish structure plans altogether and to replace them by development plans that would not have to be approved by the Secretary of State. This would make it easier to challenge their policies. Despite some welcome changes the government's policies for farming and forestry remain in conflict with social and environmental objectives, and receive entirely disproportionate financial support. Rural services of all kinds – education, health, transport, local shops – continue to decline. The county council elections of 1985 were a massive vote of protest against the failure to integrate rural policies.

THE MACHINERY

The strength of the contending interests and fossilized thoughts behind sectoral policies suggests to us that although adjustments in the machinery of central and local government are desirable, even essential, they are unlikely by themselves to solve the problem of integration at government level. It might be more useful to introduce a rule that Ministers of Agriculture must not be farmers or landowners or to eliminate the unhealthy influence of the NFU in that department, than to devise a new departmental set-up. Some landowning and farming interests would like to see the Ministry of Agriculture transformed into a Rural Affairs Department with responsibility for the Countryside Commission, the NCC and the Development Commission. But this is transparently designed to preserve the entrenched position of the NFU and the CLA, and to retain Ministry of Agriculture officials in commanding positions. Conservation and recreation interests instinctively suspect any such move.

A key element in the Labour Party's new environment policies (several of which have much in common with those presented in this book) is the machinery the Party proposes for getting things done. At the top level a Minister of Environmental Protection, possibly with a seat in the Cabinet, would be responsible for promoting conservation as an integral part of all government policies and programmes. Two new conservation agencies would be responsible to him. Countryside conservation would be the responsibility of an agency created by merging the NCC with the Countryside Commission and giving it more powers and money. An Environmental Protection Service would be given the job of enforcing standards on public bodies and private companies or individuals alike. The Liberal–Social Democratic Alliance also seems to favour establishing a Department of Environmental Protection.

Some such machinery is necessary if integration is ever to be achieved, or even attempted. But reorganization often causes as many problems as it solves, and can achieve nothing by itself unless there is both commitment and understanding in the Cabinet and in the individual departments and agencies. Committed, able people can make an inferior machine produce the goods; hostile, resentful, unskilled or poorly motivated people can turn a theoretically good arrangement into a shambles. Not even a super ministry can guarantee a reasonable 'balance' in terms of policies, funds or personnel. Sectoral policies and separate departments will never disappear, for government cannot be carried on without them. The key question is how far the spirit of integrating conservation with development on a sustainable basis informs the policies of every department. A Minister of Environmental protection could achieve little, especially if he were outside the Cabinet, unless, for example, the Minister of Agriculture was totally committed to the environmental, agricultural and forestry policies that Labour has proposed. Established departmental interests and habits of thought, and the pressures of the vested interests in farming and forestry, will not be overcome without a long and a tough struggle.

We welcome the Labour Party's recognition of the need to establish a stronger, unified conservation agency by merging the Nature Conservancy Council and the Countryside Commission, for which we argued in Chapter 9. People in both agencies increasingly accept the principle. The NCC's policy statement of 1984, *Nature conservation in Britain*, conceded that the lack of a 'closely integrated joint effort' prevented the two agencies from exerting their combined strength to oppose developments that were highly damaging to both nature conservation and scenic beauty. The existence of the Countryside Commission for Scotland presents a problem, for a merger would be unacceptable to Scottish opinion if the Scottish region of the NCC were merged into a united conservation agency for Britain. The regional organizations for Wales of the Countryside Commission and the NCC should also be merged, but whether as a separate Welsh Agency or as a regional branch of an English and Welsh Agency should be for Welsh not English opinion to decide. The mergers might be traumatic, and would certainly cause some loss of momentum for a short time. But that would be a small price to pay for the long-term benefits to be gained by uniting the nature and landscape conservation interests. We do not share the English establishment view that Scotland and Wales cannot be trusted with nature conservation. We take the opposite view that devolution would give these countries a better chance of developing responsible attitudes and policies, and of securing more popular support for nature and landscape conservation.

AREA PLANS

Integration is often conceived as a somewhat paternalistic, top-down approach, by which the mandarins of Whitehall and the politicians agree among themselves how to achieve a mutual accommodation between their rival interests. But the success of integration can only be measured by its achievements on the ground and in local communities. It can only be achieved if local people, with diverse interests and habits of thought, begin to think and act co-operatively. Conflicting government policies place serious obstacles, sometimes insurmountable obstacles, in the way of integration at the local level. As Michael Dower, now the National Park Officer in the Peak, said in a perceptive article in *Landscape Research* in the summer of 1985, it has proved relatively easy to do small things that fall within one of the competing sectors, such as farming, forestry or tourism. Success has been achieved by the Farming and Wildlife Advisory Group in, for example, persuading farmers to leave the headlands of fields unploughed, or to plant trees in unwanted corners or to value small woods or wet places. But, Dower added, the changes that really matter are those which cross the sectoral divide.

The national park authorities, although handicapped by their lack of powers in social and economic matters, are nevertheless uniquely placed to take a comprehensive view of the problems of their areas, and to devise comprehensive plans for tackling them. As they have tried to get more done on the ground they have had to move more and more into area-based policies and management plans which cut right across the single-purpose approach that characterized their earliest efforts to control afforestation or moorland reclamation. These plans provide a basis for promoting the multiple use of land on a sustainable basis, and for integrating conservation and recreation with measures to promote the prosperity of local people. They can be developed at almost any scale. They embrace at one end the comprehensive farm management plans being promoted by the North York Moor and Lake District authorities, and at the other plans for whole estates or valleys, of which the plan for the Duchy of Cornwall's Dartmoor estate is certainly the largest and sets a new standard for a public agency. The main credit for the plan must go to the late Sir John Higgs, the Secretary to the Duchy, who saw

conservation as an integral part of land management. Its management objectives are taken from the Council for National Park's
study of hill farming, *New life for the hills*, written by Malcolm
MacEwen and Geoffrey Sinclair.

What can be achieved in practice depends very largely on land
ownership and the readiness of the owners to co-operate. The
national park authorities have the greatest opportunity on the land
they own, but they have only recently begun to make imaginative
use of their estates. Partly through lack of resources, and partly
because it was deliberate policy for many years to give priority to
investment in visitor services, the park authorities often neglected
the land they had acquired to secure access or to ward off some
threat. A major impetus towards positive management was given in
1979 by the Peak Board's acquisition of the Roaches, a popular
climbing area in the Staffordshire moorlands. It was the Board's first
major land purchase, and there was an urgent need not only to
guarantee public access to the climbs but also to bring the heather
moor under sound management after it had been fenced and
overstocked with sheep by the previous owners. The Board decided
to prepare a comprehensive management plan, and it has now four
such plans, one for each of the estates it has acquired. It has estimated
the cost of the work on these estates to overtake the backlog of
neglect and to manage them soundly at £1.4 million over the four
years 1986–9.

Most national park authorities have now grasped three basic
truths. One is that they cannot acquire land management skills
unless they own a modest estate. The second is that they are in a
weak position to advise anybody else unless they set a good example
on their own land. The third is that buying the land does not by itself
achieve the national park's long-term aims, without a comprehensive management plan. This can be achieved either by the park
authority as landowner, or on common land through a commoners'
association (as in the 9000 ha of common land bought by the Brecon
Beacons in 1985), or by selling land to a private owner under
positive and restrictive covenants (as the Exmoor authority has done
at Warren Farm). One of the reasons now given by three park
authorities – Dartmoor, North York Moors and the Pembrokeshire
Coast – for wanting to acquire more land is that they need to be able
to demonstrate good farming and woodland management practice,
in the last two cases by setting up demonstration or experimental
farms.

The park authorities have also made considerable progress in
recent years in developing management plans in partnership with
other public landowning agencies. The water authorities and the

Forestry Commission have begun to overcome their long-standing reluctance to co-operate with the park authorities since they were given more positive duties towards conservation and recreation. The National Trust, too, although always committed to conservation and public access, has shifted away from the patrician aloofness that in the past led it to take major management decisions without consulting the park authorities. A turning point was the condition imposed by the Countryside Commission, when it grant-aided the purchase of Kinder Scout by the Trust in 1982, that the Trust would prepare a management plan in consultation with the Peak Board. The Kinder Scout management plan has been followed by others, notably in the Peak, the Lake District and Snowdonia. It is now the Trust's policy to consult national park authorities in preparing plans for individual estates and even farms.

We were enchanted and impressed by the sensitive management and rehabilitation scheme carried out by the Lake Board and the National Trust at Rydal Woods and White Moss Common in the Rothay Valley. Here is a microcosm of the elements that give Lakeland valleys their unique qualities – riverside walks, views over Grasmere, broadleaved woodland on the rocky hillsides and in White Moss Common a wetland conservation area – but all were being eroded or degraded by lack of management and a good footpath system. By phasing out some paths and skilfully improving others visitors now find it easy to enjoy the landscape and wildlife, and are unobtrusively persuaded not to enter the quiet or vulnerable areas. The Lakes Board intend to prepare more valley plans, if possible at the rate of two a year.

The Brecon Beacons have published studies for the management of two large areas heavily used by visitors: the Beacons mountain, with its associated valleys, and an area on the southern flank of the park. The Welsh Water Authority, the Forestry Commission and other landowners were involved in these studies, which appraised the entire landscape from the mountain tops to the valley bottoms, and developed appropriate management policies. The question is whether the Brecon Beacons authority has the resources fully to implements its plans. Management plans for Haweswater and Thirlmere in the Lake District have been prepared by the North-West Water Authority and the Lakes Board. A joint management plan for Ennerdale involves the Board, the Water Authority, the Forestry Commission and the National Trust. But both plans raise some difficult issues. For conservationists and the Lakes Board, Ennerdale is a 'quiet area', but Copeland District Council and some people in West Cumbria see it as the ideal place for the active (and sometimes noisy) water sports that the Lakes Board has had some success in regulating in Ullswater and Windermere. However, the taking of difficult decisions is unavoidable if sectoral policies are to be replaced by integrated land and water management.

INTEGRATED RURAL DEVELOPMENT

There has been a spate of initiatives since 1984 to stimulate jobs in the rural areas, many of them in remedial work for conservation or recreation. Of these the more important are the Manpower Services Commission's community schemes for the long-term unemployed, the Development Commission's Rural Development Programmes for Rural Development Areas (RDAs) and the Tourist Board's Development Action Programmes, all of which have been referred to in earlier chapters. Our impression is that the Rural Development Programmes (RDPs) have brought to light a wealth of jobs that need to be done, and an enormous potential in local communities for getting them done and raising part of the money. But if, as seems likely, the money is not forthcoming for most of these projects, the people who have made immense efforts to set the projects up will be soured by the experience. A study of RDPs by Chris Green (in *The Planner*, May 1986) found that they had been highly successful in generating excellent new ideas and projects and stimulating local initiative and enthusiasm. But the author feared that frustration and disillusionment would set in as it became apparent that an under-staffed and underfunded Development Commission, with a budget of £25 million for the whole of rural England, must turn down or delay most of the projects put up to it. Similarly, a new 'farm and countryside' initiative, announced with a fanfare by the Ministry of Agriculture and the Department of the Environment in 1986 provided no new money. It simply made use of the existing Manpower Services Commission's community scheme.

The Forestry Commission, with the Countryside and Development Commissions, decided in 1986 to finance an experiment in integration initiated by the Dartington Trust. This experiment, known as Project Silvanus, offers a first glimpse of what could be done by combining the top-down approach of official agencies with the bottom-up approach of local initiative, and treating existing small private woodlands as a resource for timber, for landscape, for nature and for jobs. It aims to bring a quarter of the two counties' neglected small woodlands in Devon, Cornwall and the Exmoor National Park under management by providing the financial, technical and managerial help needed to make them self-financing within ten years. Extracting timber and marketing timber products is tied into the conservation of the woodlands as habitats and landscape features. Farmers would be invited to form co-operatives, and to acquire new jobs and incomes by managing their own woodlands or by acting as contractors for others.

An Association of Co-operatives to be managed initially by the Dartington Trust will run the project, but it will be transferred to the farmers as they gain experience. The Association will employ skilled staff to inspire, train and advise farmers in woodland skills, timber crafts, contracting and marketing, and will set up an alternative contracting and marketing network, run by the farmers themselves. The cost to the Trust is estimated at £100 000 a year, which is expected to generate a turnover of £1.6 million a year and about 100 jobs after ten years. But the immediate gain in money and jobs in a limited experiment is less important than the gains that could be obtained, not only in money and jobs but in beauty, wildlife and recreation, were such an approach to woodlands to be developed on a national scale.

Project Silvanus has been welcomed by the Exmoor National Park Committee, which is bidding for substantially more money for the management of its own extensive woodlands, but sees no prospect of offering substantial help to the much greater area of privately owned woodlands in the park. But, in welcoming the project Dr Curtis, the Exmoor National Park Officer, expressed two serious reservations. He wanted to be certain that no attempt would be made to include Exmoor's nationally significant ancient woodlands in the scheme, as in his view ancient woodlands should neither be cropped nor planted, and he was seriously concerned that the project was primarily dependent for finance on the Manpower Services Commission community scheme. Having had eight years experience of running MSC schemes with unemployed labour in Exmoor's woodlands, he foresaw a 'terrific headache' in managing a ten-year project with a continually changing labour force over a very much wider geographical area. As with so many other government initiatives, like the Project 2000 programme to 'clean up Britain', there is no real new money in the MSC allocation – it has to come out of the existing MSC funds. Dr Curtis thought it would be ironic if one consequence turned out to be a reduction in the help he was getting to manage the national park authority's own woodlands. Our own conclusion is to welcome the Silvanus experiment, but to deplore its dependence on MSC funding.

A TALE OF TWO VILLAGES

Whereas Project Silvanus is still, as we write, a hopeful but untried intention, the Integrated Rural Development Programme in the parishes of Longnor and Monyash in the White Peak is a going concern. It has five years of lessons to pass on from its experience, and it was extended in 1985 to a third parish. The programme, an EEC-sponsored experiment, was originally given a 50% grant by the EEC, the balance of costs being shared by the Development Commission, the Ministry of Agriculture, the Department of the Environment and the NCC. The Peak Board provided secretarial and administrative services and an officer to co-ordinate the project, which combines the top-down with the bottom-up approach. The Board published a report on the experiment, *A tale of two villages* (1984), which identified three key factors in its success. The first was the involvement of local people. Instead of imposing the ideas of the Board or of other public agencies the project team involved local people in devising alternative grant schemes. It encouraged them to take all the decisions on which specific schemes would be carried out and how. The second key factor it called individuality. Each parish developed schemes adapted to its own (very different) circumstances, and the ideas (and prejudices) of the people.

A third factor, which the report called interdependence, was the combination of economic, social and environmental projects in a single grant scheme. A crucial element was the partnership that developed between the different public funding agencies. Although each of the two alternative grant schemes had such headings as 'community projects', 'new business developments' and 'farming or land management', a single piece of work could include elements from all of them. A single application, for example, could cover building work, planting trees, maintaining farm walls, providing tourist accommodation and developing a business. In submitting applications people were encouraged to use existing buildings. Instead of fixed grants based on a percentage of the money spent there were flexible arrangements which took into account the villagers' own labour. The general principle was to reward effort or success, but never to compensate for profit foregone or to pay people to do nothing. A rates relief grant for new businesses, for example, was paid in proportion to the number of new jobs created.

The scale of the experiment is tiny. The project fund for 1983 and 1984 was only £60 000 for the two villages, in addition to which the agencies and authorities participating in the project contributed the salaries and expenses of some very able and committed people. But the main inputs of time, labour (often unpaid) and much of the money came from the people themselves. In three years the IRD created 35 jobs. It provided business premises, introduced new businesses, and revived old crafts, such as making spining wheels, and old customs, such as well-dressing, in Longnor. In the blizzard of 1986 a firm specializing in the micropropagation of plants, working from a small factory converted with an IRD grant, exported 10 000 pineapple plants from Longnor to Senegal! The scheme has helped to provide community facilities, such as a village hall and a folk museum. New community institutions were formed and an amazing range of activities (including musical events, craft demonstrations, a school conservation area and a newsletter) developed. The IRD fostered pride in people's surroundings, and this was reflected in village enhancement projects.

The main innovation of the IRD was the decision in Monyash to make the offer of the alternative grant to farmers conditional on their agreeing not to take any Ministry of Agriculture grants that were incompatible with conservation. Maintenance work was encouraged and farmers were paid annual grants for well-maintained walls, varying with their length, height and condition. It cost the IRD about £36 in grant for each mile of wall maintained – but £4377 in one case to rebuild less than half a mile of new wall. Grants for managing flower-rich meadows and dalesides were related to the diversity of typical dales plants. In Longor the scheme on offer was different, partly because (according to the report in *A tale of two villages*) key members of the High Peak Livestock Society expressed strong hostility to the alternative grant scheme just after it was published. Several months passed before many farmers in the area would discuss the project. The Longnor scheme did not ask farmers to forfeit headage payments (as the Monyash scheme did), or offer specific grants for conservation works. Farmers were offered support if they developed conservation management plans, but none have taken up that option so far.

The IRD demonstrated the feasibility of integrating conservation with environmental improvement and development at the local level. But it also showed how great are the obstacles to be overcome if the seeds sown in Monyash and Longnor are to be transplanted on a large scale to other areas. Half the farmers in the two parishes took up the alternative grant scheme, those who did being largely dairy farmers who did not rely on headage payments and those who did not being largely beef and sheep farmers who relied on them heavily. The IRD brought home to those involved the bureaucratic complexity of the existing grant arrangements offered by different agencies, and the need for flexible schemes administered by officers with defined discretionary powers. It suggests that big opportunities are being missed by the application nationwide of standard rates and conditions for grant favoured by central government. The report concluded that if the experiment were to be extended on a wider scale a single 'lead' authority should co-ordinate an integrated grant scheme, in the management and promotion of which people from all the relevant agencies would be involved. There would be a single application for grant, and the scheme would include elements devised to meet local needs and opportunities as well as elements drawn from the existing, separate grant schemes. But there are no signs, as yet, that the Peak's initiative will be taken up by government, although the Snowdonia National Park Committee would like to initiate a similar experiment.

Chapter Seventeen

Broadland breaks the mould

THE BROADS AUTHORITY

The Norfolk and Suffolk Broads have been in all but name the eleventh national park since the Broads Authority was set up on an experimental basis in 1978. The government and the Countryside Commission formally recognized its national park status in 1985 when farmers were required to notify grant-aided improvements to the Broads Authority, as in a national park. The Broads had figured in John Dower's 'reserve' list of national parks in 1945, and in the list of 12 recommended by the Hobhouse Committee in 1947. But the Broads were not included in the ten parks designated between 1951 and 1957, and after that the resistance to further designations brought the process to a halt. By 1976, when the Countryside Commission proposed the designation of a national park, the Broads were facing progressive ecological deterioration caused mainly by water pollution from domestic sewage and farm wastes and unrestrained recreational use. It took another ten years to secure agreement on the need for a fully effective authority, and there are still some tricky problems to be resolved before it can be said with certainty that the Broads have been saved.

It has to be remembered that the national park system was not designed for crisis management. The park authority's role in conservation was thought to be passive, because farming and traditional land management would conserve the countryside. But by 1976 modern agriculture had been identified as the most destructive force in the countryside. When it was finally recognized in the 1970s that disaster stared the Broads in the face the traditional remedies on offer from the Countryside Commission and the NCC were either unacceptable to local interests or irrelevant. John Dower himself had recognized in 1945 that the standard model of a national park would not fit a river and wetland park heavily used for boating and fishing.

Initially the running was made by the Nature Conservancy Council, which pioneered the diagnosis of the Broads' problems and was shocked by the deterioration of the wetlands and their wildlife. But although an NCC study had suggested a special authority in 1964 the NCC's tradition has been to focus on protecting specific sites. It has no designation appropriate to large areas of countryside in multiple use. The Countryside Commission's options were to designate a national park or an Area of Outstanding Natural Beauty. But a national park authority would have no control and little influence over water management, water purity, land drainage or agricultural practices, and an AONB even less. The split between the two conservation agencies inhibited the emergence of a solution that would achieve the aims of both.

The Countryside Commission realized that a Broads National Park could not be the complete answer, but in the hope of breaking the log jam that had stopped progress for 30 years it formally proposed the setting up of a national park committee of the county councils in 1976. The proposal was unacceptable to the district councils which, at that time, had no statutory right to be represented on a national park authority. But the NCC and others had given so much publicity to the crisis facing the Broads that the local authorities were under great pressure to do something constructive. The Broads Authority, ironical as it must now seem, originated in the local authorities' desire to frustrate the national park proposal. They countered the Commission's proposal by suggesting the formation of a joint planning committee of the local authorities, on which the Countryside Commission and the water and navigation authorities would also have representatives.

The Countryside Commission wisely agreed, and the Broads Authority was established in 1978 on the lines suggested. The county councils only had seven of the 26 places on the Broads Authority, the district councils 12 and the Countryside Commission three (the 26 members represent Norfolk County Council (5), Suffolk County Council and the six district councils (including Norwich City) (2 each), the Great Yarmouth Port and Haven Commissioners, and the Anglian Water Authority (2 each), and the Countryside Commission (3)). The Broads Authority was funded by the local authorities in rough proportion to their membership, with 50% grants from the Countryside Commission towards the staff establishment and special projects, together with small contributions towards administrative costs from the water and navigation authorities. The authority was, therefore, funded less generously than a national park authority and it could only exercise the planning and other powers delegated to it by the local authorities. Neither the water nor the navigation authorities could delegate any powers, and figured in the scheme as consultees. It was clearly a temporary arrangement but, after considerable teething troubles (it took two years to appoint a chief officer, Aitken Clark), it worked.

The experiment made such good progress in research, management and public relations that by 1985 the case for giving the Broads Authority the autonomy, the powers and the funding it needed had become almost irresistible. The Commission, after reviewing the experiment, concluded that an orthodox national park was not the answer, and recommended legislation to establish a permanent authority with appropriate powers. The local authorities, with Norfolk County Council in the lead, agreed to promote a private Bill, but it became clear that no solution could be found unless the government itself promoted the Bill. It took another year for the county councils and the Countryside Commission to overcome the resistance of the navigation authority and to persuade the government. The government's Norfolk and Suffolk Broads Bill was given an unopposed second reading by the House of Commons on 1 December 1986.

BROADLAND AND WATER QUALITY

The boundary of the Broads Authority's executive area is tightly drawn to embrace the low lying land in the valleys of the rivers Waveney, Yare and Bure, and the Bure's tributaries the Ant and the Thurne. On the map (Fig. 24) it resembles a hand whose fingers poke up along the river valleys inland from Great Yarmouth and Lowestoft, the palm being formed by a large block of grazing marshes – the now famous Halvergate marshes and Haddiscoe Island. The 'broads' themselves, which provide the only expanses of open water, are shallow lakes formed by digging for peat in mediaeval times. They now form part of a unique river, drainage and navigation system. The Broads' 28 322 ha are a cluster of linear parks that can only be fully experienced by boat, whose open country is largely water (although there is considerable scope for opening up more walks of extraordinary beauty and wildlife interest), whose main recreations are boating, fishing and nature watching, and whose landscapes have been fashioned over centuries by man and nature working together. Rivers wind slowly between

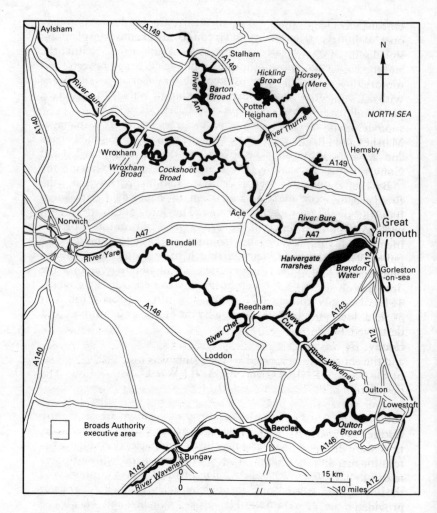

Figure 24   Area of the Broads Authority.

embankments high above the grazing marshes and fens, cattle graze on a seemingly endless plain beneath the open sky with an occasional sail, windpump or clump of trees on the horizon. The rivers and the larger broads are thronged in season with sailing boats and motor cruisers. But one can also find peace, remoteness and contact with nature at its most intimate and inspirational. It is so rich in bird, plant and insect life that the NCC has scheduled 22 SSSIs, and will soon designate seven more. The National Nature Reserves at Bure Marshes and Hickling Broad are of world significance as wetlands, and have been listed under the 1971 International Wetlands Convention.

By 1982 the draft strategy and management plan *What future for Broadland?* was able to unravel the tangled chain of cause and effect. It did this so clearly, and with the aid of such lucid drawings, that the problems were immediately comprehensible to the Authority's members and officers, all the interested parties and the general public. The key to the future of Broadland is water quality. By 1982 phosphate in domestic sewage, agriculture fertilizer run-off and gull droppings had enriched the water to the point that only four of the 41 broads could support the traditional range of aquatic plants, and 31 had lost virtually all of them. As the aquatic plants were destroyed by nutrient enrichment, the once clear water became cloudy. By this process of eutrophication the water lost its oxygen and the animal life supported by the plants was lost. Fish died, loss of the reeds and other plants exposed the banks to erosion. The destruction of the banks was accelerated by the wash of motor boats in ever increasing numbers. As the banks crumbled the water authority resorted to steel piling, which turned rivers into dead, featureless canals. As traditional fen and marsh management practices were dropped, the reeds were no longer cut for thatch or the fens for marsh hay. The scrub advanced and the fens receded. The marsh dykes, which became the major reservoir of aquatic plants as the broads died, silted up. As the marshland was drained, with funds provided mainly by the Ministry of Agriculture, the landscape lost its traditional character and wildlife was impoverished.

The Broads have the largest hire-boat fleet of any waterway system in Europe, and the boat-building industry has a thriving export trade. But the boat hiring and tourist industries were slow to recognize that their activities had been steadily killing the resource on which they live. The farmers, who control the internal drainage boards, had been seduced by drainage grants, high, subsidized cereal prices and the prospects of big profits and higher land values if they could switch from the traditional livestock grazing to cereals. The water and the navigation authorities each concentrated on their

statutory functions, but neglected the wider social and environmental costs and consequences of their neglect or their conventional
attitude to environmental issues.

PROGRESS, PROBLEMS AND RESEARCH

It is too early to say that the Broads Authority has saved the
situation. What is certain is that had it not been set up the situation
would have been lost. The credit for this must be shared between the
authorities and many others – not least the NCC and the University
of East Anglia for their original research, the Countryside Commission for its tenacity and flexibility sustained over a decade and the
local authorities for putting up a workable compromise and making
it work. The Council for National Parks and the CPRE played a
major role by exerting pressure on government to switch its
resources from subsidizing destructive land drainage schemes to
providing positive support for traditional farming.

What immediately strikes anybody familiar with national park
plans is the emphasis given in the Broads Strategy and Management
Plan to the conservation of natural or semi-natural systems. Nearly
half (44%) the Authority's gross expenditure of £948 000 for 1986–7
is spent on conservation, because safeguarding the resources must
take precedence over everything else. A high priority is also given to
information and interpretation, because success in conservation
depends upon the support and understanding of the public and of
interested parties. Recreation is by no means neglected, but for the
time being at least it takes third place.

Perhaps the Authority's most important achievement in restoring
water quality has been to dissuade the Anglian Water Authority
from dropping its experiments in stripping phosphate from domestic sewage and to persuade it (with some financial encouragement)
to extend these experiments to other areas. This work has already
proved that it is possible to achieve the required levels of water
purity, although the cost of phosphate stripping on all the Broads
rivers will be high. Stripping alone, however, is not enough.
Enormous quantities of phosphate-laden mud from the decay of
generations of algae have been deposited over the years to a depth of
several metres on the bottoms of the rivers and the broads, and
prevent the revival of aquatic life even when the water entering
them is clean. An experiment at Cockshoot Broad has been dramati-
cally successful in bringing the Broad back to life by shutting off the
polluted river water and pumping out the mud. The crystal clarity
of the water now contrasts sharply with the cloudy water on the

other side of the barrier separating Cockshoot Broad from the river (Plate 29).

Water purity is so central to the solution of the Broads problem that a lot of thought has been given to the relationship between the Broads Authority and the Anglian Water Authority. The relationship is not an easy one, not least because the Broads Authority's area is but one part of the river basin and only a tiny part of the vast territory for which Anglian Water is responsible. Anglian Water made £39 million profit in 1985–6 (60% up on the previous year) but it has other priorities. It will be very reluctant to find the large sums (running into several millions) required to achieve a complete solution of the Broads problem unless it is firmly required to do so by the government, or unless the funds can be provided by government or by the Broads Authority (which can only get the money from government). The problem will be exacerbated if the water authorities are privatized, for the last thing that a private water company would want to do would be to spend large sums unprofitably on achieving high standards of water purity in the Broads.

For these reasons the Broads Authority wanted the Broads Bill to impose a duty of environmental care on both the water and the land drainage authorities. It wanted to have a right to be consulted over any proposals for water supply, water quality or environmental protection that affect the Broads. In the event of disputes it wanted a right to put its case to the Secretary of State at a public inquiry. It wanted farmers and others to be required to observe a code of environmental management. But the government's Broads Bill, as drafted, conceded none of these requests.

The Broads Authority wants to tackle the problem of river bank erosion at source, first of all by reducing the water pollution that is killing the reeds and other plants that hold the banks together. It is also devising techniques for retaining and restoring the bank vegetation and dealing with the wash from motor boats, which is the main force removing the bank material. This involves reducing the speed of boats, controlling their numbers and loading, and designing hulls that minimize the wash. For these reasons the Broads Authority has insisted that the Broads Bill must also make it the navigation authority in the upper rivers with responsibility for licensing boats and regulating navigation. The Great Yarmouth Port and Harbour Commissioners held up the Bill for many months by refusing to surrender these functions, or even to discharge them as agents for the Broads Authority. It was a classic instance of institutional inertia, with those in charge hanging on to power and distrusting the expertise of those who would replace them. But as we go to press it is certain that the Broads Authority will be the navigation authority for its area.

Scientific research has not, until very recently, been seen as a normal part of the work of a national park authority, although the need for research is now being recognized and some is under way. But from the start the Broads Authority has directed about a third of its project budget towards research, because it could not develop sound policies or programmes, or win support for them, unless it was confident that it understood the causes of the problems and had tested the remedies. Its research programme, into such matters as reedswamp dieback, marsh dyke management, river bank erosion, vegetation mapping, the recovery of polluted broads and the hull design of boats, is complemented by a number of experimental management projects, of which pumping the mud from Cockshoot Broad was one of the earliest. There are conservation projects for fens and the management of open water. Environmental programmes include the production of a guide on building design and landscaping, some landscape enhancement schemes and a fund to preserve derelict windpumps.

HALVERGATE MARSHES AND ESA DESIGNATION

The most decisive achievement by the interim Broads Authority has been the successful resolution of the crisis that developed in the Halvergate marshes soon after it had been set up. The crisis could easily have broken the Authority, many of whose members and staff were unfamiliar with the issues and had not been through the learning process that subsequently sharpened their perceptions. It could have resulted in a disastrous, open conflict with the farmers, or at least with the bigger, expanding farmers backed by the Ministry of Agriculture who controlled the Internal Drainage Boards. Their financial interest lay in the installation of more powerful pumps to lower the water table and facilitate conversion from livestock grazing to heavily subsidized cereal cropping. Those who are interested in the details of this fascinating story should read the full account of it written by one of the main participants, Timothy O'Riordan of the University of East Anglia, in *Countryside conflicts* (Temple Smith Gower, 1986). Professor O'Riordan, an environmental scientist, as chairman of the Authority's Strategy Committee was at the centre of the Halvergate negotiations, and succeeded in winning the confidence of the elected members by his combination of knowledge, tact and good humour.

The Halvergate marshes assumed national significance because it proved impossible (as we said in Ch. 12) to find a solution by negotiating management agreements with compensation for profit foregone on the Wildlife and Countryside Act model. Some farmers went to the length of defiance, and the Authority had to invoke the rarely used power to make an order (an 'Article 4 Direction') under the planning acts forbidding a drainage project. The Direction had to be confirmed by Patrick Jenkin, then the Secretary of State for the Environment, who felt obliged to consult Michael Jopling, the Minister for Agriculture, who objected. The issue was decided by Mrs Thatcher, who came down in favour of confirming the Direction, which was duly made on 25 June 1984.

The confirmation of the Direction proved that agricultural engineering operations could be controlled, but it did not resolve the basic dilemma. The NFU and CLA, backed by the farmer-controlled Internal Drainage Boards, wanted to negotiate a deal at the local level, based on the principle of compensating for the profit foregone if they agreed not to lower the water table or to go in for cereal production, but to continue traditional livestock grazing. They did not want to involve Whitehall or Parliament, or to let it be thought that the Wildlife and Countryside Act's 'pay through the nose' approach did not work. The Broads Authority refused to pay exorbitant sums, and the local negotiations were stalled. The breakthrough came when the Broads Authority realized, by personal discussions with the marsh graziers, that the NFU and the CLA did not represent the views of the majority of them. On the contrary, the NFU, and CLA and the Internal Drainage Boards were speaking only for the big arable farmers in pressing for very high levels of compensation. The majority of graziers, many of them in small enterprises, feared that they would be forced either to sell up or go into arable farming if the NFU/CLA view prevailed. They preferred a solution that would help them to continue to graze the marshes in the traditional way, and were less greedy for money. It was this knowledge that enabled the Broads Authority to convince the Countryside Commission and then the Government that the payment for compensation for profit foregone was intolerably costly, and would not solve the problem.

Another solution had to be found. The Countryside Commission then had the idea of making use of a new power, given to it by Section 40 of the Wildlife and Countryside Act, to finance experimental schemes for the conservation of the countryside. The Broads Grazing Marsh Scheme was the result. It is a three-year experiment from 1985 to 1988 administered jointly by the Commission and the Ministry of Agriculture's advisory service. It pays a flat rate of £124 a hectare a year (much less than payment for profit foregone) to every farmer who agrees not to plough the Halvergate marshes, to maintain limits on stock numbers and nitrogen application, and to take only one cut of silage a year.

The success of this scheme can be measured by the fact that over 90% of the farmers accepted its terms. The designation of the Broads in 1986 as an ESA (see Ch. 12) enables the grazing scheme to be continued after 1988. However, the Broads Authority believes that a flat rate payment per hectare is too crude. It would like to be able to offer one or more higher rates to those farmers who would accept stricter conditions, eliminating silage cutting and fertilizer application altogether, on the more sensitive parts. Whether the ESA scheme will allow this degree of flexibility remains to be seen.

BROADLAND'S SIGNIFICANCE

What seems certain is that by 1988 a statutory Broads Authority will have taken over. It will enjoy national park status, and it will have the same autonomy in finance, administration and policy as a national park board. It will be the navigation authority. It will be financed by a 75% grant from the National Park Supplementary Grant fund. The balance of expenditure will be met by the constituent authorities in the same proportions as before, but the Authority will be able to levy a rate and the individual local authorities will be unable to withdraw from the scheme or withhold their share of the money. The Farm Grant Notification Scheme, by which farmers in national parks have to notify grant-aided operations to national park authorities, has applied to the Broads since 1985. The new authority will consist of 35 members, with a majority from local authorities. The water and navigation authorities will continue to have two members each. The remainder, about a third, will be appointed partly by the Secretary of State for the Environment and partly by the Countryside Commission. The NCC, for reasons that we cannot understand, seems unlikely to appoint a member directly. But the Authority will include representatives of a very much wider range of interests than any national park authority, including boating, fishing, tourism and the voluntary conservation movement. The new Authority strikes us as too large, but the Board's officers believe that the benefits of wider representation outweigh the disadvantages of excessive size.

The crisis from which the Broads Authority has emerged was caused by 30 years of administrative bungling, during which all the separate interests pulled in different directions. There is now an opportunity to solve the basic problems, and to restore Broadland to ecological and economic health. But success is by no means assured. The ESAs are as yet untried. Neither the essential resources nor the whole-hearted co-operation of the water or navigation authorities are assured. And the government's Bill, as drafted, fell short of what was required. It did not give the Broads the title of 'national park'. The purposes of the Broads Authority were ambiguously drafted as 'to develop, conserve and manage the Broads for the purposes of navigation, preserving and enhancing natural beauty and public enjoyment'. This seemed to give priority not to conservation but to development and navigation. The Authority was given no powers to stop damaging farming or drainage operations, beyond the proposed Landscape Conservation Orders (see Ch. 15), and no additional conservation duties were imposed on the water or drainage authorities. The Authority would be advised by a Navigation Committee on which its representatives would be outnumbered by representatives of the navigation and boating interests.

Nevertheless, the significance of the Broads Authority is that it broke the mould that has confined the system for 30 years to the ten parks established in the 1950s. By doing so it has opened the door both to the strengthening of the existing national park authorities, and to the extension of the system to other areas where the county council national park committee is unacceptable or irrelevant.

Chapter Eighteen

Greenprints for the countryside, if . . .

THE PARTING OF THE WAYS

The year 1987 finds the national park system in a strangely paradoxical situation. Any threat to the national parks is guaranteed to generate a powerful political and emotional response, and the ten existing parks have all been able to consolidate their position. But they are still regarded with so much suspicion or jealousy by county and district councils, by farmers, landowners, timber growers and the Forestry Commission that for nearly 30 years it has proved impossible to extend the system even to areas that fully satisfy the criteria for designation. Since the designation of the Brecon Beacons was confirmed in 1957 only three areas have been seriously put forward as national parks. The Cambrian Mountains in mid-Wales were peremptorily rejected by the Secretary of State for Wales in 1973 without a public inquiry. The Countryside Commission did not even consider designating the North Pennines as a national park and designated it as an Area of Outstanding Natural Beauty. This robbed the North Pennines of the benefits of national park status, but did nothing to diminish the resistance to the less effective AONB designation. The Broads did not achieve national park status until, after 30 wasted years, both the title and the statutory model prescribed for national park administration had been abandoned. The Countryside Commission has announced its belief that the New Forest merits national park status, but it is inconceivable that any of the interested parties would accept its designation as a national park under the 1972 Local Government Act. This would require it to be administered by a committee of Hampshire County Council, which is promoting a Parliamentary Bill (opposed by the Countryside Commission) to drive the Lyndhurst bypass for 1½ miles through the open forest. The national park system was held in a state of inertia by the balance of antagonistic forces and by the rigidity and even irrelevance of the statutory administrative model, until the Broads Authority broke the mould and opened up new possibilities.

The situation in the national parks is also paradoxical in another sense. Those responsible for running them hardly know whether to hope for the best or to anticipate the worst. For at this moment in time it is impossible to say whether the collapse of the Common Agricultural Policy over the next few years will open up unprecedented opportunities for creative, integrated land management or let loose forces that could be even more destructive than those of the past 30 years. The park authorities are stronger and more confident than they have ever been, and are well placed (if given the powers and resources they need) to grasp new opportunities with both hands. The multiple use of land in national parks, the authorities experiments' in integrated land management since 1974 and the new flexibility brought into the system in the Broads all suggest that the parks can provide what we call 'greenprints' for the management of other areas – if government, in particular, is prepared to take the necessary action.

The fact has to be faced that the national park system is still a cosmetic one. For no system of local administration, however well endowed with money and power, can stand out against powerful economic trends, promoted and usually financed by government, that are literally changing the face of nature. Governments are responsible directly or indirectly for the overall policies for farming, forestry, nuclear power, military training, highways, mineral extraction, water management, the sale of public lands and the integration (or disintegration) of policies and planning for rural areas. The key to the future of the national parks, the uplands and the wider countryside lies, therefore, in Brussels and Westminster. Their future depends, first of all, on the British government translating its verbal commitment to the integration of conservation with development into deeds; and secondly, on the decisions that will be taken by government within the framework of a new Common Agricultural Policy designed to eliminate costly food surpluses.

There is a fundamental philosophical and political conflict here, which rages over the healthiness (or otherwise) of the food we buy and the increasing evidence of malnutrition or underfeeding in the midst of plenty. Put at its simplest, the choice lies between two ways of eliminating food surpluses. One is to grow food by intensive, high input, high technology farming on an ever smaller area of land, while 'setting aside' the 'surplus' land for other purposes. The land set aside is permanently lost to food production if it is afforested or built on. The other way is to adopt less intensive, lower input and more environmentally benign technologies that employ more people and use much the same total area of land as now. To cultivate land in this way provides reserve capacity to increase food production in times of need, and is the more prudent way in a politically and financially unstable world.

The food surpluses of today could well become the food shortages of tomorrow. Let us consider the 'worst case' and the 'best case' scenarios that might result from the 'set aside' and the 'lower input' approaches.

THE 'WORST CASE'

The worst case that can be envisaged is a combined assault on the countryside, by the commercial forestry interests in pursuit of their expansionist planting goals and by farmers either selling out to forestry companies or larger farmers and planting the most 'economic' tree species haphazardly across the land as a farm crop. It would be a rerun of the devastation let loose by intensive high-tech farming, but dressed up this time as the integration of farming with forestry, and speciously justified on the ground that it provides farmers with incomes, the nation with timber and (in time) a landscape with beautiful trees. The combination of 'set aside' and aggressive tree farming, encouraged by subsidies and tax concessions and subject to no serious control, would re-create the antagonism between conservation and recreation interests on the one hand, and farming and forestry or timber interests on the other; a conflict that was diminishing as the impending collapse of the CAP began to create a common interest in conservation. The Council for National Parks, the CPRE and the Countryside Commission had every justification for expressing their concern to the House of Lords at the extremely serious consequences that could flow from ill-conceived programmes to 'set aside' farmland.

The 'worst case' scenario for the uplands is already discernible. The Thatcher government intends to weaken strategic planning and the control of development. The inevitable reduction or withdrawal of the price guarantees for sheep and beef could precipitate the collapse of hill farming – unless the EEC and the British Government have the foresight to turn the Environmentally Sensitive Area Programme from a minor, ill-considered experiment into an effective system for supporting lower-input, multi-purpose farming. Falling profits on hill farms and declining land values are the classic signals for a new wave of afforestation, as farmers sell out for the higher prices the forestry companies can offer. The surviving hill farming communities in the national parks have been so reduced by the policies of the past 40 years that many of them no longer have the resilience to withstand another severe trauma.

Afforestation is not, however, the only alternative land use in the uplands. Some conservationists have welcomed 'set aside' because it would allow the least productive land to go out of production. Why waste public money subsidizing lamb production in the uplands, they ask, if it can be produced more cheaply in the lowlands, and if sheepmeat is moving into surplus? Why not let the uplands revert to wilderness in whatever way nature dictates? In this scenario the most productive farmland round the cities, where the people's need for easy access to nature and open country is greatest, would become the factory floor of an ever more intensive agricultural industry, and impoverished in terms of landscape and wildlife. The uplands would cease to be an open, accessible, richly varied, inhabited, managed landscape. There is a case, as part of a well conceived, integrated plan, to allow a part of the uplands in carefully selected areas to revert to wilderness. But no such planned approach to 'set aside' is in prospect. The danger is that if the rug is pulled from under the hill farming economy, and coniferous afforestation moves indiscriminately down the hill, the hill farms in the remote valleys or even the dairy farms in the White Peak would gradually be ranched or abandoned. The process would be haphazard, insidious and progressive and would not arouse the same immediate protest as would be generated in response to blanketing the hills with Sitka spruce. It would be a social as well as an environmental disaster, and would destroy the unique partnership between man and nature that gives our uplands their most precious qualities.

'Set aside' could have other damaging consequences. We have drawn attention to the White Paper of 1985, *Lifting the burden*, which urged local authorities not to let their structure plans stand in the way of economic development. The Countryside Commission and the Nature Conservancy Council were excluded from an inter-departmental working party on Alternative Land Use and the Rural Economy (ALURE) set up in 1986 and co-ordinated by the Ministry of Agriculture. The Forestry Commission and the departments interested in development were represented, however, and the report, although discussed by Cabinet committees, was not published. The Director of the CPRE, Robin Grove-White, had earlier expressed fears that policies to 'set aside' so-called surplus agricultural land could 'knock the bottom out of the planning policies that have controlled development since 1947'. The ALURE study, he said, 'heralds huge changes in British farming, new developments on hitherto greenfield sites and major expansions of forestry in all sorts of unlikely places'. And this study was undertaken without the advice or even participation of the government's conservation experts.

The 'worst case' scenario may well be the most probable outcome of the present confused debate, unless public opinion can be mobilized to prevent it. People will certainly begin to react powerfully when the first signs of a random bombardment of the landscape becomes visible. But creeping development and the abandonment of the uplands could go quite a long way before the visible and the social damage commanded national attention. Even if the worst is avoided there is all too likely to be enough fudging in the legislation to allow a lot of damage to be done. It will take time to expose the specious justifications about the supposed benefits for jobs, incomes, landscape and wildlife that are currently being used to cover the proposed assault. It would be tragic if time and effort had to be diverted into new conflicts instead of being used to realize the immense opportunities that could be created by a conserving agricultural and forestry regime integrated with social and economic development.

THE 'BEST CASE'

If the EEC is prepared to shift substantial resources from costly and destructive price guarantees for surplus commodities into the guidance of farmers towards lower input, more conserving farming and land management practices a 'best case' scenario could emerge. The EEC cannot be written off as hopeless, for there are good ideas as well as bad circulating in the present confusion in Brussels, and a determined British government that was willing to take the lead could get some results. The EEC Council of Ministers is formally committed by its Third Action Programme on the Environment to promote an overall strategy in which environmental policy is a part of economic and social development. When the present government, however reluctantly, pressed for ESAs it got them. There is also a growing recognition in the EEC that the immense variations in the landscapes and farming conditions in Europe make it increasingly difficult to impose a uniform policy straightjacket on individual countries as different as Greece and Britain. The EEC Agricultural Commissioner is known to favour giving individual governments far more freedom to interpret broad EEC policies, in ways that suit national conditions.

This could enable the British government to replace all the destructive price guarantees and subsidies, and to use both EEC money and British funds to develop a sophisticated, refined, well monitored and far more widely applicable scheme for Environmentally Sensitive Areas. This should give farmers an acceptable income from lower-input farming, while conserving landscape and nature and opening up new opportunities for countryside recreation. It should be a condition of grant under any such scheme that enough people are employed on the farm, for the much diversified tasks of land management and helping visitors, in accordance with an appropriate farm plan or guidelines. In the uplands such a scheme could incorporate ceilings on the headage payments to larger farmers, higher rates for the socially and environmentally disadvantaged, and controls to bring stocking levels into line with ecologically determined limits, as suggested by Sinclair and others (see Ch. 14). Every national park would be within an ESA.

If the 'best case' scenario were to be realized more people would work on the land, many of them as skilled workers in a wide range of real jobs. There would be homes for them and for local people in the country too, provided at low rents or prices by housing associations or by local authorities – even by national park authorities. Farming would demand more skill, not less. If our horizon could be extended to land reform, it would be possible to see the over-large farms being broken up to provide smaller but viable farms for the many young people who would like to get into farming, but are now excluded from what is virtually a closed profession open only to those who qualify by money or inheritance.

Nature and landscape conservation would move beyond the limited perspectives of FWAG, with its concentration on planting trees, and conserving ponds, field headlands and the other odd corners that are surplus to intensive farming. Conservation, as we have said, would be the common thread running through every aspect of management. There would be a reversion from monocultures to mixed arable and livestock farming, and a rapid development in organic farming. These trends would be encouraged by substantial investment in research, marketing and advisory services. The use of artificial fertilizers and other chemicals would be reduced, and technology developed in ways more sympathetic to natural processes. The UK could follow the lead already given in some other countries by banning the use of dangerous or dubious chemicals. The disposal of slurry and the management of silage would be strictly controlled, and the conservation of soil fertility would be the duty of every farmer. Afforestation and other damaging operations would be subject to appropriate controls. Farmers would lose their privileged status in regard to water and air pollution; straw burning would be banned. They might reasonably be expected to pay local rates, like other business people. But in return they would be guaranteed stability and a reasonable return for their labour, and they would be respected as key partners in a vital national enterprise.

All the remaining ancient woodlands, wetlands, mires, bogs and other surviving natural or semi-natural features, and historic landscapes, would be conserved. A start could be made to bring back heather to overgrazed, neglected or converted moorland. A better balance between sheep and cattle on the hills would hold back the spread of bracken. Recently drained farmland of inferior quality could revert to wetland for light grazing and to harbour wildlife. New woods and trees, planted or naturally generated but sensitively located, would enrich the landscape and wildlife of both uplands and lowlands. In some areas a conscious attempt could be made to create Nan Fairbrother's 'man-made wild'. It might take 150 years, Oliver Rackham says, for downland that has been cropped for cereals to revert naturally to its former condition. It could be transformed into open country if suitably grazed, with rich mixtures of grasses, flowers, and broadleaved trees in much less time. Quite large areas of down, heath, woods and newly created nature reserves, open country and water space could be opened to the public for fresh air and exercise – often, as Marion Shoard and others have urged, close to the conurbations and accessible from the inner cities. Nature could be brought within everyone's reach. It is to local countryside near the towns and cities that the great majority of countryside trips are made.

GREENPRINTS FOR THE COUNTRYSIDE?

If the 'worst case' scenario is all too credible the 'best case' is not so remote from reality that it can never come true. Important parts of it are now within our grasp. But most of the participants in the debate on food surpluses and 'set aside' are still so strongly attached to the technology of intensification that they are unable, or unwilling, to see that there are other ways. They cannot see that what we call the 'greenprints' for a better managed countryside everywhere already exist in the national parks, albeit in imperfect forms. The national parks are, of course, prototypes in course of development, not the perfected model. We have not glossed over the defects of the park authorities, the conservation agencies or the government. In the next chapter we will be discussing how the system must be strengthened if it is to realize its immense potential, and how it can be extended to other areas. But the national parks are the nearest thing we have in this country to the 'best case' scenario for countryside management.

The low fertility of the uplands saved them from the worst effects both of the enclosures of the eighteenth and nineteenth centuries and of high-technology farming in the twentieth century. The basic characteristics of multiple land use, low-input and labour-intensive farming systems survived. So did semi-wild landscapes and habitats and their wildlife, and widespread opportunities for people to walk over and through the countryside and to seek recreation there in many ways. These characteristics have been impaired in recent years, but their essential qualities remain. It is precisely in the national parks that the greatest efforts have been made to retain these qualities, and where possible to enhance them. The national parks demonstrate, in a living way, that it is wrong to despise the multiple use of land as agriculturalists have done since the Parliamentary enclosures of the eighteenth and nineteenth centuries. Multiple use and lower inputs enable the land to yield a wider range of products and of benefits, including the aesthetic, the cultural and the social, and to do so on a sustainable basis.

The national parks have established some important principles. The idea that land ownership confers an absolute right to do what one pleases with one's property is of comparatively recent origin. It is incompatible with the national park principle that the land and the landscape are a common heritage, to be managed by their owners or tenants (whether private individuals or public or semi-public bodies) in ways that promote the common good as well as their own. Another principle, which follows from the first, is that there must be a measure of social control over land management decisions that affect the public interest as well as public initiatives and the investment of public money.

The principle of social control over land use has been extended in national parks by such means as the Farm Grant Notification Scheme, the Landscape Special Development Order (controlling farm and forest roads and buildings) and (if government goes beyond its consultation paper of 1986) Landscape Conservation Orders. Both social control and social initiative are essential because countryside conservation and recreation are not marketable products and are open to destruction by market forces, particularly if these are stimulated by public money. The present degree of social control over farming and forestry is too weak, but it is stronger in national parks than anywhere else outside SSSIs, which are a special case. It would perhaps be more accurate to speak of social influence, backed up by what Peter Melchett calls bribery, than of control. But farmers and landowners have become very conscious of the need to clear their proposals with the park authorities despite the authorities' lack of legal bite.

The national park management plans were landmarks on the road to the integration of conservation and recreation with economic and social development. They were tentative, exploratory, and experimental, but they have led inexorably into the new initiatives that we have described in recreation management, in integrated development and in landscape and nature conservation. Research, experiment and monitoring are increasingly part of the normal work of the national park authorities. There is still a very long way to go, but a range of greenprints for the integrated management of the countryside can be derived from the best of the national park experience, and from the possibilities that would emerge with greater resources, powers and commitment.

Other countries are beginning to take an interest in the national parks of England and Wales, precisely because they are not wilderness national parks in the internationally recognized meaning of the term, but are experiments in achieving national park purposes in inhabited, developed, man-managed landscapes. The International Union for the Conservation of Nature recognizes our national parks as 'protected landscapes', and the Countryside Commission is acting as host to a world conference on protected areas in the Lake District in 1987. Adrian Phillips, the Commission's Director, identified four interlocking principles for the management of national parks at the Jubilee Conference of the Council for National Parks in 1986. These are: sustainable development; the integration of national policies as they affect the local environment; the multipurpose management of rural land; and a partnership between local and national interests. He sees these principles as being equally appropriate for 'protected landscapes' in other countries. But the lessons start nearer home: they need to be more fully applied within our national parks, and extended to the rest of the countryside.

Chapter Nineteen

National parks tomorrow

MORE NATIONAL PARKS

It is beyond the scope of this book to review the overlapping and proliferating, even bewildering, system of designations for protecting nature and landscape in the countryside. Two more, the 'section 3' maps of open country in national parks and the Environmentally Sensitive Areas, have been added in the last few months. Areas of Outstanding Natural Beauty, which cover areas as extensive and as beautiful as some national parks, are denied the resources and the integrated management they need, and in theory have no recreational, or even nature conservation, purpose. The Countryside Commission would support a government-sponsored review of designations, if it encompasses nature conservation as well as landscape designations. The proposed SSSI and AONB for the Berwyn Mountains near Snowdonia, for example, virtually overlap. One designation is enough. The national park designation must stay because it has proved itself, and the breakthrough in the Broads has reopened the possibility of extending national parks to other areas in a form that is adapted to their special needs.

The criteria for designating national parks should remain unchanged. They must include extensive tracts of beautiful, semi-wild country of national significance, where the recreational and other uses require the establishment of a unified land management authority. The first purpose of designation, the conservation and enhancement of natural beauty, should be amended to place the emphasis on the conservation both of nature (which includes natural systems and resources) and of beauty (whether 'natural' or the result of human intervention). Promoting the enjoyment of the park by the public should remain the second purpose, but a third should be added: the improvement of the social and economic conditions of local people. If, in addition, the park authorities get the autonomy, the finance and the powers they need, and a constitution tailored to the needs of a specific locality, many interesting possibilities emerge.

Scotland is beyond the scope of this book, but the first place where we would look for new national parks would be in Scotland's superb National Scenic Areas, some of which clearly need the help, management and protection that a stronger national park system could provide. In England and Wales the Countryside Commission should designate national parks in the Cambrian Mountains and the North Pennines. Commercial afforestation has already bitten deep into the Cambrian Mountains, but the North Pennines are still almost unscathed. In the words of the Countryside Commission's evidence to the public inquiry into AONB designations in 1985:

> it contains the largest continuous block of land in Britain over 2000 ft outside the Highlands of Scotland. It is a big, high, open landscape modified less by man than probably any other of a similar size in England and Wales ... The area contains important physiographical features and a unique collection of flora and fauna of the highest national importance ... The moorlands are of international significance for their bird population and Upper Teesdale is similarly important botanically ... The North Pennines is the pre-eminent example in England and Wales of an upper moorlands plateau ... The dales, too, are of a high quality ... The absence of large scale afforestation over such an extensive area is now probably unique in England and Wales ... [but] there is a steady flow of applications for planting grants from the Forestry Commission.

The area is underused for recreation, but the development of tourism is hindered by its division between nine local authorities and two tourists boards. Unfortunately the government, in confirming the designation of the North Pennines as an AONB, reduced its area by 15%.

The establishment of national park authorities armed with the wider powers we have suggested, and perhaps with a novel mix of membership, could be the only hope of saving the Cambrian Mountains and the North Pennines and putting new life into their economies while conserving and enhancing their landscapes. Such areas as the South Downs, high on the lists of national parks drawn up by John Dower and the Hobhouse Committee in the 1940s, should also be looked at again. If the taxpayers of Europe and the UK are no longer going to subsidize the growing of cereals on former heath and downland, the way is open for national park authorities to begin the long job of restoring the diversity of their flora and fauna, and restoring public access. If these areas were also given ESA designations on the improved model we have suggested (as should all national parks), agricultural money would begin to support farmers, the environment and the public's enjoyment of increasingly interesting landscapes.

The Countryside Commission has formally recognized the national park status of the New Forest, which is probably the only significant part of England and Wales that would satisfy the international criteria for recognition as a national park. It is unique both as a historic landscape, whose management has been documented for 900 years, and for its mosaic of deciduous woodlands (said by the NCC to be the finest relic of undisturbed forest in Western Europe), timber enclosures (now predominantly coniferous), open heath and grass lawns grazed by red deer and ponies. It is more heavily used than any national park, with more than six million visitors a year in an area of 145 square miles, which is smaller than Exmoor. It owes much of its interest to the extensive commons, managed by a statutory Court of Verderers which acted as an essential check on the destructive policies pursued in earlier years by the Crown (which owns three-quarters of the land) and the Forestry Commission, which has managed it since 1919. Since the government gave it a mandate in 1971 to manage the Crown land as a 'national heritage', the Forestry Commission has done a great deal to bring cars, camping and caravans under control and to have a more sensitive regard for ecological and landscape considerations. But the New Forest is continuously threatened, by visitor pressures, the Lyndhurst bypass, oil exploration and other developments.

The New Forest is still a long way from having the appropriate protective designation or a management authority that represents the diversity of interests directly interested in its management – above all the Nature Conservancy Council, the commoners through the Court of Verderers, the local authorities, the users and local conservation interests. The Crown's ownership of land is supposed to present some tricky constitutional questions, but if Crown ownership could permit the Forestry Commission to wreak havoc in the past we can see no constitutional reason why it should not welcome the formation of a national park authority, whose composition and powers would be tailored to the special needs of the New Forest. The Forestry Commission is reviewing the management of the Forest, and the Countryside Commission is reserving its position in the meantime.

A NEW LOOK AT OLD PARKS

Another area that is crying out for the establishment of a unifying management authority is Hadrian's Wall, about 15 miles of which lies in the Northumberland National Park. The National Park Committee does a useful job within the limits of its powers and territorial reach in interpretation, transport and planning control. But national park designation is of little relevance to the real problem. For Hadrian's Wall is uniquely important on an international scale, both as an archaeological monument and a historic landscape. The Wall with its associated forts, ditch, vallum, roads, related landscapes and SSSIs is a broad strip several miles wide in places, and 75 miles (with gaps) from coast to coast. Impressive though it is as an ancient structure, its magic also lies in its magnificent natural setting along the Whin Sill, and the contrast that can still be felt between the friendly, fertile lands to the south and the bleaker moorland and marsh to the north.

The problem is divided responsibility. For the Wall lies within the administrative areas of three county councils, six district councils, two regional tourist boards and a national park authority. Key sections or features are owned by the National Trust, English Heritage, the Vindolanda Trust and individuals. Co-ordinated management is the responsibility of the Hadrian's Wall Consultative Committee, which was set up in 1977 on the initiative of the Countryside Commission, and consists of representatives of no fewer than 32 bodies. It took the committee seven years to prepare a Strategy, which was published by the Countryside Commission in 1984. The Strategy contains so much good advice about what *should* be done that we call it 'The Should Report' but it is advice and nothing more. There is no programme of action, no budget, no corporate funding; and the Committee is incapable of giving firm direction or control. English Heritage has begun to take its responsibilities for the Wall more positively and imaginatively, but even were it to acquire new portions and develop a more enlightened attitude both to conservation and to visitor management it is not the right body to manage the entire corridor. The publication of the Strategy confirmed us in the opinion we expressed in 1982, that a special trust (on which both the National Trust and English Heritage would be represented) should be created by Act of Parliament to acquire such land as is necessary and to manage the Wall, the related landscapes and SSSIs as a special kind of linear national park.

The detachment of Hadrian's Wall from the Northumberland National Park would open the way for another novelty on the Anglo-Scottish border. The Otterburn and Redesdale ranges may be compatible with a nature reserve, but they are incompatible with a national park and should be phased out. But if the military refuse to go it would still be possible for England and Scotland to co-operate in the creation of a Cheviot National Park on both sides of the border, from which the ranges would be excluded. Having visited the Glacier International Park managed by the Canadian and United States Governments in the Rocky Mountains we think it is about time that the Scottish and Welsh borders ceased to be obstacles to national park designation. The Brecon Beacons National Park could be extended to include the eastern slopes of the Black Mountains that lie in Herefordshire. Is it really unthinkable to have an Anglo-Scottish or an Anglo-Welsh national park authority bridging a divide that makes no sense in landscape, ecological or recreational terms?

The Countryside Commission is currently reviewing the boundaries of all the national parks over a period of five years, but it seems unlikely that it will go much beyond ironing out local anomalies. There is a strong case for including the superb mountains of the Howgills and Mallerstang which the Commission excluded from the designated area of the North Pennines AONB, in the Yorkshire Dales National Park. Now that the park authorities are being seen as generators of income rather than a drag on local funds there may be less resistance than there was in the past to the inclusion of such enclaves as Whitby in the North York Moors, or Blaenau Ffestiniog and the coastal towns of Barmouth and Tywyn in Snowdonia.

The boundaries of the Pembrokeshire Coast National Park are far too tightly drawn. We are more convinced than ever that they should be extended seawards to facilitate integrated coastal management by the park authority, and landwards to give it planning control over land where development can create serious problems in the coastal strip. It is, perhaps, characteristic of the present division of responsibilities that in 1986 the NCC, in announcing the impending designation of Britain's first Marine Nature Reserve at Skomer Island, failed to mention that the island is in the Pembrokeshire Coast National Park. The representation of the NCC on the park authority is long overdue. But we would add that all the national parks with coastal strips or extensive inland waters are handicapped by lack of powers and divided responsibilities.

STRENGTHENING THE SYSTEM

The national park system should be strengthened in several ways. The first, and much the easiest, is to give the national park authorities the money they need. The trend is upwards, but it is not rising fast enough and the Countryside Commission is still reluctant to encourage the park authorities to bid for what they really need. Its advice to them in 1986 was to bid for cash increases of between 12

and 18% for 1987–8. Our assessment is that if the park authorities' resources are to match their needs, and to replace temporary
underpaid MSC labour by full-time workers in real jobs, their
incomes should be at least doubled or trebled over the next three
to four years. In addition to raising the total of National Park
Supplementary Grant, the government should lift the poorer
parks like the Brecon Beacons out of their poverty trap by
paying grant to them at, say, the 90% rate already paid for
moorland conservation in Exmoor. None of these changes need
legislation.

We have already suggested that the national park authorities
should be allowed to spend money on improving social and
economic conditions in their areas. They would not take over the
housing or other functions of the local authorities, but could
intervene positively in job creation, housing, rural transport or the
support of local services. This, in turn, would enable the national
park authorities to become what one national park officer calls 'the
front-line agency' in rural land management, recreation and social
and economic development within the park. The national park plan
is the only policy document that takes a comprehensive view of the
park, and pulls together the strands of policy affecting it. The
national park officer should be in a position to co-ordinate the
resources available from all the agencies or authorities operating in
the area, in an agreed programme of benefit both to farmers and
other residents and to the national park. It is absurd that a farmer, for
example, who is interested in woodland management or tree
planting has to seek for money and advice from several official
agencies, whose officers in many cases are not based in the park. The
park authority is based in the park and has (or should have) more
people on the ground. It is more aware of local needs, is more
accessible and is uniquely placed to act as a catalyst, integrator,
pump-primer and co-ordinator.

The national park authorities should become what we call 'Rights
of Way Authorities'. So long as footpaths, bridleways and RUPPS
(Roads Used as Public Paths) are in the same hands as roads for
motor traffic they will be underfunded and neglected. The principle
applies throughout the countryside, but in national parks responsibility for rights of way – including both the legal aspects and
construction or maintenance – should be the exclusive responsibility
of the national park authorities. It is grotesque that, as we write, the
Brecon Beacons Authority in its bid for grant for 1987–8 has had to
protest that, although 'it has a wealth of local knowledge and
contacts, experience and expertise . . . and detailed priorities for path
improvement', it cannot do the work unless it is given the necessary

funds, and responsibility is delegated to it by the highway authorities.

The government's decision to circulate a consultation paper on Landscape Conservation Orders in national parks may prove to be a step forward. But LCOs as currently envisaged appear to be essentially 'Stop Orders', available in emergency to avert an immediate threat to some valued landscape feature. They will be of limited value unless part of a wider reform. They will, for example, be too costly if the park authorities have to pay through the nose for profit foregone, as they have to do for management agreements and, it seems, for Tree Preservation Orders. Compensation, if paid, must be related to actual not hypothetical loss. LCOs could be too negative, if there is no provision for continuing management, and ineffective, if the landowner or farmer is uncooperative.

The park authorities need the power to make LCOs but they also need the power to buy land compulsorily, for any national park purpose. The 'section 3' maps of open country that the park authorities think it is 'particularly important to conserve' should be extended to include any other valuable landscapes or features. The maps could then provide a basis for developing the present Farm Grant Notification Scheme from grant-aided farming operations to any operations that would adversely affect landscapes or features recorded on maps. Without notification the park authority may not know of the operation until it is too late. Most important of all, the park authority (not the Forestry Commission) needs the power to control afforestation above some very small area, perhaps one hectare.

A further essential reform is to free the park authorities from the control of their policies, finance, administration and staffing by the county councils. The earliest opportunity should be taken to give national park committees the autonomy of the Boards. Government could advise county councils to concede autonomy in these matters. If structure plans were abolished as Government proposes, and park committeess became development plan authorities, there would be a strong case for giving committees board status. Should a future Government decide to abolish the shire counties and to replace them (as Labour may propose) by regional assemblies or councils, it would be essential to replace the present county council committees by autonomous boards. It would be a positive advantage if national park authorities could levy a rate over a far wider area than a county, and include some members to represent the big cities. But to have a national park run by a committee with a majority of members from a remote regional council would be unacceptable to local or conservation interests.

Local government reform would, therefore, reopen the whole question of the composition of the national park authorities. If the new Broads Authority were taken as a model, there would be a majority of elected members drawn from the local authorities (50% plus one) and a minority of appointed members (50% minus one) representing a wide range of interests. Instead of a majority of county councillors there would be a majority of elected members, including a greater number of district councillors. The risk that district councillors would put job creation and local interests before the priority national park purposes has to be accepted. The national park authorities cannot win the local confidence they need in today's circumstances unless they are in the business of creating jobs, and are more representative of local people than they are now. We are still attached to our earlier idea that some of the local members should be directly elected by residents of national parks. But, however elected, the elected members should be counterbalanced by the appointed members, the proportion of whom should rise from a third to very nearly half. The appointed members should also be better qualified than today. The Secretary of State should be required to choose his appointees from people who have some prescribed skills, knowledge or experience. Some members could be appointed by the two conservation agencies (or, better still from the united agency we have recommended) or even by such bodies as the National Trust and the Forestry Commission, provided they manage their estates in ways that are compatible with the national park plans.

THE POLITICS OF CHANGE

The most fundamental reform of all would need no legislation. It would be a commitment by government to national parks of a kind and a degree that would make it unthinkable in the future to drive bypasses through them, or to site nuclear power stations in them, or to use them to manoeuvre tanks or fire artillery, or to remove high quality limestone from them by the truck-load, or to destroy their open landscapes or woodlands. True commitment would ensure that individual departments were not allowed to wage a guerilla war against the conservation and recreation interests. Farming and forestry money and Treasury tax concessions must not be used as battering rams to knock down the weak defences erected by the national park authorities. A cease-fire should be declared, and the resources diverted from the assault into a constructive collaboration in the integration of conservation with national park development.

The obstacles that lie between the present day and the realization of these hopes are not to be underestimated, even if they are a good deal less formidable than those that Christian had to overcome in *Pilgrim's progress*. Faith can indeed move obstacles, but it would be foolish not to recognize the inertia that is inherent in established sectoral habits of thinking, and firmly embedded in the structure of central and local government. These habits are reinforced by the British tradition of secrecy, which not only keeps outsiders in ignorance but shields the insiders from new ways of thinking about old problems. Once we enter the arena of land and property rights we are entering a political and emotional minefield. More farmers and landowners are indeed beginning to see themselves as custodians of the countryside, but behind the policies of their unions and associations lie the harsh facts of property rights and self-interest. The future lies in co-operation, but co-operation is rarely achieved unless those who are challenging an established order or interest have confidence, strength and political clout. The process of change will be accelerated to the degree that the smaller farmers, in particular, are given the help and the encouragement they need, and encouraged to identify their interests with those of conservation rather than with those of the bigger farmers who are gobbling them up. We question whether the trend towards the concentration of land in ever fewer hands and ever larger units can be reversed without intervening in the land market and inaugurating what in other countries would be called a land reform.

Whether national parks are extended and strengthened, and become greenprints for the management of the wider countryside depends, in all probability, on the strength of the voluntary movements for conservation and recreation and on their ability to influence the political parties. The signs are, on the whole, encouraging, but the achievement of the broader national park purposes we have suggested is dependent above all on radical changes in the direction of government policies and economic trends. The conservation of nature and natural resources may be irrelevant to the outmoded economics of a society whose goal is ever-increasing material consumption, but it is central to the economics of sustained continuous yield. Conservation, in the sense in which we use the term, combines a conservative approach to land management with a revolutionary challenge to the established habits of thought and the entrenched interests of contemporary society.

It will also be objected that many of our ideas and even the general direction of our thinking are unrealistic in the light of current political and economic trends and the strength of the interests to which our approach presents a challenge. We live in an unstable and unpredictable world, within which the movement for conservation will have to struggle very hard if it is to influence events. But the conservation movement will never achieve its objectives if it tries to rely entirely on goodwill and persuasion, evades the conflicts of interest and denies the political nature of the issues it is raising. The future of the countryside may ultimately depend on whether it remains a political backwater in which the ideology and interests of the rural establishment go unchallenged, or whether it becomes a focus of political debate and action.

Further reading and useful information

The most recent descriptive account of the national parks of England and Wales is *Britain's national parks* by W. S. Lacey & B. Gilchrist (Windward Press). The story of the struggle to create and protect them is told in *Fifty years of the national parks* (Council for National Parks). The standard academic work on the national park system, which we modestly believe to be highly readable, is our own *National parks: conservation or cosmetics?* (Allen & Unwin 1982). It contains a much fuller account of the history of national parks and of the critical conflict over moorland reclamation in Exmoor than does the present book. Those who are looking for a fuller account of the hill farming support system, which is criticized in this book, should read *New life for the hills* by Malcolm MacEwen & Geoffrey Sinclair (Council for National Parks 1983). W. M. Adams' *Nature's place* is an up-to-date, well researched and stimulating study of wildlife and nature conservation (Allen & Unwin). *Countryside conflicts* by Philip Lowe and others (Gower/Temple Smith 1986) provides many insights into the politics of farming, forestry and conservation, and detailed accounts of the conflicts over the Halvergate Marshes in the Broads, Exmoor, the Somerset Levels and the Berwyn Mountains

The Countryside Commission (John Dower House, Cheltenham, GL50 3RA) has a very wide range of interesting publications on countryside topics. The most relevant to this book is the highly readable report *The changing uplands* (CCP 153), which is itself a summary of the more specialized *Upland landscape study*, edited by Geoffrey Sinclair (Environmental Services, Glebe House, Martletwy, Narberth, Dyfed SA67 8AS). Her Majesty's Stationery Office publishes official guides to each of the national parks, all of which contain some excellent articles by specialists, but are now getting out of date. They are being replaced by a more popular series, to be published by the national park authorities themselves, obtainable from the addresses given below.

Those who wish to take a closer interest in national parks, or to join the movement for their conservation and enjoyment, should join the Friends of the National Parks, sponsored by the Council for National Parks (45 Shelton Street, London WC2H 9HJ; Tel. (01) 240 3603). Membership entitles subscribers to two issues of *Tarn and Tor* each year, an interesting annual report and discounts at a number of national park information centres. The Council for National Parks publishes a very well illustrated educational pack, *Know your national parks* whose profiles of each park and fact sheets are obtainable separately. Those who live in or near one of the national parks (or have developed close links with one) may wish to join the local society or association formed to mobilize public support and (where necessary) criticism. The Brecon Beacons, Pembrokeshire Coast and Northumberland still lack such organizations, but contact can be made in the other parks at the following addresses:

The Dartmoor Preservation Association: Margaret Davey, Crossings Cottage, Donsland, Yelverton, Devon.
The Exmoor Society: Parish Rooms, Dulverton, Somerset.
The Friends of the Lake District: Michael Houston, Gowan Knott, Kendal Road, Staveley, LA8 9LP.
The North Yorkshire Moors Association: Don Tilley, 7 The Avenue, Nunthorpe, Middlesbrough, Cleveland.
The Sheffield and Peak District Branch, CPRE: 22 Endcliff Cresent, Sheffield, SID 3ES
Snowdonia National Park Society: Capel Curig, Betwys-y-Coed, Gwynedd, North Wales.
The Yorkshire Dales Society: 152 Main Street, Addingham, via Ilkley, LS29 0LY.

The national park authorities all run information centres and publish and sell a very wide range of publications, from leaflets and walk guides upwards. Most of them publish information about where to stay, and organize guided walks. Information is obtainable at the following addresses from the park authorities:

Brecon Beacons: 6 Glamorgan Street, Brecon, Powys, LD3 7DP.
Dartmoor: Parke, Bovey Tracey, Newton Abbot, Devon, TQ13 9QJ.
Exmoor: Exmoor House, Dulverton, Somerset, TA22 9HL.
Lake District: Busher Walk, Kendal, Cumbria, LA9 4RH.
North York Moors: The Old Vicarage, Bondgate, Helmsley, York, YO6 5BP.
Northumberland: Eastburn, South Park, Hexham, Northumberland, NE46 1BS.
Peak District: Aldern House, Baslow Road, Bakewell, Derbyshire, DE4 1AE.
Pembrokeshire Coast: County Offices, Haverfordwest, Dyfed, SA61 1QZ.
Snowdonia: National Park Office, Penrhyndeudraeth, Gwynedd, LL48 6LS.
Yorkshire Dales: Yorebridge House, Bainbridge, Leyburn, North Yorkshire, DL8 3BP.

Index